TRAVELLING
LIGHT

TRAVELLING LIGHT

*Journeys Among Special
People and Places*

ALASTAIR SAWDAY

Little, Brown

LITTLE, BROWN

First published in Great Britain in 2017 by Little, Brown

1 3 5 7 9 10 8 6 4 2

Copyright © Alastair Sawday 2017

The moral right of the author has been asserted.

Extract from 'Home from Abroad' by Laurie Lee on p. 7 reproduced
with permission of Curtis Brown Group Ltd, London on behalf of The
Beneficiaries of the Estate of Laurie Lee. Copyright © 1959 Laurie Lee
Lines from 'Le Métèque' by Georges Moustaki on p. 92
© Georges Moustaki 1969
'To a Friend in Search of Rural Seclusion' on p. 124 by Christopher Logue
© Christopher Logue 2012
A version of the text on pp. 265–7 was first published in 'Cool oases'
by Alastair Sawday, *Guardian*, 6 August 2005

A CIP catalogue record for this book is available from the British Library.

ISBN 978-1-4087-0852-1

Typeset in Bembo by M Rules
Printed and bound in Great Britain by Clays Ltd, St Ives plc

Papers used by Little, Brown are from well-managed forests
and other responsible sources.

To Em

Travel makes one modest: one sees what a tiny place one occupies in the world.

Gustave Flaubert

CONTENTS

Introduction

It was 1954. Britain was exhausted and broke. Rationing was only just coming to an end. Floods had killed hundreds. Travel abroad was unusual.

It seems astonishing now but we took our car, a Ford Consul, with us on the plane from Lydd airfield in Kent. Father wore a flat tweed cap, his usual tweed jacket and brown leather brogues. My mother, gaily dressed, had the twinkle in the eye of a woman ready to zoom along a corniche on the Med. I was in grey shorts, an Aertex shirt and Clarks shoes; my older sister Auriol in pigtails and a summer frock. Our luggage was a few leather suitcases squeezed into the boot. Father drove the Consul into the nose of the Bristol Freighter to join two other vehicles. This was an adventure for anyone, let alone an impressionable young boy. The passengers sat behind the cars while the aircrew climbed a ladder to the flight deck above us. The plane was noisy and shuddered horribly; a friend remembers his own Bristol Freighter flight across the Channel being draughty

and cold until his mother stuffed a handkerchief into the
hole in the floor.

As we drove out of the tiny Le Touquet airport we came
to a halt – and waited. Before and aft there were other cars,
unperturbed; no bleating of horns, no curses. My father
ambled down the road to see what was up and reported that
a lorry driver had stopped in the middle of the road for a pee.
My mother told us 'He is just being French' – a hint that
France would be different in unexpected ways. Something
in me thrilled to the idea.

My parents later took us often to France and I was
enchanted by the village scenes: a café/bar, a pissoir, the
mairie, the shabby Hôtel de Sport, the pétanque pitch. *La
France profonde* was visible everywhere and I revelled in it.
My mother had once loved a Frenchman, and she taught
me to love his Loire. Later travels revealed to me the canal
system, Burgundian villages, Norman farms, cycling in
the Vosges, the châteaux of the Dordogne, walking in the
Luberon. I was hooked.

Spain worked its magic on me too, starting as a teenager
with an evening of raw flamenco. The country villages
later revealed wooden barrels of wine in rows, the Guardia
Civil wearing strange three-cornered helmets, old men on
drooping, heat-drenched donkeys. All were the backdrop
to a developing fascination.

Italy was a late discovery, but no less intense for that.
Hurtling from one medieval town to another as a tour
manager, in a heady confusion of history and astonishment,
I relished newly revealed differences, layer unpeeling from
layer. A familiar place might emerge freshly understood.

I found the tourism industry to be a shallow beast that

turns a blind eye to its own excesses: Ronald Reagan's famous description of the American public – as a small child keen to absorb everything at one end and oblivious to the results at the other end – could be said to apply. Years later, in 2007, I read a brochure for a company called Airtours, advertising a round-the-world flight: twenty-three days, ten countries. There was a glowing passage about the virtues of the trip: 'The airline is currently tailoring a special in-flight menu with meals reflecting the local dishes of the countries visited.' Local food at its best, of course, and all at a cost of about seventeen tonnes of carbon emitted per person.

Our books set out to open eyes to the special places and special people that provide nourishing, and less destructive, travel. My dismay at the ravages of tourism has been tempered by the delight people have taken in those books.

These are stories of our search for people ploughing their own furrows: a mix of travellers' tales, stories from the front line of my publishing experience, ruminations and reflections about places, people and ideas. I explore, too, the value of travel. Laurence Sterne, the Irish author of *A Sentimental Journey Through France and Italy*, suggested that we travel for one of just three reasons: imbecility of mind, infirmity of body, or inevitable necessity. One might add envy, curiosity – or just too much bloody rain at home. Escape, in other words. But there are positive things such as intellectual and cultural hunger, the longing to be with people who do things differently.

The man who fired my further curiosity was H. V. Morton. He was a matchless story-teller, weaving a little history into whatever he observed. A ginger cat slinking across a piazza in Venice in pursuit of a pigeon might remind him of a ginger-haired doge malevolently stalking a rival. A chat with an old man in a café would trigger memories of an elderly pretender to the Spanish throne who had died drinking chocolate. He encouraged his readers to look up and notice details on a building while he painted its colourful history. We are now so focused on the present, and on ourselves, that our landscape of people and places is no longer populated by the events and characters of previous centuries. Our cultural references have, I think, shrunk. So I still treasure H. V. Morton.

Our language, too, was once more evocative. Read a travel brochure to see what I mean. Robert Macfarlane, author of *The Old Ways: A Journey on Foot*, has sought out the regional language that once added colour and nuance to everyday things. In *Landmarks*, he wrote: 'it is clear that we increasingly make do with an impoverished language for landscape. A place literacy is leaving us. A language in common, a language of the commons, is declining. Nuance is evaporating from everyday usage, burned off by capital and apathy.' Macfarlane discovered, to his delight, hundreds of 'lost' words that might be revived – such as 'zwer', an Exmoor term for the noise made by a covey of partridges taking flight. Many of us can add our own. But to his shock, he learned that the Oxford University Press had deleted life-enhancing words from its *Junior Dictionary* that it considered irrelevant to a modern-day childhood, including '*acorn, adder, ash, beech, bluebell, buttercup, catkin, conker, cowslip, cygnet, dandelion, fern, hazel, heather, heron, ivy, kingfisher, lark, mistletoe, nectar, newt, otter, pasture* and *willow*'.

The words taking their places included '*attachment, block-graph, blog, broadband, bullet-point, celebrity, chatroom, committee, cut-and-paste, MP3 player* and *voice-mail* . . . *For blackberry, read BlackBerry.*'

The richer our imaginations and the language we have to set them free, the richer our travel experience. We British do things one way, the Spaniards another; there are unlimited ways of doing everything. Kindness is found everywhere, and in unexpected places, as is eccentricity. Eccentrics are an endangered species and need as much protection as does the house sparrow.

I have also written of my pre-publishing careers: teaching, politics, environmental campaigning, organic agriculture, volunteer teaching abroad and the travel business. Some of them were short – as with Oxfam's disaster relief team, and with Ugandan refugees for the Quakers – but they helped shape me. For a year Em and I ran a four-pupil home school, and I have entangled myself in a host of other projects. Em, Toby and Rowan have been wonderfully tolerant, though this book has, perilously, revealed to them quite how much fun I have had. Continuous threads have been a quest for purpose and the pursuit of unusual ideas. Sometimes others followed me, but often they have just looked on bemused.

I write about my gradual awakening to the fragility of everything we love. Every visit to Europe, to rural Britain, reveals loss – whether of woodland, flora, fauna, views or silence. We have become used to change, used, for example, to massive loss of wildlife since the Second World War. We forget our own role in it and must learn. Another writer who made me look more deeply into the shrinking pond that is our countryside is Roger Deakin, who swam his way across England through every pool, river, stream and pond he encountered.

I have fought many campaigns and admire those, like Greenpeace activists, who have risked life and limb. I have tried to be, in the words of George W. Bush, a 'pitbull on the pant leg' of environmental idiocy. From whaling to recycling, nuclear energy to organic farming, I have spoken, written, urged and argued – rarely with visible success. Those with money and power do not let go of it willingly, and never has there been such concentration of both.

Like so many of my age, I see how little I have achieved. I have climbed no mountains, discovered no rivers, created no great institutions, powered no legislation and changed hardly anything. Aware of the need for simplicity and contact with nature, yet fully plugged into the wider world, I am still angry. I have spent forty years trying to understand the mess we have made and making inadequate attempts to provide solutions.

One weekend in September 2016 I camped on Dartmoor with thirty others, on a course run by two young civil servants alarmed at their disconnection from the natural world. Most of us were flagging in our working or personal lives. We were fired up by the prospect of re-ignition, and we got it.

We handed in our mobile phones, which were put in a locked box. Tents were pitched among beeches that soared high above us, their trunks as smooth and grey as elephants' skins. The stream, clean from the moor, gave us all our water. After a surprise gin and tonic, supper was served around the camp fire. We talked of nature, our weakening contact with her and of how vital it was to regain it. We discussed the pitiful plight of our wildlife. When had we last seen a sparrow? We swung into the trees on a long rope.

Through listening, walking and playing we slowed down. None of us wanted our phones back.

The day after leaving the camp, I was dragged – against all my instincts – into a vast supermarket, a brightly lit temple to consumerism near Penzance, and wandered from aisle to aisle in confusion. At a point where the aisle stretched mockingly away from me, I gave up, close to tears of rage. The gulf between the community among the beeches and where I stood was unbearable.

When we travel we follow a single line between A and B. This book follows a wandering path through my life and cannot see, over the hedges, most of the people who have mattered to me. I hope they will understand.

We once had a well-educated and eccentric tramp living with us. He was a gifted traveller. Learning that the hedge-row flowers in North Wales would be at their finest that week, he set off from Bristol on his elderly bicycle, penniless and with no more than he was dressed in. He returned a fortnight later, a smile from ear to ear. I am still impressed.

A Suffolk Childhood

There is a line in Laurie Lee's poem 'Home from Abroad' that melts me at every reading. It is the last line of the last verse, which goes like this:

> So do I breathe the hayblown airs of home,
> And watch the sea-green elms drip birds and
>   shadows,
> And as the twilight nets the plunging sun
> My heart's keel slides to rest among the meadows.

I know that the countryside he loves is not East Anglia, but I cannot help thinking of the keel of my childhood's dinghy sliding softly along the grey mud of the River Alde until it comes silently to a halt.

I grew up in Saxmundham, a Suffolk village which now

looks far prettier than I remember it. All my childhood was spent there, in a wisteria-covered Georgian farmhouse with views across pasture to distant woods. A house can shape a childhood; ours was filled with gaiety, light and play, love and imagination. Places shape personalities, and Carlton Rookery's optimism spread through me like a drop of indigo in water.

It was a comfortable, kindly world. My father, a country solicitor, deeply traditional and the son of a dentist from Weybridge, was the placid backdrop to our lives. How calm and kind he was is illustrated by his response to my first car accident. In the family's Austin van I raced off to meet a friend five days after passing my driving test. Hurtling too fast around a corner, the van continued through and over the hedge and ended upside down in a field. Unhurt, I tramped across the field to a nearby farm and used their phone to ring my father, who was unfazed: 'Don't worry, old boy, I'll be with you soon and you can go on in my car.' I left him standing in the field awaiting the rescue truck, and was more affected by his gentleness than I would have been by a stern lecture.

I later discovered that there was more to his own father than mere dentistry. He kept a lady friend in a flat in London and experienced the classic philanderer's disaster: a ball-gown intended for this lady sent home in error and unwrapped by his wife. She stormed out, and when she finally returned he was as putty in her hands. One day, coming back from London, perhaps after a tipple, he slipped under the train and lost an arm. He continued, with impressive panache, to practise as a dentist. We always thought his one-handed driving was immensely exciting, but his one-handed dentistry must have been even more so.

My mother was happy to play a traditional role but she must have strained at the rural Suffolk leash for she had a streak of daring and enjoyed unusual and maverick friends. So life at Carlton Rookery, already enriched by the company of my three sisters – Auriol, Dinx and Fiona – was given extra colour by a stream of guests and local characters. Mr Geeter was the only First World War survivor in the neighbouring village of Kelsale. Tiny, immaculate, and always with polished leather gaiters, he kept his pony and trap in our old stables and would take us trotting down to Saxmundham. In his cottage up the road, with its outside privy, there was always a welcome and perhaps a toffee from the tin on the mantelpiece. Next door was a mixed farm run by Mr Delf, who every morning led his cattle to pasture. Chickens perched upon cows, cats prowled, guinea fowl screeched and ducks waddled. I would often wander over just to be on the farm, soaking up the atmosphere. Now it is gone, sold to the Mormons, who have huge land holdings in East Anglia. Only a large concrete pad remains where a flourishing farm once stood. Many of the trees are gone too, and the fields opposite the house are sown with wheat. The stream running past Carlton Rookery, once constant, now flows only when it rains because the compacted soil structure around it cannot hold water as it used to.

It is a constant reminder of the calamity that is modern intensive farming: jobs gone, habitat gone, animals gone – a monoculture instead of a mixed field pattern, and heavy use of herbicides, pesticides and fertiliser. We the taxpayers subsidise this grim destruction by paying at least £2.5 billion a year for the external costs: cleaning up rivers, dealing with health impacts, supporting unemployment and thus enabling the big farmers to make a profit. It is the business model for an age of catastrophic environmental degradation and inequality.

Like so many of my generation, I have an idealised view of childhood. I can remember no unhappiness at home (though my sisters recall my mother's wailing distress at my departure for prep school). On the wall in the lavatory was the Irish blessing, whose optimism and love sum up the mood in our house:

> May the road rise up to meet you,
> May the wind be always at your back,
> May the sun shine warm upon your face,
> The rain fall soft upon your fields,
> And until we meet again
> May God hold you in the palm of his hand.

The wider family – my mother's three sisters and their many children – would spend holidays with us, for foreign travel was then exotic and rare. Summers were filled with picnics, barbecues on the Minsmere cliffs, sailing, reading on the lawn after lunch, playing kick-the-can and cocky olly. We had chickens and pigs, doves, dogs and a cat called Monty who, while usually unseen, once interrupted Sunday lunch with his foot dragging a mole-trap. Much of our food was grown in our garden and my mother made the most of life with a gaiety and sense of fun that were indomitable.

From the age of five to eight I was at a local school in Saxmundham run by the Misses Henderson and Partridge, both war spinsters. The sadness of those many women whose hopes of marriage had been dashed by the Great War hung over us all. I was warily fond of them, and of the pink satin bloomers that we could see beneath Henny Penny's voluminous skirts as we lay reading on the floor after lunch. Those bloomers are my most vivid memory of that school.

I was then sent to a preparatory school near Norwich. Ketteringham Hall was a beautiful house in beautiful grounds, but the headmaster was a cruel, toad-faced man called Mr Rattles. He was supported by a tall, handsome Latin master, Mr Crowther, whose head of tightly curled white hair gave him a benign, paterfamilias look. They both delighted in beating us. Rattles would pronounce the punishment, and its execution was shared with Crowther.

At the corner of a courtyard was a little building that housed the school boiler. There I would be summoned to take my beating, entering the smelly, dark room with a giant boiler humming in the background. A smaller, throbbing pump served as the execution scaffold, building in my fluttering guts a sense of impending doom as the low throb fell into synch with my by now tightened heart. The pain was always intense, but I bore it with grim fatalism. Most of us did; what else were we to do? Three strokes were the norm for such crimes as talking after lights out; an extra fourth was dreaded, and six were reserved for serious crimes.

Once I was sent to select my own length of bamboo from one of the many clumps that decorated the stately garden, a cruelty that added to the punishment. One boy, condemned to this selection of his own instrument of torture, hid, weeping and terrified, in the garden all night rather than return with the cane. He became a bed-wetter, a grim burden to bear in a tightly knit boarding school.

Two incidents of harshness and injustice remain with me. I loathed pilchards, and still do, but they were a feature of school lunches. My solution was to wrap them in a handkerchief and smuggle them out of the dining room.

'Sawday, I saw you slip something into your pocket. Empty it.'

'It is a handkerchief, sir.'

'Don't lie to me, boy. Empty it out. So, I see you have stolen some of the school lunch. Wretched boy.'

There was a stunned silence in the room, then nervous chatter. 'Silence, the rest of you, and line yourselves around the walls. Sawday must be taught to eat his lunch.'

The boys shuffled nervously towards the edge of the room. I was then beaten in front of them all, a bizarre ritualistic humiliation, and all for a couple of pilchards. Those email enquiries one receives before dinners and conferences – 'Do you have any dietary requirements, sir?' – I always respond to with 'Yes: no pilchards, please.'

Mrs Rattles, however, wasn't interested in punishment, an obsession of so many male teachers, and she became a heroine to us small boys for her wartime exploits in France. This small woman told us how, as a *maquisarde*, she had ambushed Germans in a night-time attack. I could imagine the scene only too vividly because I devoured cartoon books about the war, and the brandishing of Mrs Rattles's revolver in class had an intoxicating effect on me. She could do no wrong, and I rather wished she would use the revolver on her dreadful husband. My longing to learn French from her was unquenchable and I sailed through our lessons. I also learned ballroom dancing from a music mistress whose bosom would send me into transports of delight. She would have a bath just across a tiny courtyard from our dormitory, but so far below us that I couldn't see in. One evening I attached a mirror to a long bamboo pole. It worked! She came in, turned on the taps and went out again. But the windows quickly steamed up, so I hurtled in my pyjamas out of the dormitory, along a corridor, down some stairs and along another corridor into her bathroom, and frenziedly cleaned the windows. I returned to the dormitory and tried again. She entered the room in her dressing gown, excitement mounted – and the windows steamed up again.

Such incidents, and some kindly teachers, helped me to bear the cruelty. There is a supportive camaraderie among boys; the well-thrashed were briefly elevated to hero status. However, our society now better understands the impact on children of this sort of harshness and abandonment. Em has introduced me to the therapeutic concept of the wounded leader, a type commonly found at the head of organisations but so wounded that he or she never fully develops emotionally. We 'abandoned' children closed down emotionally at school in order to survive. I am, I confess, still shy of revealing vulnerabilities, but I am working on it – with Em's encouragement. She can hardly wait for the improved version.

I recently met someone who had been sexually abused at Ketteringham and never really recovered. I wonder how many others suffered the same fate. Perhaps many, for soon after my departure the parents began to get wind of the beatings and abuse, withdrew their children and the school had to close. For years – even when both he and Mr Crowther were long since dead – I harboured longings to return and punch Mr Rattles. I had survived, I think, thanks to a strong sense of family. Yet my parents' generation, who

banished so many of us to boarding schools, had themselves
been emotionally crippled by the deprivations and losses of
war. Their own parents, too, had closed down emotionally
after the Great War, unable to express its horrors. So the
fifties – my childhood, following another war – existed in
the wake of that period of sadness and unutterable loss.

Ketteringham also introduced me to nature's curious ways.
An annual event was the spring migration of thousands of
mating toads (or frogs?) across the school courtyard. I had
to step carefully lest I squash them underfoot, each one
with another on its back, clinging on for dear life – or,
rather, for dear love. They would get into the classrooms,
and under desks. I was both delighted and disgusted by this
invasion, but have seen nothing like it since, as both toads
and frogs have been deprived of the ponds which once
dotted the countryside. How I miss those ponds, each one
a little world unto itself. There was an old one edged with
bull rushes at the top of the hill above our Suffolk home,
next to another farm. Frogspawn was a regular feature of
the spring; every pond would fill with those glistening
baubles of promise. We would take the tadpoles home in
glass jars, but the cause of their decline was not us but agriculture itself, entering a post-war phase of intensification
in a country shocked by near-starvation during the U-boat
blockade. The rush was on to produce more, but it came
at vast hidden cost: hare, water voles, beetles, butterflies,
most farm birds and their predators. The slaughter was
immense. Ponds were a waste of space if one could grow
more crops by filling them in, and there were fewer farm
animals needing a drink, let alone farm horses. So ponds

were filled in or left to wither. Where were the frogs to breed?

The slaughter continues apace. Since the last war we have eliminated roughly half of our wildlife. A beautiful book, *The Moth Snowstorm*, has been written by Mike McCarthy, the former environment editor of the *Independent*, in which he rails about the loss. He suggests that our society should rebuild its image of itself, its narrative. We still think of the Earth as something to plunder, rather than as our home to be nurtured. He reminds us that decades ago a car journey would be hampered by blizzards of moths and other insects glued to the windscreen. What can be said about a society that calls itself civilised yet eliminates more than half its wildlife?

I am helpless when faced with the need to name a flower or a bird, but childhood experience of a richer wildlife doesn't go away. I strolled this summer past that old pond and saw a clutch of poppies, some nettles and a scattering of wood pigeons in the vast fields of wheat. It was a thin pretense at nature. 'Isn't Suffolk a rural paradise?' Well yes, but a faint reflection of what it once was. Reading *Akenfield*, Ronald Blythe's story of an East Anglian village, is a reminder of our loss. As a young teenager I had cut hay with National Servicemen: sweating backs, the growing pile of hay on the cart being hauled up by the man on top of the pile, chaff in one's eyes and ears, rabbits scudding across the fields, a stop for sandwiches in the heat and then more cutting and hauling. This scene survived until long after the war and I regret now the loss of local work, community, a sense of human pace. It was a hard life for many, but we have lost much more than we realise, including our autonomy and security. I commend, too, *Ask the Fellows Who Cut the Hay* by George Ewart Evans. East Anglia has produced many gifted literary observers of the rural scene, and painters too, such as John Nash, who was a close friend of Ronald Blythe.

The Suffolk countryside was the lens through which I would later see the world. All of us are shaped by minor events and encounters, and one such event for me was a long walk through the snow from Ketteringham to the neighbouring village of Wymondham to get bread for the school. The old word 'crump' is perfect for the sound the snow makes as one walks. The snow was deep and the cold intense, and I walked, those crumps breaking the silence, in a trudging line of small boys, each of us there to carry a load back for the others. This was April 1958, thirteen years after the war, and I don't remember snow so late in the year since then. Weather patterns have altered, the climate is changing, and the memory of that trudge through the snow hardens my resolve to do something about it all.

At thirteen I was sent to Charterhouse, the handsome public school where my father had been. It is a curious survival, this dispatching of young boys, and now girls, to a school because of family tradition. I have hoped that society would move on, but the tradition has staying power, as have so many other bad ideas.

I settled well enough into Charterhouse. I liked my housemaster and many of the staff, and I am a peace-maker, so I conformed, becoming head of house and deputy head boy – enough to get by. But I was cooped up again; the rebel in me began to awake. For a time I slept in the Wingate dormitory, and Orde Wingate duly became one of my heroes. At Charterhouse he was disliked by his peers as difficult and non-conformist. Later, at Woolwich Academy, similarly disliked, he was summoned to a meeting of trainee officers, who had gathered to 'show him'. They stood in two lines, each with a wet, knotted, towel. At the end of the lines was an ice-cold pool into which Wingate was to be thrown after a humiliating towel-whipping. About to be forcibly stripped, he slowly undressed and then strolled down between the lines of waiting trainees, eyeballing each as he passed. Untouched, he dived smoothly into the pool.

Wingate went on to help the Ethiopians rid their country of Italians, and accompanied Haile Selassie on his triumphal return to Addis Ababa. In the early forties he set up the Chindits to operate behind Japanese lines in Burma. Inspired by such tales, I joined the Scouts. Our leader was modest, tough and driven. He, Wilfrid Noyce, had been on the 1953 Everest expedition as part of the support team for Hillary and Tenzing's last push to the top. Wilfrid died climbing in the Pamirs, exactly where he would have wanted to die. Curiously, George Mallory, another Charterhouse master, also died climbing – in the Himalayas. Traditional rumour at the school had it that scoutmasters were 'gay' and the boys wet and whimsical, but we enjoyed a freedom that the rest could only dream of: weekends in the Welsh mountains, canoeing down the River Wey in pursuit of Girl Guides, camping in the woods.

Another outlet for me was my treehouse, built in the Scout woods and with running water, a window, furniture and a few modest cons. Once this treehouse was built, another project beckoned.

'Sir, do you have a bed-frame and mattress you can lend me?'

'Sounds suspicious,' said Mr Rowan-Robinson, my long-suffering housemaster. 'What are you up to?'

'I would like to create a peaceful revision place for my exams, sir.'

'I don't follow.'

'I'll lash the bed to the top of a tree, sir. In the Scout woods.'

'Of course, why didn't I think of that?' he offered ironically.

The housemaster had a fine instinct for what made boys tick, and soon tracked down a spare bed. I hauled the mattress and bed-frame to the top of a tall tree on the edge of a valley in the school grounds. Lashed by its four corners, the bed swayed gaily with the breeze and collected 180 degrees of sunshine. It was a bucolic place to revise, in happy nakedness and entirely undisturbed. The sunshine browned me and I would return to school flushed with good health. I expect my friends thought I was cavorting with the girls from nearby Prior's Field School, but up on my treetop bed I innocently read Molière, Racine, Cervantes, Unamuno and Lorca – all now forgotten but all, surely, influential on a teenage boy. The slow corrosion of my respect for authority and convention was encouraged, I like to think, by Molière. How he would rage against injustice, our bankers and our bureaucrats, our technocrats and regulators. 'If everyone were clothed with integrity, if every heart were just, frank, kindly, the other virtues would be well-nigh useless for their chief purpose is to make us bear with patience the injustice of our fellow man.'

Perhaps that tree-top haven was an early sign that I needed to do my own thing. I co-founded in 2010 a tree-house company called Bower House. We built a luxurious tree-house in the gardens of Harptree Court, a Sawday's B&B in the Mendips, and later built a five-room treehouse in a mighty oak by a pub in Devon. As well as being sustainable, treehouses appeal to something primitive, perhaps even prehensile, in man.

Down to Earth by John Stewart Collis is a book to inspire anyone to love trees and the natural world. Collis spent a year after the war thinning a fourteen-acre wood with the simplest of tools. His writing is a paean to trees and woodland, suffused with poetic and spiritual love. Our conquest of nature has, of course, resulted in near-defeat for civilisation. Collis learned his priorities while working in the woods. 'That foxglove with its series of petal-made thimbles held up for sale to the bees, puts me at ease upon the subject of — progress. It is quite obvious that the foxglove cannot be improved . . . There is no point in our gazing raptly into the future for paradise if it is at our feet.'

For all its petty cruelties and rigidity, school did me little harm – other than emotional stiffness, perhaps – and nurtured my confidence. Indeed, when years later I was offered a teaching job at Charterhouse I seized the chance. The tree-top haven was still there.

2

An American Spell

I left school with a place to read law at Oxford and an English Speaking Union scholarship to a school in the USA. I sailed on the RMS *Queen Mary*, wallowing in absurd and voluptuous comfort. Arriving at Tabor Academy in Massachusetts I was met by a wall of ice-cold January weather. But this was the sixties, when the Beatles were in full swing and any Englishman carried with him an implied whiff of Liverpool's genius. So I was a curiosity, the resident limey, which helped with the cold.

Tabor is in a beautiful setting, on its own harbour across the water from Martha's Vineyard. It is one of the few American private boarding schools, even more of an oddity in the USA than they are in the UK. But the students and staff were kinder to me than I could have expected. Americans emerge from the womb primed to be one-person self-promoting PR experts, but they puff others up too. I was no athlete, but chugged around the athletics track at my usual speed and was astonished to be given prizes. I played ice hockey and nobody mocked me for playing with the thirteen-year-olds – who just skated around me. After ice hockey had humbled me, I tried wrestling, but an afternoon with my nose in the ripe armpit of another boy was enough. I did well in class, however, and was given a cum laude award; I shone as I had rarely shone in England. Happily, the school also had a fleet of boats, including a square-rigged schooner, the *Tabor Boy*. I became a crew member and sailing was my summer sport.

The US navy subsidised the boat, so we were officially US navy sailors, with pork-pie hats and those flapping bell-bottom trousers, and we were taught to drill with rifles. I learned the eighteen-point manual of arms, the nine-point manual and other comical manoeuvres. We even marched past an admiral, flanked by my bemused father, who had, ignorant of the naval threat, come to visit me and been hauled into this unexpected ritual. A tall man, he seemed small alongside the admiral and the other officers. Americans ate steak and drank orange juice and milk in those days, which added inches to their height. My Spam fritters and spotted dick hadn't done the same for me.

Summer weekends were spent on the *Tabor Boy*. My mother, sidelined at the parade, inveigled her way onto the annual fathers and sons' cruise, the first woman to do so. Captain Glaizer, our short, pugnacious professional skipper, found himself under her orders.

'Oh, Captain, do go to starboard so we can see that whale. Whoops, sorry, better to port, and harden in the sails.' His face, initially rigid with disapproval, cracked into a grin as he relaxed into the fun of it.

During the long vacation we cruised down to the Bahamas from Virginia, where I nearly missed my ship. I was arrested by US navy police for wearing brown Hush Puppies instead of regulation black shoes.

'Hey, buddy, what's your ship?'

'The *Tabor Boy*.'

'What the hell ship is that?'

'A square-rigger.'

'We don't have no square-riggers in the US navy.'

'Yes you do – sort of.'

'No we goddam don't. Where is your ID card?'

'What is an ID card?'

'What sort of a goddam sailor do you think you are?'

'Well, only a part-time one and . . . '

They were not trained to deal with this sort of encounter, so threw me in a van and took me to HQ. There, a bemused petty officer, attempting to make sense of an English boy in US naval uniform and crewing a sailing ship, suggested that the MPs take me back to where they had found me. I was clearly a harmless, if disconcerting, oddity – best discarded.

Sailing the *Tabor Boy* was two parts magic and eight parts tedium. I would lie out on the netting beneath the bowsprit above arching dolphins, scrubbing their backs with a long-handled broom, the ship surging forwards as if towards me. But scraping paint off the bilges while feeling seasick was grim and I didn't enjoy being at the whim of the petty officer and captain.

'You've got more of that bilge paint to chip.'

'But I'm feeling sick.'

'Tough shit, limey!'

The ship looked magnificent under full sail. We were on watch for four of the wee hours, under stars and on a heaving black sea, detached from the real world. In this bubble of ship, wind and water, so far from ordinary experience, we were almost out of time. One of the watch duties was to be at the helm, and when there was a big following sea and a full set of sails fear and exhilaration tugged at my guts; a moment of neglect and the boat could swing round broadside to the waves and wind, with disastrous results. Yet it is that desperate tumult – of wind, wave and fear together – that lures so many to the sea. I had read *The Last Grain Race* by Eric Newby, and our total dependency on the helmsman, in our plunging and bucking, canvas-hauled vessel of wood and steel, was vivid to me. But the skipper knew how much leeway to give us. If the boat began to swing away from the wind too alarmingly, he was at our side, a strong hand on the wheel.

Newby had felt every terror of the sea, beginning with his arrival on board. The skipper made him climb the rigging to the top of the mast, in his street shoes. Once at the top he had to go further, to stand on the 'button', the deck distant below him. When we climbed the rigging on the *Tabor Boy* to haul the sails in I had Newby's tales of occasional disaster ringing in my head. We would step out along a rope slung beneath the yard-arm, the rope passing through a ring on the mast. Our arms clutched at the smooth wooden spar, legs swinging back and forth, and then the rope would suddenly tighten, threatening to push us over into the void as someone stood on it at the spar's far end. We balanced on our stomachs across the spar, arms reaching down to haul up a fold of canvas, but the danger of falling to the deck below was electrifying.

We sailed in to Miami to be met by a full-on version of the American dream. Miami Beach is not a pretty sight: a dense wall of hotels and apartments behind the beach; ranks of bloated, sun-tormented bodies squeezed onto the sand like toothpaste from the high-rise tubes behind them. I retreated to the boat.

America caught up with us again in Nassau. Every day a cruise ship from Miami would disgorge its vivid hordes: multi-coloured shirts, peaked caps, belly-filled shorts, chaotic regiments of camera-wielding invaders. My visceral loathing of cruise ships, however, has more solid foundations. Having seen them in Venice, I sympathise with Venetians who feel that their paradise is being overwhelmed. Paradise can, apparently, be bought, too: some cruise companies have bought their own tiny Caribbean islands, set up shops and staffed them as if they were local. The spending money thus remains within the company.

My time at Tabor ended with a grand dinner. I was asked to make a short speech, and I ended with 'Let me once again say how kind you have all been to me. Thank you!' Polite clapping, before the head of the class of '64 took his turn at the podium: 'You are the most wonderful bunch of guys a man could dream of being with for these five long years. My heart has been touched by your unswerving friendship and support. America will be a finer country when you leave this great school of ours and start your journeys towards the building of a greater nation.' Shades here of 'making America great again', and riotous applause. English understatement is under-appreciated in the USA.

We also ended with that American institution, the prom, which gave us rare contact with the opposite sex. My formally arranged date was a gorgeous blonde girl called, improbably, Bambi. Infatuation followed, and I wheedled my way to Colorado, once I had left school, to stay with her and her family. Soon after my arrival Bambi seductively chirped, 'Honey, do you want to take a ride in my car?'

'Yeah – of course,' I said, looking as cool as I could. 'I'll hop in' – and headed for the passenger seat. 'Take the driver's seat,' she said, 'and let's go!'

The driver's seat was like the cockpit of a fighter jet and just as intelligible to me. The car was a Corvette Stingray: low, fast, open – a beast whose three hundred horsepower made me nostalgic for our forty horsepower Austin A40 van: nought to sixty in fifty-four seconds, and maximum speed sixty-two miles an hour. Was I to bluff my way around the controls, pushing the wrong buttons, with calamitous consequences? Or should I confess? I confessed. Bambi laughed and showed me how to drive the thing, and we spent days cruising through the Rockies.

I enjoyed pioneer generosity in many American homes but in none did I experience a sit-down family meal. With my European approach to meal-times and conversation, I was dismayed. The urgent activity of life was more important than being together as a family. This is strange, because kindnesses and generosity are part of being American, and family is important. A Californian policeman gave me the key to his flat for the weekend when I had nowhere to stay. So did a priest in Michigan. I only had to strum a chord on a guitar for campers to offer me a meal.

Of all my memories, the most enduring is that of the

'strips' that stretched like slug trails out of every town and city. Advertising signs rose higher than their neighbours to trumpet the benefits of a cheap burger or cocktail, each a call to slavish consumer obedience. Since then those strips have become brasher and uglier. For me they stained America, as the bungalow growth has stained Ireland, and as similar 'strips' are beginning to stain Europe.

America has been brought up on fairytales of salvation: by the cavalry, by God, by technology, or by Washington. With its open spaces and vast resources and its freedom-loving and dynamic people, it has had good reason to believe the narrative. I met few Americans back in those days who questioned their culture, apart from a handful of early hippies. I was alarmed by it then, and even more so now, centred as it is on consumerism of the harshest and blindest kind. The growth of American alternative culture has been a positive outcome, however, with a long reach into Europe and beyond. The anti-Vietnam war movement, together with the bubbling cauldron of creativity that was California, tempered my cynicism.

Flying over the Midwest, if you look down you can see, for endless miles, huge rings covering the land like circles drawn by aliens. They are made by the outer wheels of immense irrigation arms, giant hands of a watering clock. The water is pumped from the Ogallala Aquifer, an underground supply of geological age that stretches through a vast corn-growing belt under eight states in the central USA. It has irrigated these lands since white man settled them. What will happen when the aquifer is pumped dry? Can it happen? Of course, and it is happening. In Kansas, the ground-water level has dropped at least 150 feet; many farmers have abandoned their wells. As water levels fall, there will be global grain shortages, for this is where the world's grain reserves are. The farmers have done what mankind is doing throughout the world: opted for short-term profit at the expense of long-term stability, or sustainability. It is a Faustian pact, and we are all colluding.

America has, of course, produced many of the finest thinkers, activists and writers about the environment, such as Rachel Carson, whose *Silent Spring* alerted the world to the impact upon nature of the use of DDT and other substances. But America does, and dreams, everything on a vast scale. When her dreams fail, others lose theirs too.

I returned to England both inspired and disappointed. As an environmentalist it is hard to go back, for any hope I might cherish that progress is being made is quickly dashed by the vastness of America's commitment to doing the wrong thing. Yet if they were to change their ways they could amaze the world.

3

'Come and have a rum'

Three years of law at Oxford had convinced me, and my tutors, that a legal career would be, at best, unwise. So I had to ponder other options. Many of my fellow graduates sailed straight into lives of inevitable prosperity as bankers or lawyers. My father hoped that I would join him in his quiet country legal practice, but a life of wills, conveyancing, probate and local litigation beckoned more like the Grim Reaper than a career. I needed an alternative acceptable to my parents, different but useful. Voluntary Service Overseas, combining the exotic with a touch of missionary zeal, was the solution, and would give me thinking space.

Asked what my preference would be, I suggested a French-speaking country with a coast – and I hoped to end up in Africa. But I was sent to St Lucia, in the West Indies, and was to teach French in a secondary school. This was hardly the tough posting I had expected.

At the training course in Cardiff I met Em. She was refreshing: devoid of social pretension, talented and committed to teaching. She bubbled with infectious vitality. I was immediately attracted to her, though I was too noisy for her to take seriously. She and I were clearly very different, she with her passion for theatre, poetry and yoga, while I, though keen to learn from her, always had my eye on the horizon. To this day, we chuckle when we observe how we hike together: I stride ahead, keen to see what is round the corner, enthusing about the general picture and the views, and planning how to get there. Meanwhile, oblivious to my pace, Em has stopped to pick flowers, to admire an orchid, to marvel at a rock's colour. Our hiking, as well as our marriage, displays an unpredictable mix of perspectives and styles.

We flew out to Barbados in September 1967, and then on to our respective postings; Em was destined for Guyana. In *The Traveller's Tree*, published in 1950, Paddy Leigh Fermor described how Barbados had revealed itself to him: 'Looking backwards we could almost see, suspended with the most delicate equipoise above the flat little island, the ghostly shapes of those twin orbs of the Empire, the cricket ball and the blackball.'* White dominance was ebbing from the West Indies, though still the whiter your skin the better off you were; England remained the mother country. In spite of

---

* White and black balls were once used in voting for membership of gentlemen's clubs. One or more black balls dropped into the box excluded you. Exclusion was the lot of black West Indians.

all this, St Lucia revealed itself as a tolerant and welcoming island.

We four volunteers arrived in Castries, the capital, a deep-water port and a town that had several times been consumed by fire. Leigh Fermor suspected that the inhabitants had grown tired of rebuilding it: for him it was 'a brisk and shoddy piece of work. And yet, in spite of its ungrateful appearance and the swarms of beggars . . . it fails to leave a disagreeable impression.' Faint praise indeed. The journey to the south, where we were to work, took us twisting through cane plantations and then lush tropical mountains, through villages of tin shacks and wandering infants. Pigs scattered, boys scampered away from their games of cricket in the road, others stared in bemusement. But the mood, to us after a damp stay in the capital, was exuberant.

Vieux Fort, our destination, was ramshackle and clustered around a sheltered bay, wooden shacks with tin roofs, a few shops, the Cloud's Nest Hotel, a jetty and fishing boats – dug-out canoes with built-up timber sides – drawn up on the sand. We were given two houses – unexpected comfort. Ian and I shared a bungalow up the hill behind the docks. Katherine and Sue shared another house a mile away, behind a wild and windy beach. Ian was an experienced, no-nonsense Baptist teacher from Liverpool, while Sue and Katherine had both been secondary school teachers. I was the only teaching virgin, but they were all supportive.

The headmaster awaited us, impatiently slapping his hand with a leather belt. A hurricane had prevented the staff returning from other islands, so for a while the four of us would form the main teaching body. French classes found me in front of sixty children hanging on every word; in

England they would have been hanging from the windows
and doors. The island had been colonised alternately by the
French and the English about fourteen times, so with their
French patois to draw upon they took quickly to the subject. 'Ou fou' was 'you're crazy', and 'moi cai aller en ville là'
was 'I'm off to town'. Even more delightful was 'elle doudou
mweh' – 'she's my darling'.

Our students treated us with undeserved affection and
respect. Many of them, as so often in developing countries,
sacrificed much for their education. I once gently chastised
Céleste for not doing her homework:

'But it is difficult, sir'.

'Why? You've had two days to do it.'

'Well, not so much time really. I get up at five o'clock and
must bathe my mother and feed my sisters.'

I was mortified, especially when I learned that her mother
was bed-bound and that Céleste also fed the pigs and walked
three miles to school – and back.

The return of the missing teachers gave the staffroom a
buzz. Keith, from Grenada, was charming, but hostile to
the idea of foreign volunteers teaching in the islands. For
him, VSO was another form of colonialism. There was little
purpose in arguing that we were there to help, to atone;
reminders of slavery were in every face. Vestiges of more
recent dominion by whites, or by their proxies, were in the
fabric of island culture: the big estates, the prosperous families with part-white heritage, the exaggerated respect for us.

We wrestled endlessly with the conundrum of post-
colonial benevolence. We accepted that we were there for
our own good, but were keen not to be robbed of a sense
of purpose. The end of colonialism had left the islands to

shape their own future with scant resources. Our role, we felt, was to help as best we could, and, given the island's history, people were kind beyond measure. Nature, too, was generous: a bread fruit plucked casually from a tree could feed a family all day. We would reach for mangoes and guava as we wandered down the road, and a slight lean from our verandah yielded paw-paw for breakfast and the lime to squeeze onto it.

I was intrigued by the two other white men in Vieux Fort. Dirty Dick was from Essex, and ignored me. So did the other, also English, the owner of a fishing boat and a devout Christian. After a month I went up to Castries to buy an old whaling boat and then sailed it down the west coast, past the twin Pitons of Soufrière, a tourist beauty spot, round the corner of the island, along the southern beach and into the bay of Vieux Fort. As I pulled up to the wooden jetty, Dick stood alone, sun-dried and spare under a battered and filthy straw hat.

'Slip me the line, bor, and I'll tie you up.' Bor! I'd never heard that outside East Anglia. 'And come and have a rum.'

That was the beginning of an unusual friendship: young English school teacher and feral émigré. Dick had fled the depressed England of the fifties in search of sunshine and sex. Both were in rich supply here: the Americans had abandoned their local airbase, leaving behind their female acolytes in large numbers and without a role. Dick had them to himself and was a busy man. He had built a fishing boat and laid some lobster pots, then built a simple shack with just two rooms, one for a big bed and the other for his fishing kit. His life was divided into easy fishing in the morning and lazy fornicating in the afternoon. He was the happiest of men; returning to Essex just wasn't on the cards. I was, of course, fascinated by this free-roaming, exotic creature who had created such a simple and carefree life. He had greeted me on the jetty because I was a fellow sailor. Perhaps he thought I might help him out with his life's work.

My parents joined me for a few weeks and Dad met Dirty Dick, an unusual encounter: the free-wheeling fisherman-fornicator emerging from the sea in his underpants to meet the staid English country solicitor. One day Dad didn't return from the beach, where he had last been seen in deep conversation with Dick. My mother was worried. Would he be influenced? Would he stay here and abandon his solicitor's practice? The crisis passed, and I never asked Dad how close he had come to a major life change. Who knows? He may have regretted the missed opportunity for the rest of his quiet life in Suffolk.

Perhaps there is just a thin divide between fisherman and country solicitor. I once met a bronzed and healthy-looking solicitor at a party in Cornwall. I found it hard to believe that he could be a solicitor; they rarely see the sun. Then he revealed that he spent only two days as a lawyer; the other three were devoted to lobster fishing. He had, enviably, what we now call work-life balance.

I used to anchor my boat in the little bay below our house. The water was clear blue, the beach long and palm-fringed, the trees giving enough shade for lazing, and I would go there to recover from a day's teaching. One day I was caulking the upturned boat when two women sashayed along the beach and, removing most of their clothes, lay on the sand near by. I caulked more vigorously and pretended to be unaffected. They made the tooth-sucking noise – 'shtoops' – that St Lucians make to attract attention or show disapproval. I could hardly lie down on the beach with them, I thought. They giggled, squirming their magnificent bodies around on the sand as temptingly as sirens. Odysseus had his men, their ears blocked with wax, lash him to the mast so that he might hear the sirens' calls but avoid being drawn by them. I tried to imagine icebergs, being hit on the head with a hammer, finding myself in a coffin buried alive, or assaulted by angry ants. I felt for Odysseus.

I gathered later that the locals thought that I was gay, and I can't blame them.

The tantalisingly available sex on the island was a challenge. St Lucian women were, to me, provocative, attractive and easy-limbed. The slave trade had actively dismantled tribal groups and scattered them. The slave-owners had then encouraged intercourse between slaves from different tribes, further to break down traditional values and bonds and thus reduce the likelihood of rebellion. Loosening ties further, in the sixties, was mass unemployment on the island. Few men had permanent jobs. The women did most of the work, bringing up large families, running smallholdings. Once a week, on Thursdays, the Geest banana boat would put in below our house. It was the women who loaded it, giant stems of bananas on their heads and collecting the 'tally' from the 'tally man' (as in 'Come, Mr Tally Man, tally me banana' of the 'Banana Boat Song'). It was back-breaking work; I tried to join in one day and staggered helplessly under the weight of a stem.

Added to the palpable sexuality of the island was the fact

that my whiteness was an attraction. The girls in my classes were wide-eyed and delicious, but I was a school teacher and I intended to be a model of rectitude. I was also a model of steaming frustration. But my primness eventually cracked and I embarked on a relationship with tall, half-Indian Teresa, the waitress at the Cloud's Nest Hotel. The puritan parrot on my shoulder insisted on secrecy, so I would arrange to meet her at dead of night on the end of the jetty. I would row us across the bay to a beach, and we would settle down on my main-sail.

Twenty years later I was at the World Travel Market at Olympia in London, and spied the St Lucia stand. I recognised the man running it and he recognised me. Over the heads of the crowd he shouted:

'Man, is Alastair – nah?' It was Charles Augeeste, my neighbour in St Lucia. 'How you doin', man? And how Teresa?' I was stunned.

'How did you know about Teresa?'

'Man, whole village watchin' you.'

My nocturnal 'sailing' with Teresa didn't last long, so I had to fill my head with other activities – a boys' camp, for example, in the wilder north of the island.

I was determined to ensure a supply of food, so I took several uncomfortable lessons in how to slaughter and butcher a goat. The sacrificial beast was loaded into the boot of my car and we departed for the north, an advance party of boys having set off earlier. I hoped they had enough basic food to sustain them, yet we arrived to the unmistakable whiff of barbecued pork. The boys had captured a 'wild and dangerous boar', as they referred to it, slaughtering and butchering it with practised skill. 'Man, it wild!' The owner of that missing, now barbecued, domestic pig, which had carried a huge wooden triangle around its neck to stop it running far, haunted us with his suspicion-laden visits for days. The goat was, I hope, grateful; I hadn't the heart to kill it.

The local economy was dependent on fishing and bananas. Most fishermen would operate close inshore in long canoes with outboard engines. (The USA had given them engines as part of a post-war economic recovery programme, but the boats had not yet been reinforced to take the extra strain; most of those first engines carried the sterns away and were lost. Some of the boats, too.) My old whaling boat gave me natural contact with Jim, the one remaining whaler in the island, and my first thrilling but traumatic encounter with whaling.

For millennia, whales of many kinds had drifted through the islands, but few had survived the industrial slaughter of the late nineteenth century. In the twentieth century there had been hunting of sperm whales and humpbacks, and now only short-finned pilot whales survived in any numbers. Jim, his crew and their families could live off the meat of a pilot whale for weeks, and I joined them for an unforgettable day. We bobbed about on the ocean swell in the lug-rigged, open wooden boat, one man perched on the bow with his eyes peeled. St Vincent, another poor but beautiful small island, lay a few miles to the south, and the sun beat down upon a lazy blue sea. The boat's wallowing was tinged, however, with urgency, for another day without a whale would be tough on the fishermen and their families. Then the man on the bow shouted 'Dere she blows' and we set off in pursuit, the distant pod of whales arching away from us.

An hour passed before we were close enough to fire the first harpoon, a ramshackle apparatus of old twelve-bore shotgun, harpoon and rope. The harpoon wobbled towards the whales, the boat corking up and down as the whales dived and rose. Time and again we missed and would head into the wind to haul the rope back in, coiling it neatly back into the barrel amidships. While we coiled, the boat stationary in the wind, the whales would be swimming away – so the urgency was intoxicating.

In the late afternoon our harpoon finally hit a whale. A general exultation was followed by an urgent, disciplined routine: down came the sail, then the mast and all the rigging in a few quick moves. The sail was furled along the boom in a trice, the whole paraphernalia laid neatly along one side of the boat. The decks were now cleared for action, the crew lined up to haul on the harpoon line while I took the tiller. But we had to wait now, wait for the whale to tire itself as it pulled us through the water at speed. Now and again the skipper would yell 'Heave!' and the crew would pull in the line a few feet. Had this been a sperm whale there would have been the terror of the boat being pulled into the depths. We just had to wait, the primeval struggle between man and beast tipped inevitably in our favour.

As the whale tired we hauled ourselves closer, then close enough for a gaff to be plunged into its flank to draw it alongside. Blood reddened the sea around the boat, dramatising the exhaustion and death throes of the whale before it was lashed to the side of the boat and the head cut off. I don't know why it was cut off. I had to sit on it all the way home, an eye gazing up at me from between my legs, the fishermen grinning at my discomfort. Turning away from

the crimson sea and heading back for the island was a relief.
No more blood and struggle, just wind and boat and carcass.
It was a slow sail, now more sad than triumphant for me,
the evening drawing in as we drew up to the jetty and the
waiting womenfolk.

Memories of that day have haunted me ever since, and
energised my campaigning against whaling in the eighties.
Whale-watching is now popular in the islands and an alternative source of revenue for the fishermen. Em and I went
back to St Lucia in 2005 and found the harbour transformed:
huts for fishermen and their gear, an enclosed harbour and
concrete slipways. All had been financed by the Japanese,
for this enabled them to count on the island's votes on the
International Whaling Commission. The cynicism is sickening. This process continues, and explains the success of
the Japanese in getting away with their 'scientific' expeditions to hunt whales.

My own boat, decrepit as it was, gave me solace. An
hour at sea would lift me after a heavy day's teaching. The
sails could be repaired by a Vieux Fort seamstress using the
bags in which US Aid flour was sent to the island. One lazy
Sunday I sailed along the coast to see my friend Ravenscroft
for lunch. He was an old-fashioned Englishman who had
lived on the island for most of his life and was much loved
locally. He swam naked below the house in all weathers,
was generous to everybody and was determined to finish
his life in St Lucia with nothing material left other than an
empty house. He also kept a wine cellar stocked informally
by boats passing by from Martinique, the French island to
the north. Lunch was good, and I sailed away in the late
afternoon back towards Vieux Fort, feeling that life could

not get better than this. Then a resounding crack broke my reverie: the mast had snapped in two. I had to paddle, drift and swim back a couple of miles to where I had started. It was now dusk. I anchored, put my clothes in a bucket and swam ashore. The path to the house was steep and my underpants wet. I knocked, shivering slightly, at the door, holding my bucket. 'Hullo, old chap,' said my host, only slightly surprised to see me again so soon, 'you are in perfect time for dinner. I'll get you a tie. See you in ten minutes in the drawing room.'

I took my parents to lunch there; a French yacht was due to arrive from Martinique with some wine, and they dressed for the occasion. After a couple of weeks of simple living with me they were looking forward to it. The yacht was becalmed, but the wine finally arrived with the French crew, who had been so bored that they had drunk all but one bottle. I treasure the memory of the bronzed and unrepentant French skipper, in the tiniest of swimming trunks, chatting amiably to my father in his formal tropical suit.

What did we achieve as volunteer teachers in St Lucia? We taught well and hard, but perhaps we unwittingly conveyed too much of the seductive mother country image, encouraging the children to want what we had. None of us left feeling that we had made a difference, but we did learn humility, affection for the islanders, absolute rejection of racism, and to enjoy simplicity. Another pace of life was possible, and the lives of us all were irretrievably changed.

Kenny Anthony, one of my favourite students, became Prime Minister of Saint Lucia, and Em and I met him when we returned to the island for our thirtieth wedding

anniversary. I don't envy him his job, for the island has
struggled since the crash of 2008 and the banana industry
has been devastated. They still export some bananas, coconuts, vegetables, citrus, root crops and cocoa. There is a tiny
industrial sector that makes clothing, corrugated cardboard
boxes, assembles industrial components, processes lime and
presses coconuts. Tourism is the biggest sector and is fickle:
clients stay away on a whim, revenues flow abroad to the
foreign hotel corporations, and people abandon stable jobs
such as fishing and subsistence agriculture. Little is left in the
local economy. The finance sector has grown, but this rarely
benefits ordinary people. Globalisation is hard on small,
vulnerable and dependent communities like this.

The Caribbean seems a long way away now, though that
return for our wedding anniversary swept us back into our
old enthusiasms. But we are unlikely to go back; Europe,
closer and more richly textured, beckons more seductively.

4

Up the Orinoco

I sailed away from St Lucia in 1968 on an island trading schooner, across a clear, calm blue sea to St Vincent. Many years later I was offered a job skippering one of these schooners, and often wonder what would have become of me had I accepted. Perhaps I would have followed Dirty Dick's route to contentment.

I island-hopped my way down to Trinidad, through Bequia and the little Grenadines to Trinidad. Although carnival – a joyful riot of music, costumes, carousing and dance, shot through with sexual tension – was months away, the mood had already begun. I felt a frisson of excitement upon docking in the town's ramshackle harbour, with its chaos of masts and hulls, hubbub and people from many islands. I pressed through the crowded streets, inhaling the smell of rum, vegetables, fish, fruit, straw, wood, animals and people.

It was alive with jostling, bantering humanity, and I had the electric expectation of a young traveller. I found a place to stay with a kindly old lady, in her two-roomed shack up the hill from the centre. She treated me like a long-lost son, which suited me fine for I am drawn to older, motherly women. I couldn't stop her doing my washing – a touch embarrassing for a newly self-aware white man with others looking on – but the warmth of the community was palpable. All around us things were hotting up for carnival. Bands practised, dances were perfected and costumes submitted to feverish alterations. Carnival seemed to be just around the corner: if the islanders are not celebrating carnival, they are preparing for it; for the rest of the year they gossip about the previous carnival. In the days of slavery, carnival encouraged potentially rebellious subjects to let off steam. It now, perhaps, diverts them from protesting against other things, such as poverty and corruption.

While in Port of Spain I met, and swooned over, a tall and beautiful Indian girl called Shoba, who was from San Fernando in the south of the island. The Indians had made their way to the Caribbean as indentured labourers once slavery was abolished, and had flourished. Shoba's family was prosperous and protected by a zealous father, but undeterred (and even perhaps stimulated), I made my way south and dossed down in a sleazy hotel in town. At every turn I bumped into yet another woman; there were a lot of them. I then made the nervous first phone call to Shoba's dad. He questioned me politely and was glad to hear that I had been to Oxford. I had got off to a good start.

'And your father: what work does he do?'

'He is a lawyer.'

'Will you be a lawyer too?'

'Possibly.'

'Excellent. And where are you staying?'

'In the Hotel Capri.'

The line hummed with silent tension. There was a pause, then: 'You will not see my daughter and you are not to come to my house.' The phone was put down. Stunned, I managed to get a message through to Shoba to ring me, and she told me that I was staying in the town's brothel. Thus ended a promising courtship, or perhaps just a hopeful one. But then, I was supposed to be en route to stay with Em, with whom I had already begun a relationship and who was awaiting me in Guyana. What was I thinking of?

I left Trinidad in a battered old freighter, heading for Guyana. I perched on the bow, where I spent the whole trip trying to ward off seasickness and scanning the horizon for signs of South America. The low coast crept into view after a few days and we sailed into a river system to the south-east of Georgetown. I took a bus to the capital, a small town of wooden shacks, muddy streets and colonial buildings, and immediately liked it. Em lived with another teacher, and there I took root while I worked out how best to continue my South American journey.

Life in Georgetown was livelier than I expected, for Em had a lot of friends there, partly through her work as a schools' radio broadcaster and partly because she had immersed herself in the acting community. She was, and is, a gifted actress, and her Ophelia was a big hit in Georgetown. Clairmont Taitt, a well-established broadcaster, had been her Hamlet, so she mingled with the Guyanese glitterati, including the young Derek Walcott, who eventually won the Nobel Prize after writing his epic poem *Omeros*, set in a fishing community in St Lucia.

Em was busy and I needed a job, so in a town that was largely illiterate I became an encyclopedia salesman – an early sign of my perennial optimism. Pedalling around Georgetown with a bag of books to sell was fun but doomed to failure, so I wangled a role as interpreter at a conference on foot-and-mouth disease.

I sat behind the Guyanese agriculture minister as he welcomed the delegates from Venezuela, Colombia, Chile and Brazil. I stood to translate. Then my stomach turned as I stalled at the words 'foot-and-mouth disease'. Desperately, and hopefully, I ploughed on with '*la enfermedad boca y pata*', and when I sat down the amiable, and unforgettably kind, Chilean delegate leaned across and whispered, 'Don't worry, señor, I speak excellent English and can take over your role if you wish.'

This he did, yet the minister nevertheless invited me to tag along as they flew up to the Rupununi for a tour of the cattle ranches. Perhaps they felt that I needed a little help to recover from my humiliation.

Guyana is a vast and neglected country. As with St Vincent, I have rarely heard or read its name since I was there. It was first colonised by the Dutch, who drained the coastal swamps, as the Dutch do. Once the Dutch had done the digging the British soon took it over, followed by the French, then the Dutch again and finally the British – enough change to confuse anyone. The architectural legacy includes St George's Cathedral, made of local hardwood and the tallest wooden building on the continent, and fine wooden colonial houses, as well as parks and markets. But Georgetown is not on the route to anywhere.

The country, a little smaller than Britain, consists of a high-plateau hinterland and a narrow coastal strip, with a vast rainforest in between. It is a thin slice of British imperial ambition in a continent largely ruled by either the Portuguese or the Spanish. Alongside Guyana are two other anomalous slivers of Europe: Dutch Guiana (now independent Suriname) and Cayenne, still part of France and used for storing high-security prisoners and space rockets. Five European languages betray the vast reach of the slave trade in this long coast hugging the shoulder of South America: Portuguese in Brazil; French, Dutch, English and then Spanish in Venezuela.

Guyana is the anchor at the southern end of the string of islands that form the Caribbean. The culture is Caribbean, but one wonders why the British hung on in such a remote place. The answer, as usual, lies in raw and cultivated materials: bauxite and sugar. From bauxite is made aluminium, and so for decades it was one of the world's most valuable minerals. Sugar is no longer so important, but was for a long time the staple export. So Guyana was important – important enough for the CIA, fearful of communist influence, to care who was in charge. They made it impossible for the government of the left-wing Cheddi Jagan to remain in power. He threatened their bauxite interests, so the British intervened militarily.

The rainforest is huge: 450 miles deep towards Brazil and 270 miles from the eastern border with Suriname to the western border with Venezuela, with a few great rivers as the only highways. The Amerindian tribes have had long contact with outsiders, and one of Em's jobs was to putter on her VéloSoleX into the villages upriver from Georgetown and run drama and English workshops for teachers in the more remote areas.

Once back from the five thousand square miles of grassland and cattle ranching that is the Rupununi, I spent more time with Em in Georgetown, exploring on her VéloSoleX. This loveable machine was a bicycle with an engine perched over the front wheel, and attached to a lever. To go, one lowered the lever, lowering the engine and its moving roller on to the tyre. The latter had no choice but to rotate too. It was noisy, fun and reliable, a feature of French life for decades after the war.

I was keen to move on to Venezuela, but the two countries were in one of their states of war. Venezuela claims much of Guyana, and occasionally slings some chains across the rivers and bars flights between the two countries. I chose to cross the frontier on the Orinoco River by canoe, after a journey through the network of rivers called the Amazonas in the north-west of Guyana.

Getting to the north-west involved taking a ferry along the coast to a river-estuary village called Morawhanna. At the river's edge I found a canoe to take me along the river creeks to the estuary of the Orinoco and thence into Venezuela. It was long, perhaps thirty feet, its sides built up to create space for carrying sacks of sugar, flour and rice, as well as tinned goods. The skipper and his wife were the crew; I was by now travelling with a young Colombian, Juan, so we were four – a bit of a squeeze.

For a long day we chugged through the jungle, a monotonous curtain of green unrelieved by wildlife. Modern tales of river exploration are often populated by birdlife, alligators, snakes and assorted jungle creatures, but ours had all fled by the time we arrived, alerted by our engine.

The skipper chose to drop us off at a tiny, isolated jetty. He had changed his mind about his route, but reassured us that another boat would soon be along. Juan and I sat on the jetty watching the canoe disappear up a creek, our aloneness slowly dawning on us. There were no other boats, just a deep jungle silence and then the sounds of wildlife taking up their chatter again. We spent a fitful night in a hut by the jetty. I am a bad sleeper, and the jungle noises were alarming. I pictured black panthers stalking me, giant spiders crawling into my sleeping bag, piranha fish stripping the flesh from my bones.

A boat appeared early in the morning, to our relief, though it was another canoe stacked with cargo and perilously low in the water. Our extra weight didn't help, but we were keen to get away. For another long day we chugged up the creek, twenty or thirty metres wide. I read *The Penkovsky Papers* from cover to cover, throwing each page away as I finished it; the Venezuelans, under the fiercely conservative government of the time, would take offence at any 'communist' Russian name. As the day grew hot we emerged from our narrow river system into the Orinoco delta.

At its mouth, much of the Orinoco flows into hundreds of rivers and waterways that meander through sixteen thousand square miles of swampy forests. In the rainy season it can swell to fifteen miles wide. To us in our tiny, low-slung craft it seemed like an ocean, but we ploughed on, heading for the invisible far side. Clouds were gathering, the sky darkened and the waters began to heave. Waves grew and came towards us, lapping at the edge of the boat and then slipping over the edge into the canoe itself. Our skipper was paralysed with fear. The waves grew higher but still he did nothing. His wife was even more terrified. Juan, bailing frantically, lost the one bailer overboard. We resorted to using our shoes to bail out the boat as the skipper got to his knees to pray. His prayers went unanswered and the bailing grew more frenzied. We were now bailing for our lives. I found a plastic pot that was bigger than a shoe and it made a difference. Praying was perhaps the only other option, as we couldn't risk turning around in those waves, though we did wish the skipper would take off his own shoes and help.

The prayers now grew desperate. '*Dios, mio, que está en cielo, que venga ayudarnos en nuestro pequeño barco. El rio está furioso. Ayúdenos!*'

I was *furioso* too, but relaxed a little as the river inexplicably grew calm – clearly a response to the prayers. As darkness fell we slipped gratefully into a tiny mangrove creek on the Venezuelan side of the Orinoco delta. The roots of the mangroves stood darkly about us as, wet and cold now, we settled down to a fitful sleep on the sacks of cargo. Sleep was broken by what sounded like hands slapping the water, closer and closer. Then they were gone. Sleep – and back they came, time and time again, in fearsome numbers. My head spun around the possible explanations, all of them frightening. I found a torch and cautiously spread the light over the water to reveal dozens of salmon-sized fish, their mouths agape, careening around the creek in search of food. Next morning the skipper explained that this was normal.

All next day we motored up the Orinoco, with me tearing pages out of my book and casting wary glances at the waves. The canoe felt less like a boat now than a doomed collection of sodden sacks. We made it to a port where I gratefully stepped ashore, avoiding the border guards who would send me back to Guyana.

So began an illegal stay in Venezuela. Leaving, without an entry stamp, was as difficult as entering, for the Immigration bureaucrats told me that I couldn't leave because I had not entered, an irresistible logic. The solution was, of course, a very traditional and even more logical one: a brown envelope stuffed with dollars.

After six months of travel through Brazil and Uruguay to Argentina, I returned to England in 1969 – and needed a plan. I still wanted to justify myself to my parents – and to myself – and a career in teaching felt like a wise response to what I had learned in St Lucia and on my travels.

My father found me a job at Framlingham College in Suffolk, and for a term I taught French while living at home and getting to know my parents better. My mother, in her fifties and as energetic and imaginative as ever, was still the engine of the family and my father remained even-tempered and sweet-natured. No wonder his housemaster had written in such glowing terms when he left school: 'I wish I could have kept him for ever as my head monitor, as it will be years before I have another to equal him and with such tact. He has the great gift of getting the very best out of others. The smaller boys always accepted his decisions as right and final, for they felt that he weighed their points of views and decided with absolute fairness.' I am touched by that report, for it is the father I knew. He was never unkind or harsh to us children.

In December 1969 I was summoned from class to see the headmaster, and there was a policeman with him. 'I have very sad news for you, Mr Sawday. Your father was found dead at the wheel of his parked car in Ipswich this morning. We would be grateful if you would come along with us to identify the body.' I was stunned. Only the evening before we had driven down from London together and had had our first open and intimate discussion, during which he had confessed that he was tired from a weak heart, in pain from arthritis and unable to enjoy walking any more. That meant that he couldn't play the golf he loved, or do anything active. 'I am so much older than your mother. I would like to leave her time to find another husband and enjoy the rest of her life. She is full of life and energy, and I am not. I am ready to go.' He was sixty-six.

That was typical of him, yet it meant that somehow he had never found enough to sustain him in those difficult later years. But I am convinced that he died a happy man. The police led me to a cold room at the police station in Ipswich and there my father lay, dignified and elegant even when drained of life. I was numb with grief, severed from a life-affirming force, angry with fate for taking him from us just as he was beginning to talk with me. The word father is heavy with expectation. Hamlet's agony over his father's death rang true: 'That it should come to this . . . so excellent a king'. So much of England's ordinary virtue in one man, but my grief was tempered by that talk the evening before.

After two years of a widowhood that was intolerable to her, my mother married a lovely man called George Sinclair and had thirty years of happiness with him. George had been a colonial officer, for many years an administrator in Ghana and a friend of Kwame Nkrumah. George had jailed Nkrumah, the revolutionary independence leader, in the fifties, but when Nkrumah became president of an independent Ghana he asked George to stay on to help, which says something about George's gift for relationships. Later he was on the Elliot Commission, which laid the foundations for the first three universities in West Africa. His next job was as Deputy Governor in Cyprus during the Cyprus Emergency, EOKA's battle for independence and political union with Greece. It is a forgotten war now, but some researchers claim that more British soldiers lost their lives in Cyprus than were killed in the Iraq War. After leaving the Colonial Service, George became a Tory MP in the safe seat of Dorking, a matter of initial embarrassment to my *Guardian*-reading family when he later married my mother. But we learned to respect him for his liberal views, not least on race relations and abortion reform. He chaired both the Family Planning Association and the Intermediate Technology Development Group, being a close friend and admirer of Fritz Schumacher. He despised Enoch Powell, was embarrassed by Margaret Thatcher and loathed the right wing of his own party, but he bit the Tory bullet when he had to. We agreed, at my mother's wise request, never to discuss nuclear power – for this was the time of the Sizewell B Nuclear Inquiry and I felt strongly about it. George followed the party line, not, I thought, without a touch of coyness. He was very much a Tory wet, along with his friends Jim Prior and John Hill. The speaker once branded him 'not only wet but bloody soaking'. He must have turned in his grave during the Brexit campaign.

In January 1971 I took a teaching job in the London borough of Brent and signed up for a correspondence course in education. Studying while working was fascinating, as the teaching was tough and I needed a wider context. As tradition has it in schools, I was thrown into the boxing ring as a novice without gloves and without a clue.

I taught Spanish to about forty boys in the bottom class. In moments of immodesty I claim to have taught two words, *holá* and *holé*, by setting up mock bullfights in the classroom. The headmaster came upon us during a bullfight and was unconvinced by my 'direct' teaching technique, let alone by my skill as matador. The children were more interested in 'bashing Pakis' during the lunch break, which they did after going home to put on their steel-capped boots.

My departure was a relief, as I was making no progress and the school was a shambles. I witnessed a visiting Catholic priest set a classroom up for Mass and then watched as the boys vanished through the broken door one by one until there were none left, the priest still intoning. Nevertheless, the school was still considered to be 'functioning', which bemused me as little seemed to be taught or learned. All political parties in the UK have wrestled helplessly with education, with none, apparently, keen to learn from experience elsewhere, as in Germany where technical education is respected and educational access is more equitable. Ironically, that system was set up after the war by Robert Birley, who later became Head Master of Eton.

My plan had been to go to Spain and live with the gypsies in Granada to learn flamenco guitar: total immersion. But my father's death intervened and I took a teaching job at Charterhouse, my old school. I had two good years there, but I was unsuited to such a sheltered existence. Asked to be a house tutor, I knew that I would be donning golden handcuffs. I might prosper but I wouldn't progress – and too many boys were bent on becoming rich. The school couldn't but reflect family ambitions.

One small success for me as a teacher emphasised the flaws in the exam system. Given the least gifted class to put through French O level, I analysed the way exams were marked and discovered that one could pass simply by failing to make mistakes. A lack of substance and style would only mean failure to get high marks. So I drilled the class for months to write faultlessly, if drearily and repetitively, about any subject. They all passed, and few of them knew much French. What spare time I had with them I devoted to the singing of French folk songs.

Some of the brightest boys I taught went on to become merchant bankers. Would the world be a better place if such talented people did different work, and if the vast sums spent on private education were invested more widely and wisely in the community?

I abandoned my teaching career after just three years, but I missed the extraordinary energy of a classroom of children, however little I missed teaching the French imperfect subjunctive.

5

The Joy of Rubbish

'Bloody fools! Not a damned one of them has a clue about Afghanistan. If they did, they'd not go to war with them. Nobody wins.'

Thus expostulated Uncle John, Em's extraordinary uncle, when he heard that the British and Americans were invading Afghanistan. He loved the country, having been on the North-West Frontier during the war, and considered our leaders criminally ignorant. Had I known about Uncle John before marrying Em I would have brushed up on my history, my Latin – and much else.

My return to England after two years away in St Lucia, Guyana and South America, was a happier one for still having Em as a friend and confidante. She was always there for me, even when I was in a new relationship. Our own relationship had drifted to a close after Guyana, but there was something magnetic about her that I couldn't let go of. She came to stay in Suffolk, met my family and my friends and was a central part of my life for the six years before we married, moving in to share a house in London. Although we are as different as lime pickle and coconut, we share values, sympathies and much else – and our VSO background is a strong bond. She is one of the funniest people I know, but hides that bright light under a bushel. She should have been an actress, but there wasn't enough money to take her to drama school. So she poured her talents into teaching, and our marriage obstructed a promising path to head-teachership.

I went to observe her classes at a Shepherd's Bush primary school, and was entranced by her radiant energy and ease with children – and by her voice. She arranged her own local version of the Notting Hill carnival and put on *Joseph and His Amazing Technicolor Dreamcoat* with her children, encouraging ad-lib performances. These two moments remain my all-time theatrical favourites:

Joseph is despatched to the fields by his dad, to pick potatoes.

''ere, Dad, I don wanna pick no bloody spuds.'

'Get in the field now before I give you a clip round the ear.'

He travels to Egypt and finally arrives at the Pharaoh's palace, hungry and exhausted, but triumphant. His passage is blocked by a ferocious-looking guard.

'Oo are yoo?'

'I'm Joseph and I'm knackered from crossing the desert. I wanna see the Pharaoh.'

'Well push off! Only 'gyptians allowed in 'ere.'

Em's own performance in Bristol as Shen Te in *The Good Woman of Setzuan* was chillingly good. It is easy to see why men have so often fallen helplessly for actresses.

Marriage came in 1975, in the Norman church of St Bartholomew the Great in Smithfield, next to the hospital where, during the Blitz, Em's father had been a doctor and her mother a nurse. Her cousin Chris married us, our friend Painton played the organ, the children of Em's primary school played the recorders as we entered, and Stelios, a friend from the LSO, played from Dvořák's Violin Concerto. It was a joyous occasion, and I can see the smile on the face of Em's mother. Afterwards we were chauffeured by Painton in our old Fiat 124 to our little house in Islington to celebrate with quiche, cake and bubbly.

Em's mother had long ago been abandoned by her GP husband for the practice nurse. It was ineffably sad. The family – Em, her brother and their mother – then lived in genteel poverty before moving in with her mother's cousin, a vicar in a poor Midlands parish. After some contented years there they had to leave again and Em's mother settled as matron at a girls' boarding school in Dorset, which Em attended. When I met Em, her mother was wheelchair-bound from a stroke.

So our wedding was a source of great happiness, and Em was given away by her irascible Uncle John, a classics teacher at the grammar school in Redruth. He was an old-fashioned pedant, once attacking me for using the word fabulous to describe a mere cake. 'More bloody misuse of language!' Nowadays, of course, everything is fabulous or fantastic, and we are excited or passionate about small things, especially if we are in PR. He was, perhaps, right. I avoided further rows by deferring to his scholarship, which was considerable; just before his death he was reading the Venerable Bede in Latin. Every book in his library was annotated with comments like 'ridiculous', or 'Pliny would disagree'. He dragged the teenage Em and her brother on an Alpine holiday, not to enjoy hiking or mountain-flower spotting but to research his theory about Hannibal's route across the Alps. He died at ninety-six, still regularly cooking chicken for his solitary Sunday lunch, for which he wore a jacket and tie, and then eking the chicken out for a week, washing his clothes by hand on Mondays and wringing them in a mangle, darning his sofa and not lighting his log fire until three o'clock in the winter, even if his hands were blue with cold. His carbon footprint was close to zero, and in a saner world we would consider him an eco-hero. His passionate teaching of Latin at the grammar school propelled many talented Redruth boys, to their astonishment, to Cambridge.

Just before our marriage Em and I had a holiday in Crete. In the river gorge of Samariá, naked upon a hot rock and with a picnic, we made the decision to live in Bristol, away from London's urban grind. Bliss was achievable, it seemed, as we dangled our feet in the cool river water. So upon our return home we bought, for a song, a huge derelict Georgian house in an elegant crescent in Clifton. With ruin on both sides of us, we set about the long task of restoring it.

The house was encrusted with pigeon shit and riddled with dry rot so we moved into the attic while we destroyed the floors below. Em would come at weekends from teaching in London. We had mattresses, a two-bar electric fire that served as a cooker, and a bath served by a hosepipe snaking up from the basement. An immersion heater balanced precariously, perilously, on a plank at the end of the bath. Our bedroom had an open fire, so we kept warm by burning the wooden partitions ripped from the house below us. Our sitting area was, for a time, the scaffolding platform outside the window. A Health and Safety expert would faint at the mere thought of it all. My amateur workforce consisted of Roger, a Bristolian VSO I had met in Papua New Guinea; Painton, my childhood friend, musician and Renaissance man; and Vernon, an east-coast bargee who did horoscopes. (For me he predicted the writing of practical guides.)

There was an orgy of destruction. Out came two hundred and fifty tons of dry rot-contaminated plaster and timber, about seventy-five ceiling joists were cut back and restored with sliced railway sleepers, and concrete was poured to make forty lintels. Our ignorance of building construction was energising but boundless, to the extent that an architect neighbour wrote begging us to replace the bricks in the walls lest the house collapse and carry others with it. In the meantime I pursued my villainous neighbour for dampening our house, and thus feeding the dry rot, via his blocked gutter. He met my request with such hostility that I took him to the High Court myself, winning a Pyrrhic but satisfying victory. He later went to prison for further villainy, and I learned that life is too short for amateur legal work. Em must have been gritting her teeth to see me yet again embarked on a mad project, but supported me throughout the case.

She escaped the worst of the chaos, however, by going to Durham University to do an MA in Drama in Education, and I followed her every other week to a rented cottage in the hamlet of Garrigill, high in the Pennines. It was bitterly cold and we were trapped on the wrong side of the hills when the snow fell. While Em studied, I made rose-hip jam and played the guitar on Sundays for the Slaggyford Women's Institute. We then abandoned Garrigill to squat, with permission, in an empty house in Durham. Em could be snow-free and attend lectures, while I scoured skips for material to furnish the house.

Durham's mighty cathedral was a brief stroll away: one of the great structures of Europe and built in just forty years, only two years longer than it took to build the equally remarkable Salisbury Cathedral. It remains one of my favourite buildings, perfect in its Norman harmony and largely unaltered. The monks' dormitory, now a library, has a timber roof to compare with that of any tithe barn.

We both wanted children and imagined that Em could complete her masters while in the early months of pregnancy. This plan went badly wrong when, having just announced to the family that she was pregnant, Em had a miscarriage at fourteen weeks. It was a huge loss.

Even more devastating was the loss the following year of our baby daughter, born prematurely at twenty-eight weeks. Despite the nurses' efforts to halt labour throughout twenty-four hours of contractions, the early birth became inevitable. The final moments of labour were chaotic; the baby was in the breech position and her feet were delivered. A paediatrician was urgently sent for and Abigail was born by forceps delivery. We had a brief glimpse of our tiny, dark-haired daughter before she was whisked away to intensive care. That delay in her birth, and her prematurity, caused brain damage which we were told was 'catastrophic', and she died two days later. We visited her twice and touched her tiny feet, but we never held her. Abigail's brief stay in our lives was a powerful experience; she has never entirely gone. In the distress of her loss we failed to ensure a proper celebration and burial, and have never been able to visit a place that is specially hers.

Toby, born in 1979, also gave Em a frightening pregnancy, but he was a May baby so she could at least lie in the spring sun like a beached dolphin. We nearly lost him, so his safe emergence was a small miracle. Rowan's birth, in 1982, was another miracle, for we were frightened of losing him too.

Back in Bristol I did a little supply teaching and helped Friends of the Earth (FOE), which functioned with a bizarre mixture of shambles and committed intelligence. They knew a great deal about the environmental issues they were tackling – whaling, resource conservation, nuclear power, recycling – but were not gifted organisationally. So, knowing little but keen to contribute, I created a recycling system for waste paper.

I printed leaflets and, with help from some children, spread them around north Bristol. Then I hired a van two days a week to collect the resulting bundles of waste newspapers and drive them, up to two and a half tons at a time, to the paper merchant, a kind Quaker called Nick. By now the house was finished and I was full-time with FOE, so the money I earned from paper sales kept me going – modestly. The vehicles I hired became bigger and bigger, the price of paper went up and I paid myself twenty-nine pounds per week. I learned to value the orderliness of those who lived neatly and wrapped their paper carefully in string.

I was now a bona fide rubbish collector, the pride, of course, of my mother's eye when she contemplated the money spent on my education. 'What is Alastair doing, Mollie? Is it the law? Or the diplomatic?' 'No, not exactly. You see, he's doing something with paper in Bristol.' Less robust mothers might have gone into therapy. She came out with me one day in the rain to collect paper, and later described it as one of the darkest days of her life.

Back in the late seventies, we in FOE were considered to be either quaint or barmy – or both. Why on earth should we recycle, save whales, conserve resources and wildlife, and promote biodiversity and green energy? Wasn't the country getting merrily richer and able to find technical solutions to any problem we created? The economy, surely, was more important than animals or forests thousands of miles away. FOE was, however, thinking strategically and now stands vindicated. The general thrust of the environmental movement has, I would argue, been focused correctly throughout its history. I offer one small example among many: for years, led by the organic movement's Richard Young, excessive antibiotic use in farm animals has been flagged up. Now there is a crisis, with the resulting rise of the MRSA super-bug in hospitals. Another example would be the long campaign against the fossil-fuel industries, now finally acknowledged as the deadliest of the contributors to climate change.

As long ago as 1969, Bishop Hugh Montefiore wrote an impassioned book, *The Question Mark*, about the environmental crisis and Christianity's potential role in tackling it.

His warnings have gone unheeded. If, for fifty years, we
have achieved so little, we now need a touch of urgency
over the next fifty.

Meanwhile in Bristol I had, with my board, created
Avon FOE as an umbrella group. It was booming, with
several new FOE groups, three ex-council lorries, more
than one hundred employees funded by the Manpower
Service Commission, and me as chairman and manager on
seven thousand pounds a year. We employed two full-time
campaigners, published the *Western Environmental Bulletin*,
founded and ran the Children's Scrapstore before it separated under the gifted Simon Hooton, ran a horse-and-cart
paper collection service, set up the Avon Conservation of
Resources Network, and established a glass recycling system
in Bristol – raising ten thousand pounds for Oxfam. Helpful
council employees would let us know when an empty building could be used to stable the horse. I loved the energy,
freedom and sheer momentum of it all. I enjoyed, too, the
pioneering, cash-strapped scruffiness. Our first offices were
in the Methodist Central Hall, a vast and forgotten building
that we shared with assorted charities, one of which, the
Cyrenians, had unpredictable 'clients'. One day I left some
suspended files unattended in the hall and one of them seized
the unusual opportunity to relieve himself on them. I chased
him down the street and made him clean up, but the deed
was done and the papers sodden.

Interviews for the cart-driver role were colourful. We
considered an elderly Pole who had managed horses on
a farm before the war and another who used horses to
shunt goods wagons behind Bristol station for the Midland
Railway Company. The man who finally got the job had

an invincible advantage: he came with his own horse and cart. The project was popular with Bristolians and modestly successful, with people queuing up to help in the stables; but it collapsed when we had to sack the driver and the female replacement ran away with her supervisor – and the horse.

At the same time I found the energy, thanks to Em's support, to try other projects. One of them was a social enterprise called Green Initiatives, running seminars on the ethics of money. I would also give talks in schools and clubs and on the radio, and when asked 'What can I do?' I would suggest that making money work ethically for you should be a top priority. Even a small sum in a bank can do harm on your behalf.

In 1984 I resigned, to Em's relief; she had had her fill of jumble sales, impecuniousness, bizarre characters and my kinetic energy. I owe her a lifetime of devotion for putting up with it. I don't remember her ever complaining, and she found time to train as a marriage guidance counsellor. Counselling has been her main work since then.

Joining the Green Party came naturally. No other party was interested in the environment, an issue which in my view trumps all others. I stood for my ward in the local elections and then for Avon County Council, both glorious failures. Further failure followed as Parliamentary candidate for Bristol West in 1992. At a disciplined church hustings, with just ninety seconds to deliver our main speech, I enjoyed William Waldegrave's humiliation as he was silenced before finishing his introductory waffle. But he provided amiable, and invincible, opposition.

At no stage was I hopeful, but the planet needed a voice. Em came to see me during the council election count, and found me ashen-faced in a corner. 'What's wrong?' The Green voting papers, lined up on the table, had at one point crept ahead of the rest and I had retired to deal with my alarm. 'I think I may be winning!'

Another disappointment was an organic food box-scheme. Given money for the purpose, we hired Eric Booth to work with a primary school in Clifton to promote and then deliver organic food. It was a grand idea, with parents popping their paper orders into a wooden turnip one day and collecting their boxes later. But we were ahead of our time. Organic food was still 'different', a curious thing when only recently all food was organic. Happily, the Soil Association inherited Eric and the scheme, and it eventually became their successful Local Food campaign.

Soon after the millennium, long after my time with FOE, the leader of Bristol Council set up Bristol's Green Capital Momentum Group, with me as chair. One day she gave me a handsome book about Bordeaux and I offered to publish something similar about Bristol. The project grew to become two books: a fat, glossy one about Bristol, and another smaller one – a practical guide to green and ethical living in the city. I pulled together a small team led by Emily Stokes, a green activist, to do the work. The *Good Bristol Guide* sold out and the *Bristol – Inspiring Change* coffee-table book went on to be a sales tool for Bristol politicians promoting the city in Europe.

A council director worked closely with the group: 'Come on Alastair, we need more vigorous kicking from you so I have an excuse to get things done.' So we co-authored with the council a report on peak oil, which inspired a commitment to a 20 per cent reduction in the city's carbon emissions by the year 2020. (That target has since been tightened.) The Momentum Group had little money but we were able to encourage projects that just needed some blessing to get going, such as Bristol's Green Open Doors project, which is now a city-wide success. These were heady days and, after I left, the group went on, with the council, to win the European Green Capital Award.

6

A Simple Story

I t all began on a whim.

At the Hay Festival in 2014 I was introduced as a man with a 'remarkable talent for trend-spotting and market research'. I squirmed in my spotlit seat, for the truth was rather different. I hadn't a clue about trend-spotting or market research. So the story of our first book, *French Bed & Breakfast*, is an encouraging one for other risk-takers.

I set up my own European travel company, Alastair Sawday's Tours, in 1983 – ten years before we began publishing – and needed a bilingual secretary. Annie Shillito was the best recruitment decision of my life, a radiant, energetic, amusing and lovely woman of twenty-eight, just back from living in France. We would work together for twenty-seven years. I loved her from the beginning, and she, in her turn, loved me, Em and the children, knowing Toby and Rowan from their toddling years. Although I will mention her only rarely, she was a key figure throughout, and before, my publishing years.

Annie and I began with a portable typewriter, a single phone and a desk on a mezzanine platform reached by ladder from the kitchen. Twelve Americans bravely signed up for our first minibus tour in the UK. Our next tour was in France. From the Lot we swept down via Cordes and Albi, through Toulouse to the Pyrenees and Montségur and its old Cathar castle. We plucked figs as we lay beneath the trees drinking wine, picnicking and collecting blackberries for breakfast. I learned about the Cathars, whose beliefs – in the duality of good and evil, the equality of women, the corruption of the medieval Catholic Church, and the requirement of simplicity – appealed to the reformist in me. They were a foretaste of the Puritans, with their rejection of wealth and their suspicion of centralised power. The Cathars even educated both female and male children. Some of their beliefs were less advanced, but the Catholic church saw them as a threat and mounted a crusade to finish them off, and did so – the last resistance being at the mountain-top castle of Montségur in 1244. About two hundred of the survivors walked, with dignity, down the mountain and, refusing to renounce their faith, voluntarily mounted the funeral pyre. It is a moving story and vests the Cathars' castles with a tragic nobility.

Exploring France with small groups of travellers was a charming way of earning a living, and I usually grew to love them. One, Alberta, in her late eighties and unusually liberal-minded, became a favourite. She had a neatly wrinkled, pert face, grey bun and twinkling eyes, and when asked how she was would reply 'I'm just perking along', an expression that endeared her to me. Then she broke her leg, a heart-breaking accident for an old lady on a long-awaited European holiday. She tearfully made arrangements to leave us and fly home early, but I couldn't bear to lose her so insisted she stay and allow me to look after her. So tiny was she that even with her plaster cast I could carry her up stairs, even onto the ramparts of the Château de Langeais. We became devoted friends and she lived to one hundred and two, perking along to the last.

Annie and I created tours in Burgundy, the Luberon, the Dordogne, Normandy and the Pyrenees, all of them based around family and friends. The focus was on interesting people, beautiful buildings and real experiences. We would picnic in fields, attend concerts in old chapels, explore churches and *la France profonde*. I grew to love those great Normandy stone farmhouses that stand enclosed behind courtyard walls, doves cooing in the ancient dovecotes. We were always received with kindness and with feasts of embarrassing generosity. Our older American travellers would be startled to be offered a cheese course before dessert: 'Jeez – how do they fit it all in and still look slim?' I still don't know the answer.

As time wore on we specialised in cycling and walking as the most environmentally benign ways to explore. Our richer American walking clients would, I felt, have been happier in sedan chairs. When they complained of having to look at their feet while walking through the Luberon ('There were goddam roots across the path') it was because their local shopping mall, where they did most of their walking, lacked roots. We kept them firmly away from the beleaguered writer Peter Mayle, in spite of repeated requests that we lay siege to his house.

Our first cycle tour was with half a dozen Americans, who I knew would be as keen as mustard. I hired bikes, attached them to a rack on the minibus and set off for the rendezvous. I arrived early, checked that all the kit was ready, checked the routes and all arrangements, briefed the crew and then went to retrieve the bikes. They had disappeared, all of them. Vanished. I raced back to the shop and hired six more, getting back in the nick of time. None of my cyclists ever knew of the calamity, but I watched the second set of bikes very warily.

My sister Dinx once came with me as the minibus driver for a group of clients so wealthy that each could have paid cash for every one of the hotels we stayed in. Dismayed by the conversational tone, she ate alone rather than with us at the fabulous Villa d'Este on Lake Como. I rather wanted to join her. This super-rich group was a one-off, and I learned that they, and others like them, live in fear of being kidnapped. Do kidnappers have any idea what they are letting themselves in for? Luckily, most of our clients were ordinary people with ordinary expectations. The very wealthy must find it hard to get excited about anything normal.

Most travellers feel occasionally lonely or out of place. There is a frisson of excitement at a warm connection with a waiter or a guide, a taxi driver or a shop-keeper. We all have sensitive antennae for these things. So to be invited into someone's home or to chat with a friendly local can add vital spice to a holiday. Our model was to use trusted friends who lived locally and would make such encounters a part of every day; so we visited farms, lunched with a bee-keeper, dug carrots, dined in old farmhouses. Concerts were arranged, cooking demonstrations and boat trips organised, doors opened and friendships made.

After ten years of this, an old friend asked me for a job. I admired her, and my instinct was to give her a try. Puzzling over what to give her, I spotted my file of unusual French places on my desk. 'What if ... ?' and the deal was done. Jane Ryder was off, clutching a map of France under her arm and, no doubt, holding her breath for she had no experience of writing or publishing. She didn't even speak French. However, she was the sort of person who might have been parachuted into enemy country as an agent during the war – a coper.

Jane, with Rob, the designer, came up with a plan: my name on the cover, lots of white in the design, a fee and a photo for each place, and some amusing symbols. Thus it began. My family and friends, mother, stepfather, aunts and cousins spread out across France to find the places that were keen to have guests and also had something special about them. We asked the owners to send their own photos.

Halfway through the project, progress seemed to slow. Jane had disappeared to Rome to make a film. An unemployed solicitor called Kryshia took over and our neighbour, Verdine, took on the admin. It now became a race against time and I would nip out of the house late at night to check that Verdine was still burning the midnight oil. A local printing company told me how to arrange a book and in what shape to deliver it. Roger Lascelles, a publisher, volunteered to distribute the finished copies. I had worn a rugged Eddie Bauer rucksack to my first meeting with him and he took a shine to it. He was, luckily for me, 'into Eddie Bauer'.

I also took advice from the legendary Richard Binns,

author of the *French Leave* series. He had been a tireless campaigner against hotel and restaurant chains, junk food and the plastic culture of the day. I went to lunch in his Cotswold house and asked him,

'Am I mad to think of publishing a book?'

'Don't be silly. If you have ever had an invitation printed, you know how to publish.'

Our timing was unexpectedly impeccable. This first book arrived when travellers were tired of being told what to do, where to do it and what to think. 'Every Englishman abroad carries a Murray for information, and a Byron for sentiment,' wrote William Wetmore Story, an American in Rome in the late nineteenth century, 'and finds out by them what he is to know and feel by every step.' Travel guides by Fodor, Frommer, the AA and others also seemed to encourage crowds to follow in each other's footsteps.

People are the key to good travel, in my view. You can wind up in a God-forsaken place and love it if the people are right. We have all experienced this. Our publishing success, I thought, would depend on connecting people properly. Once made, the connection would take off in unexpected directions, uncovering layers of texture, colour and meaning.

The making of the first book was a mix of confusion, hilarity, panic and teamwork. Photos rolled in, descriptions were written and the big wall-map of France slowly filled with black dots, each representing a Special Place. Rob, tackling the print-ready version of the maps, shooed his family out of the house for the evening, took a large swig of whisky and set about cutting them into the right sizes with a scalpel on his kitchen table. He then stuck on the hundreds of little black dots. He barely wobbled.

This first 'birth' is a beautiful moment for a publisher. To our delight, the books flew off the shelves. What had we got so right? Was it timing? Perhaps it was because we avoided travel agent-speak; take a travel agent's brochure to bed with you if you don't know what I mean. Perhaps our success was simply in introducing readers to good French people and their homes. We did, of course, set out to be different. Inside, a light touch was maintained with a list of useful phrases in French, such as:

- *Est-ce que les poules dorment toujours dans cette chambre?*
- *Notre robinet fuit.* ('Our tap is dripping.' Common in those days.)
- *Pourrais-je mettre ces restes du piquenique dans votre frigidaire?*

The introduction continued the tone: 'If you have ever woken under a plump eiderdown duvet to the lowing of Charolais cattle beneath your window and the unmistakable whiff of French coffee, you will know why I wanted to publish this book. On my last stay in France I tumbled down the creaking wooden staircase into the kitchen to find a great table sagging beneath jars of home-made jam and loaves of fresh bread. Grandpère sat in the corner nursing a bowl of coffee, beret tilted back from a bemused face, while his daughter fussed about serving coffee and greetings. A pair of ducks wandered in and helped themselves to breakfast from the floor.'

One of our early entries concerned the unusual Blitte family: 'Monsieur et Madame Blitte, in the village of Odeur-sur-Pestilence, have a goat-house. The goats provide

the atmosphere of this memorable house. Their gentle mas-
tications lull you to sleep and you awake to the hissing as
the morning milk hits the pail. Breakfast of goats' milk is
something to ruminate upon. As you leave you are helped
on your way by these gentle creatures. Don't arrive unan-
nounced; your hostess needs time to remove evidence of the
previous occupants.'

The book had several such spoofs, which soon became
a tradition. They make no logical sense: a waste of space,
confusing to some, taking up precious editorial time. But
we enjoy writing them, they fill a vacant space, and they
help to sell our books into shops. The fun should never be
driven out by the balance sheet.

For another spoof, a photo of a tiny brick outhouse was
accompanied by the following text: 'It is known as "le petit
coin" but that is to demean a building capable of so much
more. There is sitting room only, but it is deeply functional,
a place where you can off-load the burdens of your day. A
place to meditate, to rue your failures and celebrate your
successes. The mood is heavily influenced by the ebb and
flow of generations of people bent on the same task.'

This first edition had involved a rush to meet the printer's
deadline and, being short of photos, we chose a few holiday snaps: cows grazing in French fields, children splashing
in French baths, Cézanne-like baskets of fruit. One of my
nieces was embarrassed twenty-five years later to be recognised as 'the little girl in the bath'. On the day the book
reached those four hundred French owners in January 1994
I had my first, and rare, experience of an angry one. Upon
opening the book she picked up the telephone. Her smart
country house's photo had been replaced by that of another

family repainting their house's shutters. 'My husband is a lawyer and I am taking you to court.'

I had to admit that the photo made the house look scruffy. Her incandescent rage quivered down the line. At top speed, she calculated the amount of lost business and the cost of the blot on her escutcheon, and demanded damages of ten times the tiny fee she'd paid. By the third lively call we'd managed to calm her down. Then, as the summer went by, readers reported back: 'the most charming hostess', 'she's dynamic and fun', 'the room is lovely'. She stayed with us for years.

We later reverse-modelled ourselves on the AA guide, for much of what they held sacred was, to us, almost profane: 'facilities', tidiness, depth of shag on carpet, towel size and trouser presses. They, in turn, probably couldn't understand the amiable chaos, character and unpredictability of some of our places. The AA nevertheless was useful: our inspectors would bypass hotels and B&Bs that had the tell-tale AA sign swinging proudly from the building.

This first book carried our prejudices and values and quickly sold 12,500 copies; an ambitious reprint of 12,500 also sold out. We had almost forgotten the book once it was out of sight in the warehouse, but now realised we could become proper publishers. It was more fun than sending people off to walk or cycle in Europe: no punctures, blisters, complaints, sore feet, thirst or flooded footpaths to worry about.

An old friend from Suffolk, Ann Cooke-Yarborough, joined us to do the marketing and PR when her marriage broke down. Like Jane, she was, technically, short of the relevant skills. In fact, she knew nothing whatsoever about PR and marketing, but made a good fist of it before becoming an inspector and writer for us. *Special Places in Paris* was our next book and, with Ann in charge, we launched straight in: 'Your day in Paris can too easily be spoiled by a rotten night . . . We have left out the very grand, the pompous, the clinically modern, the unfriendly and the ordinary . . . But many small hotels have bravely hung on to a way of receiving people that I feared might have gone the way of . . . the old footpaths beside the Seine.'

Then came Spain. Guy Hunter-Watts lived and breathed Spain; he slept under the stars while rattling around in an old Citroën 2CV and carousing with artists, aristocracy, leftists, rightists, free-thinkers and farmers. His carousing got the book off the ground – no mean achievement when we were charging a fee for inclusion. The Spaniards who had had the imagination to create hostels out of abandoned convents, or B&Bs out of farmhouses, loved our idea.

With Spain and France behind us we could now tackle Britain, backed by *Country Living* magazine. Here is the Introduction to that first UK book:

You know the scene: the pubs are closed, lights hang limply from the lamp-posts, and you have nowhere to sleep. The only hotel in town has been taken over by Forte. There is a guest-house called Lime Villa, to which an S should be prefixed. It lurks behind a tight belt of conifers. The pub has a room but it is over the bar. All that remains is the Crest hotel, or is it a Novotel, or Stakis – or whatever – three miles away on the bypass and 'meeting the growing demand for faster access and customer-focused corporate hospitality'?

In despair, you contemplate driving home for the

night and then remember the dog-eared copy of this book that you had stuffed into the front pocket of the car . . .

The B&B scene is almost as depressing as the hotel scene. You may soon be able to travel from John of Groats to Land's End in a familiar cocoon of neat modern bedrooms equipped with trouser presses, tea and coffee-making kit and UHT in irritating little packets. But there is hope.

Since then trouser presses have given way to WiFi routers, and UHT milk survives only in the oddest of places, but our gentle railing against the tourist industry, chain hotels, chain restaurants and burger bars was well received.

I encouraged our editors to write as human beings first and foremost, even when describing something as superficially banal as accommodation, a grim word in itself. We were determined to replace travel-agent cliché with a little colour. We developed a list of banned words and phrases – such as 'nestling', 'picturesque', 'facilities' and 'a perfect base from which to explore . . .'. The list quickly grew: 'ambience', 'bygone age', 'affords', 'imbibe', 'quality', 'residence' and 'located', for example. Grammar was important from the beginning; I was pitiless with the dangling modifier, where a sentence sets off in one direction and abruptly changes tack: 'Impressively upholstered, Emily is proud of her restored furniture.' They can land you in trouble.

We worked hard to avoid dullness, even if we erred towards the fanciful at times: 'It poses above town like a venerable French gentleman: tall, handsome, impeccably dressed in a wisteria-trimmed pale suit.' But when we erred beyond the fanciful we were taken to task, once severely and properly by a New Yorker called Harry. In our Paris book we had waxed fantastical about the Hotel Pergolese: 'Once past the blue doors you forget the trumpeting sculptures of nearby Arc de Triomphe for a festival of modern design ... Edith works with renowned designer Rena Dumas ... to keep a sleek but warmly curvaceously human hotel.'

Harry wrote to complain: 'The phrase "warmly, curvaceously human hotel" has actually quite exhausted me.' I can see his point.

Gradually our collection of special places in the UK took shape. Very rarely were we refused, perhaps because we were talking with like-minded people even if some had different political views from our own. If they were too exuberant, for example, in their display of guns, sports trophies, golfing cups and such paraphernalia we would gently retrace our steps and go elsewhere. Male house-owners are sometimes happy to regale guests with tales of birds shot and animals slaughtered, mindless of the goggle-eyed vegan at their side.

We had opened a treasure trove of human ingenuity and kindness, and a rich store of architectural, and sometimes artistic, achievement. We had also found some impressively sustainable houses, with productive smallholdings, home energy generation, organic food growing and green buildings. These were especially close to my heart. I treasure the memory of an ancient motorbike harnessed to a cider mill in Herefordshire. Running on a battery and attached by a long arm to the millstone, it motored round and round the oasthouse floor in the place of the horse that once plodded there.

On Bodmin Moor, Robin and Louella generate enough electricity for thirty houses, and their solar-charged electric cars are silent witnesses to their foresight. Charles, an organic grower in Somerset, pioneered a no-dig garden system. His garden delivers superb produce to his own B&B, he runs courses, writes books and is a modest horticultural guru. I think of him every time I rest on my spade on the allotment.

Our offices were in a small terraced house overlooking Bristol harbour. When I ran for Parliament in 1992, one room was our Green Party headquarters. From another room we ran a campaign to introduce organic food into local schools, and Em ran counselling courses at weekends. We were an easy-going working community, given to celebrations and spontaneity. Eliza worked in her underwear during a heat wave; Daisy, the spaniel, rampaged from room to room; bottles were opened at all hours and neighbours were welcome. The car we used for inspections was a VW, bought for its green credentials and run on recycled cooking oil. We installed a special oil drum from which we hand-pumped the oil. This felt elegant: a waste product and local too – from Bristol fish-and-chip shops. The engine worked smoothly, with a whiff of fish and chips about the exhaust, but the oil clogged up the pumps and the fuel gauge. Being a pioneer can be expensive.

Meanwhile, *Special Places to Stay – Great Britain* flew off the shelves with its French and Spanish predecessors – and we met our first publishing disaster. Our production manager, Jules, came in to show us the first copy of our latest book, *French Self Catering*. It was our fattest book yet and we had printed an ambitious twenty-five thousand copies. Jules was cock-a-hoop and we opened a bottle. Half an hour later she returned, ashen-faced.

'What's wrong, Jules? You look terrible.'

'We have printed the wrong maps in the book. I am so sorry.'

'Oh God, that's twenty-five thousand books that are useless. We'll have to pulp them.'

I hadn't got it in my heart to be angry, for Jules had done her best. But thus were lost £45,000 in printing costs, let alone all the books. And I had spent years urging better use of resources. Annie and I were in despair and shock, unsure which of the two emotions to settle upon. At that moment an Australian friend rang; she ran a company that made artificial body parts for medical training purposes. Her humour is deadpan Aussie.

'Margot, I've had a disaster. Have you ever had one?'

'Sure. A bloke last year put in one of the best orders I have had. He did a good design and all we had to do was make the things – six thousand of them.' They were beautifully made and Margot was proud of them. Just before the warehouse shipped them out the bloke rang and said:

'We've got a problem: we got the design wrong! We can't use them.'

'What were they?' I idly enquired.

'Vaginas.'

All thoughts of our twenty-five thousand books vanished.

'What did you do with them?'

'We put 'em in the skip.' I pictured the skip-man arriving to take them away, and the manual sorters at the other end. This was a stretch too far for my fevered imagination, but I did briefly forget my own troubles.

As the business grew we moved into the countryside close to Bristol, where our landlord was known to toss the odd dead fox into his ancient heating boiler, and allow his geese to hiss our accounts department into terrified refuge. Across the yard was another barn with two young men starting an organic tea company called Pukka. From there we moved to our own barn closer to Bristol, where we created eco-offices part designed and built by Quentin, Annie's husband. The Old Farmyard in Yanley was our HQ for six years and we won a Queen's Award for Sustainability, plus other awards for sustainability, building and environmental publishing. We recycled rainwater, installed a thermal solar system and a biomass boiler, and insulated the structure to the rafters. It was a wonderful place to work: a series of light-filled rooms, one of them a green-oak barn, around a courtyard, in the centre of which was a circular pond. This was deep enough for a swim, and Annie and I would often dive in, just ten yards from our desks. Em would give lunchtime yoga classes and lunches were frequently communal.

Opposite us was an empty field which we used for free in exchange for waiving all rights – a delightful arrangement. Local people formed a rescued chicken group; Nicola, one of our long-serving staff, built pig pens and imported Myfanwy the sow for breeding – a success. I tried scything the rest of the field, but gave up and brought in a horse to plough it for the local food group. They eventually numbered about thirty and co-operatively grew vegetables. On a summer evening whole families would come up to play, harvest, dig and socialise. On our own patch of land we had an allotment that waxed and waned with the enthusiasms of the staff. This all felt, to me, like a sort of office paradise.

We also put on classical guitar concerts. The first was by Xuefei Yang, a rising star fresh from guitar studies at the

Royal Academy. Her playing that night was fresh, delicate yet robust. Her career rocketed and she is now one of the world's greatest guitarists – astonishing for a woman who was the first female guitarist ever to attend guitar studies at a specialist music school in China. This in a post-Mao China shorn of music culture. These concerts were, for me, a nourishing part of life in our barns.

We had a poetry evening, too, with our son Rowan – now known as Dizraeli – doing his early rap pieces with poet friends from Bristol, and a young jazz pianist called Rebecca Nash. I had found a pair of 'gypsy' musicians busking in Bristol and brought them out too. John Pearce, the fiddler, was to return again and again looking, in full flow, like a perspiring rugby player making love to his violin. He ranged from passionate intensity to gentle lyricism, and set our farewell-to-Yanley party alight. It ended with my last dive into the pond.

During those twenty years of publishing life, before the final dominance of the internet, we also published books on Croatia, Morocco, Greece, Turkey, Ireland and India, and a successful series on slow travel. Our eco-series, the *Little Books*, on earth, money and food, gave strong voice to our commitment to both the environment and to environmental awareness in travel. We also published a book about the Millennium window in Chester Cathedral, another about natural weddings and a book called *Stuffed* in partnership with the Soil Association. They were stimulating and worthwhile, if unprofitable, projects and I still miss that emphasis on books. But at least we'll never have to pulp twenty-five thousand of them again.

Toby, our elder son, who took over the company in 2011 and has overseen its final transformation from paper to digital publishing, was keen to be in the heart of Bristol. It was an emotional wrench for me; the barns reflected what both Annie and I cherished. We are now in an eighties office building, but our floor is filled with life and colour. There is, through windows on two sides, the whole of the harbour centre on display. We publish fewer books now, just half a dozen a year. I feel for the young staff fixed to their computers, but there is still a focus on fun; my old Bechstein piano stands proudly in the middle of the office and our first concert was by John Law, the jazz pianist, in 2016. We even have a flourishing office choir conducted by David Ogden of Exultate fame – a weekly hour of sheer delight. The company is as devoted to informality and spontaneity as ever, but Toby and his team are now burdened by the relentless pressures of internet-based work. One relief the employees have, of course, is the network of delightful people whose houses and lives we still celebrate.

7

French People and Song

O ur first book was about France, for the English find France irresistible. We managed to persuade hundreds of French people out of their reluctance to have strangers in their homes. The result has been the flowering of thousands of relationships.

Our family holidays in France, in the fifties, felt adventurous. That flight to Le Touquet I have already described now seems extraordinary. France was still recovering from the war, her economy in tatters, her rural areas limping from lost productivity and manpower. But to us she was beautiful, and my generation is understandably nostalgic about those days. Her villages had cafés, bars and shops, wine was cheap, fields for picnics were bucolic, farms were small and rural life was traditional. As British travellers, and bearers of cash, we were extra welcome and we were encouraged by my mother to speak to anybody we met. My first conversational contact with a Frenchman was in a 'pissoir' (in French, a *pissottière*; pissoir is pure English). These were available in most villages, visible proof that the French were less coy about these things than we were. So as I piddled I struggled to hold my own with a large Frenchman on each side of me.

'*Salut, petit!*'

'*Bonjour, Monsieur,*' perfectly, but fearfully, enunciated.

Then came the machine-gun-speed chatter of a relaxed pair of Frenchmen, with me in the middle. My mother heard the plaintive words emerging from the pissoir: '*Excusez-moi, je ne comprends pas. Je suis anglais!*' I escaped, a bit wobbly but pleased to have uttered some French without tragic consequence.

Since then French has been a source of confidence for me, giving my travel added layers of meaning and fun. Speaking the language usually does, of course. Samuel Pepys spoke good French and it served him well. Writing of an Oxford scholar he had encountered at dinner in the French embassy, he thought that 'though a gentle sort of scholar, yet he sat like a fool for want of French'.

On those family holidays we would stay, all of us in one room, in the hotels that once graced almost every town: the Hôtel de la Poste, or the Hôtel de Sport. Many of them are gone now, beaten into submission by the grim fortresses of incivility that are called Novotel, or Ibis, or Formule 1. Some I encountered were run by fearsome older women, but at least they were fearsome in their own way. When they were charming, they were irresistible.

As late as the nineties, before the tyranny of design magazines and the British influence on house style in France, we could still find B&Bs that fitted our childhood image of the tiny farmstead, with a dozen pigs, a cow, some hens and a few small fields. The range-warmed kitchen, with baskets hanging from the beams and preserves lined up on the shelves, was the wife's empire and the focus of life on the farm. Here the farmer and his worker, if he had one, would gather for three or four high-calorie meals a day, so Madame was constantly bustling around her hot stove.

It was fun to find, for example, a B&B where I could milk the cow by hand in order to get a decent café au lait. The old girl who ran it – this was in the sixties – was too old to do the milking quickly and would bring the café au lait too late for me to enjoy. So I resorted to the udder myself. Madame Béatrice was a tiny black-clothed widow like a darker, French version of Mrs Tiggy-Winkle. She wore a lace shawl and shared her run-down family house with myriad old photographs, assorted pieces of furniture and occasional guests. I had found a museum of immutable peasant life, the rooms just as her children had left them: rustic, ill-fitting and indescribably atmospheric. The stables were just as the cart horses had left them too, magnificent in their fluted timbers and brass knobs – a striking statement of priorities. The land was now rented out. Madame Béatrice cooked admirable country suppers and talked and talked. If you didn't understand her thickly accented French she would repeat it until you did – or could pretend to. Breakfast was minimal, though the coffee that kick-started the day came in big white bowls that you held with both hands. The bathroom was shared and it was clear even then that she and her house were, together, a dying breed. Some loved it, some couldn't stay even one night.

I was among those who loved it. I hoped that we might help people like Madame Béatrice to stay in their houses. In a tiny way we have succeeded, as handwritten letters have told us: '*Monsieur, grâce à vos lecteurs nous sommes toujours fermiers.*' Thanks to your readers, we are still farmers. That is heart-warming, but the tide of young farmers leaving the land is too much for even a thousand of us to hold back.

In the eighties, now with a family of our own, Em and I would go to France as often as possible, frequently with my sister Fiona's children for she worked abroad, and to wherever Dinx was living – usually in the Lot. On one of those journeys we returned through Normandy and spent the night in a small farmhouse, which came to play an unexpected role in my career, for the kindliness of the farmers triggered the idea of writing a book.

The farmhouse was unremarkable, but solid, handsome and welcoming. Madame, homely and dressed in a floral work dress, was the queen of the house. Monsieur was dressed in *les bleus*, the traditional French workman's blue dungarees, and wore his wellies in and out of the house. The kitchen was the beating heart of the home, chickens wandering in and out at will and even a goat nibbling at our legs during breakfast. I felt instantly at home. Em enjoyed the atmosphere as much as I did. We took a double room and persuaded the farmer and his wife to allow the boys to camp on the lawn outside our bedroom. Any alarm Em felt about their safety was dealt with by a large hand-bell, which we instructed Toby to ring vigorously if frightened. Thus assured, we slept soundly in spite of the matching vomit-green bedspread and curtains. We slept late and ambled down for breakfast to find Madame clucking about the yard with the boys obediently in tow. Chickens were being fed and cows admired. Rowan had been subdued by an encounter with the electric fence and was unusually malleable. Bless her soul: Madame had met the boys early, before they could ring the bell, and swept them up into her daily farm routine.

What a wonderful experience, we felt, and how useful it would be to share it. Surely there would be others as kind and generous to child-weary travellers. The electric fence wasn't a bad idea either. So the idea of a book was born.

We found four hundred and fifty special places for that first book. We were eclectic in our choices, tolerant of the vague and the dotty. The houses, many of which were farms, were a stimulating mixed bag, as were the owners. After an early visit to a château, however, the inspector wrote:

The couple are formal and rules-obsessed, their château an eighteenth-century wedding cake built on medieval foundations. These 'châtelains' were the best-preserved I have ever met, their silver candlesticks the most sparkling. Monsieur talked of the family's former power and glory, how they fitted into the web of the European aristocracy and how many learned essays had been published about them (not a whiff of *Hello!* magazine here). Dinner was a jacket-and-tie event, we guests struggling not to use the wrong cutlery, not to put our glasses back in the wrong spot on the table. (Monsieur had already written to us about the Brits' lack of manners.)

They only stayed with us for a couple of editions. Such social tyranny is fun to write about, but less fun to experience.

As the book grew, so did our friendships with French people and their houses. French custom has not been to receive strangers with open arms but rather to take them for a quick drink in the nearest café. But doors opened to us, and hearts too; older owners were especially rewarding. One of the first to welcome us lived in Brittany, alone in a monolithic building that echoed to our steps. She eagerly hustled us in to her small sitting room and disappeared to the kitchen to get what we imagined would be a cup of coffee. Back she came with a bottle of dark red liquid. 'I know you English drink port, for I have read it in novels.' Another, a frail lady in her eighties, had a twelfth-century château of ravishing beauty and many turrets, but she was too ancient to get up the stairs. So I made my own bed, tidied the room and nipped up and down helping her as best I could. The stairs were indeed demanding – entirely of stone and worn concave by the feet of centuries, the sort of stairs you feel your way down gingerly lest you encounter a knight hurtling up in chain mail. Having descended, I looked forward to a medieval-size breakfast, but poor Madame lay slumped in a chair near the table.

'Ah, Monsieur. Je suis tellement vieille que l'énergie pour servir votre petit déjeuner ne m'arrive pas. Mais voilà la cuisine . . . '

I was seduced, and on that day even made her breakfast – which we ate together at her oak table. Making one's own bed and breakfast was a tiny price to pay for such an experience.

Em and I, en route to Spain, once turned up at a B&B

very late, having asked that nobody wait up for us. We arrived to a fully lit house, an expectant and eager hostess bearing dinner, and a tableful of guests. They were three London cab-drivers and their wives, keen to meet the publisher of the book they always used for their French holidays. The evening was fun, though I hadn't bargained for late-night discussions of bus lanes, tipping and the mistresses of Russian oligarchs.

Those cab-drivers loved France, as do so many of us, but it is easier to love her than to explain why. Often it is the food, the wine, the markets – rarely, and strangely, the people.

My own devotion has several threads running through it, and one of them is music: the French song tradition that encompasses poetry, politics or passion – or all three together. Music is a great social lubricant and many of our owners are musical. Others just have musical dreams. At one end of the scale was the whole family in the Luberon who emerged from their kitchen after dinner to form a rock band: Mum on bass, Dad on electric guitar, the boys on drums and guitar. Their music was electrifying and ear-splitting. We were high in the hills of Provence, up a long track and with glorious views. It had, until that moment, been a place of idyllic peace but they derailed our bucolic illusions with the first chord. At the other end of the scale was the elegant hostess who played a Bach prelude on her cello while we had a drink before dinner. She was entirely at ease with it, as if cello music belonged to that moment.

There is special delight in music emerging from unexpected places. I once found myself following a small river through the Hérault on a dry, dusty day, looking for a spot where I could slip into the water. An old stone barn, tangled in the trees and submerged in ivy, windows without glass, offered rest in the shade of its broken eaves. It felt good to be alive and well as I stretched my back along the cool stone and took a long swig of water from my bottle. As I melted into the moment, the sound of piano-playing spilled out of the barn and into the trees, slow and gentle and then with gathering intensity. I was transfixed, then moved to the edge of tears. I learned later that a pianist rented the barn and kept it almost as derelict as she had found it, as that seemed right to her.

Ask anyone to sing a song, and you learn something of the country's musical tastes. Press an older Frenchman to sing and he may dip into his stock of Brassens songs. Georges Brassens captivated much of France for decades with his wry, poetic whimsy and unerring feel for the very bones of the culture. I, too, have been under his spell and have played and sung, in public, a few of his song-poems, such as 'Chanson pour L'Auvergnat'. It speaks of kindness, generosity, gratitude – and does so with a withering scorn for '*les croquantes et les croquants*', the upper crust, who couldn't give a damn.

Georges Moustaki, the poet-singer, with his wild hair and Greek–Jewish background, touched something in me too, especially with 'Le Métèque':

Avec ma gueule de métèque
De Juif errant, de pâtre grec
Et mes cheveux aux quatre vents
Avec mes yeux tout délavés
Qui me donnent l'air de rêver
Moi qui ne rêve plus souvent

There is a whiff of the anti-hero there, a nostalgia for the outsider and the romantic.

Leaving aside the ineffable Édith Piaf, I was under the spell, too, of the Belgian Jacques Brel and even volunteered to play him in the musical revue *Jacques Brel is Alive and Well and Living in Paris* at the old Arts Centre in Bristol. 'I can play the guitar, speak French, sing – I'll be fine with it.' I had forgotten about the acting bit. Em bravely sat in the front row and I can still see her squirming with embarrassment as I clumped woodenly about the stage, unsure which leg to raise first, how to move from A to B and how to express any emotion. Em knew I was not an actor, but I was worse than she feared.

French chanson conveys so much of what France is about: quixotic individualism, respect for the intellect, conviction about living and Frenchness – and irony. (Curiously, however, the French have no equivalent of the word 'silly'.) There is a sense of the ridiculous, with sexual longing, in the Brassens song about the man whose lifelong ambition is to see the navel of the wife of a policeman. But lyrics apart, the very sound of French captivates me. In my teaching days I would show children how to conquer the 'eu' sound by getting them to run around the classroom pretending to be fighter jets screaming out of the sky and descending to a perfect 'eu'. It worked for some of them. The rest just enjoyed screaming. The French way of saying 'r' I encouraged with mass gargling noises. Brassens milked the rolling, throaty 'r' with terrific effect.

Music festivals pop up all over France every summer as they do in the UK, and I had some sublime and unexpected moments with my little tour groups in the eighties: a string quartet in a Norman chapel, folk-dancing after a village fête, spontaneous Swiss oompah music on a barge on the Canal du Midi. Several times I picked up surprised buskers and brought them along to entertain us at dinner. Faced with a week leading a group of refrigerator salesmen from San Francisco, I hired a violinist from the London Symphony Orchestra and asked her to play whenever the mood felt right. She played on trains, buses, boats and in hotel lobbies, lending a touch of magic to counter the refrigerator culture.

There must be something of the impresario manqué about me. Living in a small, shared Islington house in the seventies, I organised several guitar concerts in my bedroom. We would split the cost among about fifty of us sitting tightly together on cushions. The first was with Paco Peña, now one of the great flamenco stars. With the audience so close he was as nervous as a kitten. I also persuaded the Abreu brothers from Brazil to play. They were one of the world's great guitar duos and briefly transformed my modest room into a concert hall. Dorita y Pepe also performed in the tiny space, and were magnificent. Their black hair-slicked Spanishness was a great act, for they spoke to each other in broad cockney.

France has a vibrant jazz culture, and I have written much of this book to the background sound of Michel Petrucciani playing his own compositions on piano. I know little about jazz but now think of him as one of France's greats. Burdened tragically by 'glass bone' disease, which stopped him growing beyond three feet and weighing more than fifty pounds, he died at thirty-six and is buried in the Père Lachaise cemetery in Paris – symbolically, close to Chopin and not far from Jim Morrison. His death was mourned by the nation and lamented by the President of France in a way that is, I think, uniquely French: Chirac praised Petrucciani's ability to 'renew jazz, giving himself up to his art with passion, courage and musical genius'.

In the eighties, up to 10 per cent of the country's budget was allocated to culture, much of it to jazz. How can one not admire a nation that does that?

8

Paris and Old Ladies

A Parisian café-théâtre in the sixties offered the can-can and other cabaret after dinner. Dinner was served by surprisingly elderly, coquettish women and I was on tenterhooks about the cabaret. Dinner over, our waitress sidled away and soon the stage curtains parted to reveal her and her colleagues lined up in wild, flouncy skirts and heavy make-up, poised for the can-can. I could almost hear hips squeaking as legs were raised, and feared the worst. But, of course, this was Paris so the performance was witty and knowing. Where else would a club dare such a thing? Berlin in the thirties, perhaps, and working men's clubs in the north of England?

France has a special way of being gently provocative. The Théâtre de la Pleine Lune, near the tiny Hérault village of St-André-de-Buèges, is another example. St-André is a tightly built medieval jumble of stone and river with a soaring plane tree under which Em and I ate a hurried dinner. The planes of France are the glory of many a simple village square; they often live for four hundred years and have inspired poetry, painting (they shaded Van Gogh) and countless intimacies. We dragged ourselves from the shelter of this one to get to the theatre in time, and then waited for the moon to rise. The name of the theatre barely does justice to the madness of the project. The owner, a Parisian opera manager, has created an amphitheatre on a hill behind his house. The light of the moon was to be captured and reflected onto the stage, and to this end was assembled a motley array of mirrors and their accompanying experts. Each had erected, behind the back row, a vast reflective surface. We waited and waited while the moon slowly, oh so slowly, rose. By late evening there was light enough for the Indian dance to begin.

We could barely distinguish the dancer from the trees, let alone see her intricate hand and foot movements, but she carried a candle so we knew where she was. After the interval, when half the eye-strained audience fled, the performance continued – but, to our discreet relief, with electric light. We saw now what we had been missing. The evening was judged a success by the local cognoscenti; the moon had risen to the task and this was, after all, the Théâtre de la Pleine Lune. As a demonstration of art's power of conviction, and man's eternal optimism, it was magnificent. However, we rather wished we had remained at our table under that gargantuan plane tree and watched it grow.

Not far from the Théâtre de la Pleine Lune is the little village of Brissac, another pint-sized seduction-piece of stone buildings on a dramatic hill. There, on a family holiday near by, we would gather in the evenings to drink *panaché*, the French version of shandy beloved of foreigners, and to recover from the fleas that were teasing us in our gîte. There were twenty of us gathered together in a primitive, rambling farmhouse whose owners, curiously, failed to see that fleas and bed-bugs, '*puces et punaises*', might be unwelcome. '*Eh bien* – what do you expect from a farmhouse? Butterflies?'

Criss-crossing France in those early publishing days was exhilarating. I tore myself away from one region to another; from Normandy to the Loire, for example, whose châteaux were embedded in my memory from family holidays. Chambord was still startling in its scale and magnificence, but then I saw Chenonceaux again: a sculpted Renaissance dream dancing modestly along its own bridge, mingling modesty with one flourish after another. The arches are the brows of a serene mistress; it is ladylike, intensely self-aware, built by a woman then nurtured by two of France's finest and strongest: Diane de Poitiers and Catherine de Médicis. It was even saved from the ravages of the Revolution by a female owner. Its still reflection in the water is like the mirror image of a court beauty before the ball. How, I had wondered as a teenager, and now as an adult, could anything be finer?

Yet Azay-le-Rideau, not far away, vies for admiration too. The setting on the tiny lake challenged the builders; piles were driven into the mud, as in Venice, and the stone was hauled from sixty miles away by boat. Azay suffered fire and war, but strong feminine influence gave it its present confidence. For me, oddly, the crowning glory is the inside of the roof-space – a forest of giant timbers at odds with the delicate interior below.

I have a special affection for big timber buildings. The church of St Catherine, to the west in Honfleur, is the largest wooden church in France, built by shipwrights after the Hundred Years War to celebrate the departure of the English. It is rather as if a forest had been given a new ecclesiastical role. Our arrivals in France have been less celebrated, unless you count the wine supermarkets in Calais. Perhaps, after Brexit, there is another great church to be built – in lamentation this time.

Every time I am set alight by a French town, or village centre, I wonder about the rest of the place. My vision, my narrative, of France is of houses clustered around a Norman church, cobbles and a pétanque pitch, fading shutters and church bells. But the truth is more likely to be a business park, petrol stations and supermarkets until, with massive relief, you reach the ancient heart. Most towns have now suffocated their old centres in the commercial embrace of our era. Instead of claiming, for example, that Toulouse is a beautiful city (tourist-brochure language) we might more accurately say that Toulouse is a sadly disfigured city with a beautiful old heart. We delude ourselves when ignoring the impact of the last century, for we thus turn a blind eye to our own barbarism.

I have spent most of my life among women, so no wonder I love Paris. It is a feminine city. If we ignore the suburbs and edges it is of near-perfect urban design, even if fine medieval buildings were lost when Haussmann ploughed his avenues through the city. But at least he created space and opportunity, and a certain irresistible grandeur in that age before the calamitous arrival of cement and steel. Its femininity lends it a seductive restraint. During the last war there were hardly any French men around, so the women kept the city going. Paris was lucky in escaping largely unscathed from two world wars. Often there in the sixties with my groups of obedient tourists, I would gaze across the rooftops in Montmartre from my favourite attic hotel bedroom up on the hill near Abbesses and be moved by the view: lead roofs in their hundreds, criss-crossing planes of functional beauty, a gradual fall to the city below. Nothing to mar the sense of one age adding respectfully to another.

Things were once very different. William Hazlitt, the essayist, was there in 1825 and wrote:

> Paris is a beast of a city ... you are forced to walk along the middle of the streets with a dirty gutter running through them, fighting your way through coaches, wagons, and hand carts ... greasy holes for shop-windows ... and the contents of wash hand basins pouring out of a dozen storeys ... The continual panic in which the passenger is kept, the alarm and the escape from it, the anger and the laughter at it, must have an effect on the Parisian character, and tend to make it the whiffling, skittish, snappish, volatile, inconsequential, unmeaning thing it is.

Paris still feels feminine to me, even skittish, as does France herself – and that is how the French think of it too. I have an ineradicable memory of a woman in France, one who reminded me of the Franco-Scottish 'auld alliance'. I was in the Languedoc with a small wine-tasting group, visiting a house that seemed to emerge only reluctantly from a mass of bushes, tangled undergrowth, trees and accumulated wooden sculpture. But when it emerged, it did so in unexpected splendour: a riot of arches, shutters, cellars and red tiling. Monsieur and Madame Bourgain ushered all ten of us into the kitchen and insisted that we sit down for a glass of their own red wine – even though there were only six chairs. The unseated four sat cross-legged on the floor. The kitchen's long, low beams and ponderous, dark French-rural furniture subdued us at first. Monsieur pottered – for he was in his eighties – back and forth with the bottles, which came thick and fast. We were supposed to be there for a talk about the wine, but every time I mentioned it another bottle would appear and the talk receded deeper into the distance. Madame was unexpectedly bibulous, especially for a woman in her seventies, and as the evening wore on she revealed that she had, in her youth, spent a winter in Scotland as a hotel maid. As the story trickled out we learned that she had danced every Saturday night in the village hall, and once knew how to do a sword dance. I could not let this pass, for I have Scottish blood in me and am a sucker for Scottish dancing. But a sword dance!

Madame disappeared, and we feared that she might have retired for the night. But ten minutes later she re-appeared in Scottish regalia, the dress under heavy strain from the pounds added since her time in Scotland. She meandered around the kitchen looking for swords, which came in the shape of ancient fire-pokers. With a flourish she quietened us and the room was pregnant with anticipation. There was no music, but the magic of the occasion put the skirl of bagpipes in our ears and we watched, entranced, as she skipped nimbly about the fire-pokers. She managed about one glorious, swirling minute before tottering across the room and falling, exhausted and sozzled, into the lap of one of my elderly clients. He was as delighted as he was alarmed, and it was not only he who saw that Madame's dress had finally given up the struggle to contain her fullness. The man's wife looked on aghast as her husband disappeared under the weight of a growingly exposed French farmer's wife. Monsieur, unperturbed, carried on serving wine.

The wine talk never happened, but I remembered those wonderful old ladies in the café-théâtre in Paris and quietly raised my glass to spirited French women *d'un certain âge*.

9

Provence and Rural Heroes

When José Bové, a sheep farmer in the Larzac, saw that a new branch of McDonald's, a vulgar symbol of globalisation, was being built in Millau, he took matters into his own hands. He drove his tractor up to the building site, attached a chain to the prefabricated roof of the burger restaurant, and drove away. Bové went to prison, but at his trial there was a crowd of forty thousand to greet him as a national hero, and he hasn't looked back. He is now a writer and speaker, and a leader of the French environmental movement.

Bové is something of an icon of the French resistance to alien ideas that threaten French ways of doing things. His resemblance to Georges Brassens, with his drooping moustache and pipe, must help. France has clasped tightly to its own way of ordering the world and resists the encroachment of the predatory Anglo-Saxon model. At times the attitude seems myopic, even xenophobic, but *au fond* it is, in my view, wise and far-sighted. Look where our model of development has got us. One of the attractions of France is that she ploughs her own furrow.

Dinx, the second of my three sisters, left England for ever in her early twenties, abandoning a promising career in classical ballet. Well, it had once been promising, but Dinx showed unusual spirit for a young ballerina. When she was with the London Festival Ballet she led a mutiny against the management style of the famous, but harsh, Dame Beryl Grey, one of the giants of English ballet. Dinx called in the Equity union, but Dame Beryl got in with the first blow and fired the mutineers. Dinx went to France and married an architect, meanwhile dancing a little with Jean-Louis Barrault. She divorced, and set up a dance school in Toulouse, Studio Cadence. The studio flourished and we would visit her there, enchanted by Toulouse with its great cathedral and basilica, and its rose-red brick buildings. She then married again and moved to the Lot, where we would often stay with her and her family in their old farmhouse.

On our holidays in the Lot we often canoed down the River Célé, drifting under the cliffs and across the smooth river-worn boulders, dangling hands in the limpid water and sipping wine cool from the bottom of the canoe. The river has cut deep into the limestone tableland, leaving canoeists at the feet of great cliffs one moment and manoeuvering around islets and peninsulas the next. There are churches and castles, villages of simple perfection like

Espagnac-Sainte-Eulalie and Ceint d'Eau, or the charmingly named Saint-Cirq-Lapopie (St Cyr was a child martyr
and Lapopie was a rich local family) perched one hundred
metres up on a cliff's edge. Canoeing brought us together
in the nicest way; I got to look manly, the boys spent their
energy paddling rather than scrapping, and Em, needing to
impress nobody, could choose her role.

Dinx and Bo often had guests from far-flung places. One
of them, a Japanese gentleman of exquisite dignity, spent
all day looking for snails in the garden to serve us all at
dinner. Meanwhile, our seven-year-old son Rowan, known
for his trenchant vegetarian views, was playing elsewhere.
The evening came, clear-skied and calm, the candles flickered on the outside table and, at a carefully choreographed
moment, the Japanese man emerged beaming from the
kitchen, bearing his special dish. Rowan, spotting the snails,
screamed 'Murderer! Snail murderer!' We hastened him to
his bedroom, from whose open window emerged cries of 'I
hate that man!'. To this crisis were brought the diplomatic
skills of seven adults. Rowan is now in his mid-thirties, still
a vegetarian and a man of strong views.

A few summers ago we visited Dinx in the Hérault,
where she is settled now. Like most of France, the Hérault
has beneath its skirts much to admire. The little town of
Pézénas, for example, is richly blessed with handsome historic houses and thirty official historic monuments. One of
them is a little theatre devoted to Molière, who was often
here. Ambling through the back streets makes me tingle
with happiness. On one corner rises a seventeenth-century
townhouse, its staircase cantilevered in stone on the exterior,
stepping from flight to flight as if to say 'even my staircases

are beautiful'. On Saturdays there is a lively market buzz-ing with energy, and with such delights as lime-coloured fur-lined baseball caps, mock-zebraskin bras and trainers with coloured flashing lights. I bought a bottle of ginger syrup from a sweet old lady, from whom I would even have accepted a fur-lined baseball cap. It lifted my spirits no end.

Another Hérault treasure is the old Cistercian Abbaye de Valmagne. The abbey has been in the same family of *viticulteurs* since the Revolution and they have used it as a giant wine warehouse, storing up treasures on earth in full view of the Almighty: it is known locally as *la cathedrale des vignes*. Each side chapel is occupied by a vast wooden vat, an upstaging of any Majestic Wine warehouse – Celestial Wine, perhaps. In the cloister courtyard there is a rare Cistercian fountain, and I sat there in a sun that dappled its way through the enclosing vine. Such moments are charged with meaning.

In the early days of putting our French book together I was on a trip through Provence. Staying overnight at an elegant château, I was invited to dinner. The courses came in lush succession, and with each one a different and yet more delicious wine. When I escaped to my room I had lost control of my legs and was unable to lie down in the four-poster bed for fear of it capsizing. The ceiling and walls were rolling like ocean waves, so I spent the night propped up on fine feather pillows. Waking with a splitting headache, I was relieved to be on my own for breakfast. I completed the inspection and talked to the owner about the marvels of her house without her suspecting a thing. Well, I think I did.

The following night was to be spent on the banks of Lac de Sainte-Croix, just outside Moustiers-Sainte-Marie. I

found the house down a track, built into the hillside overlooking the lake. Total magic! The house, modern, white
and minimalist with shining black floors and vast windows,
was an inspiration. No garden, just wild land and oaks
unfolding to the lakeside and a view over the water to the
hills beyond. After a wonderful evening with my fascinating and somewhat eccentric hosts, and a refreshingly simple
dinner of salad, fresh goat's cheese and a light local red wine,
I went to bed early. My plan was to leave no later than six the
next morning, in order to make my next stop for breakfast.

I rose with the sun, climbed into the car and set off across
country. Barely two kilometres from the house, the sound
of sheep bells filled the air. Hundreds of sheep, herded
by three shepherds and their dogs, appeared in the misty
early-morning sunlight as they came round a bend in the
road. Enthralled, I was soon lost in a sea of bleating bodies.
The car wobbled as the sheep pushed their way by, intent
on their journey to the hills. This was the transhumance,
when the sheep are taken up to the hilly grasslands for the
summer, something from the past and yet real, beautiful and
captivating. I felt honoured to have been witness to this old
custom and was left feeling very moved by the intensity of
the moment.

Breakfast awaited me in the farmhouse dining room, the
long wooden table laden with home-made jams, fresh bread
and croissants. The only other guests, a couple sipping coffee
from white bowls, warmly welcomed me and the conversation flowed.

They were Australian and on their way to Ireland, with
this trip a long-awaited treat. An artist, she had always
longed to see the colours and smells of Provence, the Mont

Sainte-Victoire and the landscapes of Cézanne's paintings. The journey to Ireland was a promise to her mother, who as a small child had been torn from her native land and shipped to Australia as an unwanted orphan. She was now carrying her mother's ashes back to the village of her early childhood. As she told the tale we all three were in tears.

Such warmth of human contact is inspiration to me. It is available when human beings are feeling *bien dans sa peau* – good in their skin – as they do when staying somewhere that honours their humanity.

My encounter with the sheep had echoes of lunch in the modest farmhouse of Pierre, a Provencal bee-keeper whom one of our walking guides knew from childhood. He would transport his bees from one fruit-grower to another, a sort of bee-transhumance and a tradition almost gone from France. I suspect that he earned precious little from the work, but that was where his passion lay and he would continue to do it come what may.

The interior of Provence is a relief from the bleak coastal developments, a wide-open and underpopulated land of understated beauty. Jean Giono brought it to life with his *The Man who Planted Trees* and the less-known *Regain*, a spare, restrained story of a village emptied by the Great War, with just two inhabitants clinging on: an old lady at the top of the village and a wild young poacher at the bottom. They barely speak, but she longs to bring the village back to life and he is the only man to do it. So she sets out to lure a woman to the village, and, needless to say, succeeds. The village slowly begins to breathe again. Giono is a voice for inner Provence. Another was Marcel Pagnol, with *Jean de*

Florette and *Manon des Sources*, tales of a village's simmering dispute over the local well, a story many of us know as a film. There is, as you read or watch, a lingering scent of thyme and lavender in the air, of hot pine needles, of dry earth and sea breeze. No wonder Provence nourishes dreams of a better life. We got to know many dreamers while putting our book together.

Chantal and Pierre were both social workers in Marseilles, working their way up the ladder but finding it difficult to make time for a family. They became tetchy with each other, and finally accepted that their lives were too stressful to be enjoyed. So they set out to change that by finding a house in the country. Over a few years they painstakingly restored a seventeenth-century Provençal château. We described it as 'charmingly frayed at the edges', a description that makes a house irresistible to me. Their entrance hall was twelfth century, an age almost unheard of in England, and the views were over their own lake. As I ate their leeks and salads, and raspberries straight from the bush, I felt a live connection with them and their story. Chantal and Pierre, deeply contented and no longer bickering, are among hundreds of our owners whose lives have been transformed by moving to the country.

Near to Chantal and Pierre is the Domaine Nestuby, producing organic wines. It is a gorgeous nineteenth-century *bastide*, a working farm in Provence Verte, with a spring-fed tank for swims. Jean-François runs the vineyard, the tastings and the convivial wine talk at dinner, and produces a delicious Château Nestuby Rosé: 'pale pink colour, amyl nose with blackcurrant flavour and touches of sweet vanilla and quince'. His Gourmandise rosé has a light pink colour, 'very delicate nose like a boiled sweet with intense red fruits mixed with notes of orange flowers and sugared brioche. Delicious with raspberry tart.' I admire the taster who can scent sugared brioche in a wine.

The most special of our places often only survive because of bloody-minded determination to hold on to old things, old ways. L'Hôtel de l'Orange in Sommières is such a place, the elderly owner for years resisting the relentless march of black leather furniture and television. Nothing in the hotel demands to be seen; it is understated, relying on the patina of age, beauty and good taste rather than gadgets and surprise. Philippe receives you with warm refinement and each hushed room is in *maison de famille* style: polished floors, warmly coloured walls, a piano that asks to be played. The secluded terrace garden has inimitable views over the roofs of the old town, where Laurence Durrell lived for years, and died in 1990. He loved the town and described it, in a letter to Henry Miller in 1957, as a 'medieval town asleep on its feet — a castle whose history no one knows'.

Perhaps it is because towns like Sommières, with its ancient walls and medieval atmosphere, are so seductive that it is easy to overlook other realities. France's villages are dying from the lack of youthful vitality, as the young abandon them for the towns. Family farms slowly die and others grow vast; decent milk is hard to buy, let alone in bottles; dairy farmers go bust in droves; animals are kept in conditions that we choose to ignore; chickens and cows are fed antibiotics and hormones. We watch these things with our blind eye and then dash off to the supermarket. At least in France the supermarkets are excluded from English-style dominance by the Raffarin law, which permits artisans to have a say in local planning. The impact is noticeable: independent shops thrive in France – relatively.

Another low-key hero in the José Bové mould, but English, is an old friend, Julian Rose. Trained as an actor, he was hauled back to run the family farm when his parents, and then elder brother, died. The Elizabethan house on the banks of the Thames at Pangbourne now stands in four hundred acres of organic production, Julian's priorities being wholeness and soil health rather than profit. He once delivered an anguished appeal to fellow Soil Association trustees to ban white sugar from the organic standards and also campaigned for farmers to be allowed to sell milk direct and unpasteurised from their farms, in the face of an attempted government ban. He won, but his marriage fell apart and he fell for a farmer called Jadwiga, who was campaigning to save peasant farming in her native Poland. He lives there now, with occasional forays back to Pangbourne to see to the farm, and campaigns to save the 1.5 million traditional and highly efficient Polish farmers from the fate that has befallen farmers in the UK and France. Julian, with his flat tweed cap and English face, has appeared at the head of long lines of grizzled farmer-demonstrators in Warsaw. It is a fine thing he is doing, and I pray that he and Jadwiga succeed. They have already forced a delay on the introduction of GMOs into Poland – temporary relief for those peasant farmers.

Farmers spread ideas as well as seeds. I am proud that we have so many with us in Sawday's. One of them, who had pioneered new breeding techniques for the Blonde d'Aquitaine cattle of south-west France, came to our twentieth-anniversary dinner in Bristol. Christian was bubbling with enthusiasm at the guests he had received on his farm, and was sure he had persuaded one or two farmer-guests to convert to organic cattle-rearing. Wendy from our office, at my side during a chat with him, exclaimed: 'Now I know why your name rings a bell! My father bought bull semen from you when I was a child!' Christian's happiness was complete.

10

Noble Stones
that Breathe

I was in Burgundy, looking for houses for our first book. As I peered through the windscreen, fog wrapped itself around the car and I could feel the silence. For half an hour it had been like this and I was surely lost in the hinterland of Burgundy, but my map told me I was close to the château. Slightly anxious, I reflected on what I was coming to. Mademoiselle Soisick de Champagnon would be in her seventies, or even eighties, battered by time and the long struggle to keep the family château going against the odds. It would be ice-cold and cluttered, furnished with cobwebbed antiques from a larger château that her family had once owned. Her brother would have been a resistance hero, and the old house would have been a makeshift hospital at the end of the war. She would be charming if a touch frosty and suspicious, and I would spend the evening trying to convince her that I wasn't a predatory rogue.

The fog parted to give me a glimpse of a honey-coloured building, then I crunched into a gravel yard in front of a luminous *petit château*, perfectly turreted and gabled. As I climbed out of the car the front door swung open to reveal a slender young woman framed against the light, a cigarette in her mouth and a glass of wine in her hand. Pursued by the sound of jazz piano, she came gracefully over to me, gave me a kiss on each cheek, and my critical faculties abandoned me.

Soisick had recently inherited the house and chosen to leave everything behind in Paris to make her life here. Everything was animated by her vitality and panache. Bare floorboards, elegant furniture, restored period features, whiffs of Gauloises, family portraits and Parisian theatre programmes and newspapers. Conversation sparkled late into the evening over a sumptuous dinner. Most of us enjoy good company, but where can you find yourself at the dining table sparring happily with a Senegalese chef and his lovely Parisian TV-producer wife, a former finance minister and his spouse, and a laid-back château owner? This happened for two nights running, and it was hard to leave. The world has travelled to her door and she and her husband live in a home-made cosmopolitan society. Upon our return in 2015, Em and I felt at home the minute we arrived and were soon sloping across the field in our swimming costumes to dunk ourselves in the little river. Drinks, then dinner and conversation enlivened by the wine and by gentle differences of opinion on every subject. The next day found us having lunch in Flavigny, where *Chocolat* was filmed. We finished up with a stroll around the exquisite Abbaye de Fontenay.

Soisick was the perfect hostess, and as time went by I met other remarkable characters throughout France. The elderly Madame Roget was one, another model of kindly châtelaine but in a very different mould. She greeted Em, me and the boys with rare warmth and sweetness, inviting us to share a glass of her 'special' at a table in the garden. She tottered off and disappeared down into a cellar, emerging, beaming, with a bottle of her own organic walnut wine – a rare occurrence in France, where such things are usually not considered to be wine at all. Enchanted, I took a formal sip and exclaimed: '*Ah, Madame, quel plaisir de boire du vin sans préservatif!*' She looked startled, then bemused; and I then looked embarrassed. I had just congratulated her on the pleasure of drinking wine without wearing a condom. But the encounter was delightful and we stayed the night, warmed by the wine and a sumptuous dinner.

I find it hard to resist a good château. Squat, lofty, pin-nacled, pompous or graceful – they carry an exotic whiff of the past, of royalty and nobility in the centuries before the Revolution. The aristocratic rich were out of control, of course, rampantly corrupt and reluctant to pay tax, while the peasantry and bourgeoisie had no escape from it. Louis XVI, leading the corruption but also responsible for the nation's finances, came to the edge of desperation and asked a certain Charles de Calonne to sort things out. Calonne summoned the Assembly of Notables, a grand gathering of noble tax-avoiders, and asked them to start paying. One can imagine the UK Chancellor gathering bankers, corporate

CEOs and financiers together for the same purpose, with similar results. They declined, then turned against Calonne and dismissed him. Soon came the Revolution and heads rolled, but at least we have the fruits of such rampant tax avoidance – the great châteaux – to enjoy. The British public won't enjoy Philip Green's yachts in the same way.

France has, as we all know from General de Gaulle's despair at governing the sort of country that has so many of them, about five hundred different types of cheese. Some claim a thousand, if you take local variations into account. There are as many châteaux as there are cheeses: about six hundred in the Rhône-Alpes region alone, another two hundred or so in the Loire, 120 in Normandy and many more elsewhere. The very word château can, of course, mean many things, from castle to great country house to vineyard. Our first French book, with its clutch of châteaux among the hundreds of farms and other buildings, was an introduction to a world beyond the ordinary reach of travellers.

The French aristocracy is often presumed to have died when Louis XVI was guillotined in 1793, but it thrives in the smart quarters of the main cities, in the private châteaux of rural France, in many businesses – and in the general vacuity of *Hello!* magazine. You can sometimes meet them at our B&Bs. In 1995, one of the châteaux Ann Cook-Yarborough inspected was a long stone building in northern France, which had been owned by the same family for centuries. Riddled with rot, soggy with damp, crumbling at the corners, set in a dreary wheat-growing plain, it was an unprepossessing sight. But once through the great gates, Ann was swept up by a woman of such power and passion that Ann couldn't, as she said, 'but subscribe to her ideas for the duration of my visit'. The owner's whole tribe, beautifully mannered and deeply Catholic, were rebuilding this vast pile by dint of forced weekend work parties. The six children, aged from twenty-four to twelve, were there every weekend, with press-ganged relatives and friends, to help save their family heritage. They began by doing up two bedrooms and a couple of the smaller reception rooms so that guests could have breakfast in château style, unaware of the crumbling bits. Ann came upon an unrestored bathroom that was magnificent in its disdain for niceties. Below a neglected wall-mounted cistern that competed with decaying family portraits for attention, sat a humble modern chemical toilet – the sort that needs to be taken out and emptied regularly. The clash between Elsan and Empire styles was resounding.

Madame gave Ann the grand tour, including her workroom where she was putting the finishing touches to a superb wedding gown 'for Princess So-and-So of the House of Orléans – our cousins, you know'. Every now and again she would, with an imperious gesture, brush some fallen plaster off her handiwork. Princess So-and-So might have had second thoughts, had she seen the workroom.

Over tea, Ann learned more about the intricacies of the two claimant clans and felt the full force of their blood-worship. The family had lost much of their wealth but their guts were bound up with French history, the role played in it by their forebears and their need to belong and to be seen to belong. The energy and commitment of parents and children alike was contagious: Ann could have been swept along by that power, but another château beckoned.

Here she met a more unusual type of upper-class, bloodline-obsessed landowner, large, bumbling, mild and bookish. A 'peasant peer' dressed in tweeds that had clearly fed battalions of moths, he loved farming his land and researching the nitty-gritty of his great old family and their place in history. Being neither a Bourbon nor an Orléans, he didn't think that the aristocracy should still be ruling France – a refreshing, if non-radical, point of view.

The Château Jacquot, a fortified twelfth-century jewel in the Yonne, was the one that bowled me over most readily: high, mighty stone walls under a red-tiled roof, and flanked by fortifying towers. Entering in winter, to be welcomed in front of a vast medieval fireplace by a charming couple, was a moment to soften the hardest of hearts. The one bedroom was four-postered and designed to encourage *fantaisies de noblesse*.

The Château de Béru has very different sort of magnificence, with massive, noble arches, exposed stonework and shuttered windows that survey miles of vineyards. The Comtes de Béru have been there since 1627, but the estate goes back to the twelfth century. The very stones breathe history, and Louis XIV's great-grandson apparently stayed here – perhaps as Mary Queen of Scots stayed everywhere in Scotland. This is one of Chablis's prettiest valleys, and a fitting place for Athénaïs, the daughter of the house, to establish herself as an organic wine-grower. Athénaïs and her mother are rejuvenating the *domaine* and are members of the Femmes et Vins de Bourgogne.

Châteaux, however, have always come second to great farmhouses in my affections. Some of the finest are in Normandy, where great courtyards are enclosed by high stone walls, reflecting the Normans' insatiable appetite for building – and their fear of other Normans. My first farm-love was the Ferme de la Rivière, near Isigny-sur-Mer, famous for its oysters, the 'Huitres Spéciales d'Isigny'. (Curiously, the name Disney comes from d'Isigny.) The farm also offered a *table d'hôte*, a great French institution, which meant food straight from the farm eaten with the family. I enjoyed this experience even more than a good restaurant meal. Since those halcyon days many *tables d'hôtes* have thrown in the towel, reluctant to rebuild their ancient kitchens to meet food hygiene regulations. To feast well, but simply, and then to climb a Norman stone staircase to a room with a beamed ceiling and stone walls bare of anything but a tapestry – that was the height of luxury.

Dominique is a farmer and owner of another old Norman farmhouse, which gathered together all the pleasures of staying in France. I admired her from the moment I first saw her, carrying two chickens into the kitchen, a child on one shoulder and the washing slung over the other. She had no choice but to learn the ropes as her trawlerman husband was often away on long trips and she had seven children to look after. All her children, some of them fishermen, still live in the area, and there is always fresh fish for supper. The mackerel had been caught the morning of our visit and grilled on the barbecue, sea-strong and fresh, with a mustard sauce. 'I live surrounded by nature and try to slide through it as discreetly as I can,' Dominique purred. She has been an eco-activist since she was eighteen and still makes vast quantities of jams as a practical green gesture. Her eggs come from 'our hens that peck and cackle in the fields alongside our ducks and turkeys'. Dinners are convivial, organic and mostly from the garden.

During dinner, I skirted delicately around the subject of Dominique's husband's absences, especially as his younger daughters were at the table with us. But at breakfast Dominique was looking cheerful; her husband had just sent a message announcing that he would be away for another three days. 'Don't believe those stories about heart-broken fishermen's wives waving tear-stained handkerchiefs at the end of the jetty. Behind the handkerchiefs they are weeping with relief. Time, at last, to themselves!'

Cognac is a region which I have only come to know since running mini-tours in the eighties. For me it was defined by its local building styles, with the cosiest and most French of houses: warm stone, steep roofs, tiles and blue shutters. But the region's real claim to fame, of course, is the eponymous brandy, made largely from wine rather than other fruits and usually from the humble Ugni Blanc grape – humble because it makes a wine considered by many to be undrinkable. It is distilled twice in copper pots and then aged for years in oak barrels – for about fifty years in the case of aged cognac, the stuff that connoisseurs drink, which is matured to such an extent that the oak barrels have nothing left to give, no more tannins or lignins. At that point the makers transfer the cognac to glass demijohns and store them in a room delightfully known as *paradis*.

It is a fine French tradition, to know an area for its booze rather than for anything else, and it generates extra local loyalty. We recently sent an invoice to one of our owners in the area and his reply warmed our hearts:

Dear Sawdays,

My heart raced for a few moments when I learnt you were more than doubling our subscription price. I reached for a glass of cognac to steady my nerves and read your invoice again, only to discover you had confused our five-bedroom B&B with a fifty bedroom hotel!!

What a privilege it is to live in Cognac country and to have, right at hand, and at all times, the medicinal benefits of UNLIMITED COGNAC!

I look forward to receiving something more nearly resembling last year's invoice.

Christopher

Reading the 1994 description of one of our earliest B&Bs, the gentle Villa les Roses run by Madame Christaens near Verdun in north-eastern France, I am reminded how expectations have changed. 'Beds are excellent and bathrooms are being renovated,' runs one line. French beds usually sagged, and travellers would use the traditional long bolster to protect each other from unwanted intimacy.

French bathrooms in those days were unpredictable. In the Château le Mont Epinguet in Normandy, our bedroom had a bidet that rolled on wheels from under the sink and a bath that lurked behind a screen. I was enchanted, and Em and I recently installed a complete bathroom in – rather than next to – our bedroom at home in Bristol. French plumbing has restored its reputation and is often now magnificent. The France of Billy Wilder – 'a country where the money falls apart and you cannot tear the toilet paper' – is now just a legend.

Madame Christaens is still going strong, now widowed but devoted to the company her visitors bring, especially the British. In the past twenty years France has become more prosperous, more European – and more stressed. The computer age has allowed the pressures of urban life to penetrate to the remotest corners of the countryside. But still the British keep coming, bless them, and our French owners love them for it. The *entente* is still very *cordiale*, perhaps even *chaleureuse*.

11

Barging around in Wales

Wales gave me one of the happiest encounters of my early publishing years. I set off to meet a woman whose house was set deep among the waters and valleys of the very middle of Wales, near Builth Wells. A phone call had revealed her as an American, which quickened my interest. Why would an American woman live alone in the heart of Wales?

I arrived after dark and the door opened to reveal an elegant black woman in her fifties. This was even more unexpected, for less than 1 per cent of the population of rural Wales is black. I was treated to an evening of superb food and extraordinary conversation, for there was more to my hostess than met the eye. Her story took me on a journey from the lush Welsh hills to a grim training camp and the humiliations borne by a young black female Marine. Her descriptions of the obstacle course, the mud and bullets, the vile taunts and abuse were harrowing. What sort of woman came through that with such aplomb? We talked into the small hours.

The morning found me sitting contentedly in a plastic armchair in the middle of the river that skirted the house, a cup of coffee in one hand, a newspaper in the other, my feet in the icy water that burbled over the rocks and under my chair. A kingfisher completed the picture, flying fast along the bank. This was a softer Wales than the one I knew as a boy, when I had spent sodden days camping with the Scouts, listening to sheep gargling rather than bleating, and wishing I were elsewhere. One particularly humiliating weekend had seen me lead a party of Scouts up Snowdon. Fearing for our safety, for the wind and the cold were fierce, we roped ourselves together and used ice-axes to hack our way heroically to the top. We were more than a little miffed when we got there to find a party of old ladies serenely taking tea in the café. They had come up by train.

Years later, down in the south-east corner of Wales, it was again a grey day, and the autumn colours struggled to lift the gloom. I thought of all the negativity about Wales: 'When all else fails / Try Wales', and even Dylan Thomas's 'The land of my fathers? My fathers can have it!' I was with Mike, an old friend, on a cycle ride from Newport along the Monmouthshire and Brecon Canal to Brecon, and back the next day. This would be thirty-five miles each way, a lazy and amiable ride. We parked the car on the edge of Newport and set off to find the canal.

I have a special affection for canals, cut through the

countryside with little more than shovels and often in appalling conditions. The first major commercial canal, France's Canal de Briare, was begun in 1604 with twelve thousand men digging. It is a stunning achievement and vast quantities of wine were later shipped on its gentle waters. An aqueduct that was built in the nineteenth century to connect it to another canal has fourteen piers to support a single metal beam that carries a trough of water weighing thirteen thousand tonnes. Such gargantuan effort always amazes me, an engineering innocent.

We British didn't begin our canal system until the late eighteenth century, and this little canal to Brecon is rarely mentioned. I was impressed by the locks at Cefn, fourteen of them hard on one another's heels. As Mike and I pedalled up the flight, the only slope all day, we stopped to chat to the volunteers restoring the locks. I love the way the British volunteer to rebuild assorted reminders of our past: railways, canals, bridges, dry-stone walls and footpaths. Is this harmlessly obsessive behaviour, or is it the nobility of the human spirit? Is it just, as Oscar Wilde claimed of hard work, 'simply the refuge of people who have nothing whatsoever to do'? Or is it a way of having both the satisfaction of physical work and the company of others? It is probably all these things, and those who regularly volunteer apparently tend to live longer than those who don't.

The Monmouthshire canal slides through gentle countryside, a couple of centuries away from the modern world. The flatness is attractive to a cyclist several puffs short of fitness. Along the way there are countless reminders that the canal was the main highway of its day: it has junctions with many railway and tram tracks that carried coal, iron and other goods to the canal for onward shipment to Newport and the sea. The scale of it all is impressive. At Risca, a town I had never heard of, there was once a bridge almost a thousand feet long, on thirty-two arches.

I created Barge Bookers in 1990, a casual spin-off from the tour business that I had started. I had seen barges slipping through the Burgundian countryside with effortless dignity and I wanted to be involved with them. We found a handful of bargees prepared to give us a commission, printed a brochure and sent it to all our American contacts. Eventually we co-opted forty-five barges, ranging from family-run ones to those with four-poster beds, swimming pools, Jacuzzis and other excesses. We were happy to include the latter as they were redeemed by the magnificent canals and countryside. The barge owners were all mavericks: scruffy and smart, French and English, ingenious and independent to a man and woman.

I thought that Barge Bookers was doomed when one of our clients had a heart attack. The *pompiers* (paramedics, in this case, but usually firemen) were called and arrived with a stretcher, the English patient was loaded and being gingerly carried along the gangplank when a *pompier* slipped and the patient slid straight into the canal. Happily, he was hauled out with impressive alacrity. Later, having made a complete recovery, he treated it all as an amusing incident. An American might have sued.

Gerard Morgan-Grenville was one of the barge-owners, a man of aristocratic bearing and also a committed environmental campaigner who founded the Centre for Alternative

Technology in Snowdonia. From his barge in Burgundy he spotted a foul liquid gushing into the canal from the waste outfall of a factory. Donning his pinstriped suit, Gerard presented himself to the factory receptionist as a potential client and was ushered into the MD's office, where he negotiated the purchase of huge quantities of the company's product. He insisted on speed, and the deal was mouth-watering enough to persuade the MD to draw up a contract on the spot. Gerard read it carefully, and then asked:

'Splendid. But one very minor matter, that you will surely satisfy me on immediately, is your waste. Where does it go?'

'We have, of course, a sophisticated disposal system that complies with all the EU regulations, Monsieur.'

'Excellent. I am much relieved. And the pipe that discharges into the canal: can you tell me what goes through that?'

There was much squirming and obfuscation, but the truth had to emerge. Gerard promptly tore up the contract.

Back in Wales with Mike, our cycle ride took us through woodland, along valleys, skirting the edges of villages and hamlets. Scarcely a soul was seen, other than an old man sitting on a bench watching us approach. 'You're working too hard,' he said, smiling benignly. I dismounted and sat beside him on his bench.

'I cycle along here every weekend, about ten miles each way,' he said.

'That's impressive. You must be older than I am.'

'I'm eighty-four, that's all. I need the exercise, otherwise my joints will seize up.' I asked him about his life and found that he was still, as he had been for sixty years, tuning pianos in the Welsh valleys.

The day's ride ended on a perfect note. We arrived in Brecon exhausted, clad as cyclists are often clad: unattractively, in Lycra. Peter, our host, asked what we most wanted and it was, of course, a cup of tea and a piece of cake by the stove. Moments later we had just that, in a kitchen of cultured chaos, all space for cups and saucers taken up by a motley spread of books and magazines.

As a last-minute booking, Peter had offered to squeeze us in somewhere, somehow, as long as we were flexible. The squeezing was into the old canal-boat at the bottom of the garden, in the canal. 'Damn,' said Peter, 'I didn't get round to hoovering up the leaves, but the sheets are good.' Indeed, the boat was in full leaf, but the bunk was lavishly furnished with sheets of the highest-quality cotton. I borrowed Peter's own shambolic bathroom for a long soak, a glass of wine in one hand and a book in the other. We then lit a fire in the tiny boat-stove and settled down to a drink.

Supper was with Peter: baked beans and scrambled eggs, offered when we hinted that we were too tired to pedal out for supper. After this modest feast we sank into the sofas around the fire, logs there for us to pile onto it as we wished. We drank wine and talked of books, especially *How Steeple Sinderby Wanderers Won the FA Cup* by J. L. Carr. Peter left it by my bed and insisted that I take it home to finish. It is a bizarre but amusing tale of David and Goliath, of eccentricity, native cunning and English village life. It revealed how Peter feels about the world, and why his house is such a remarkable marriage of kindness, determined chaos and cultured beauty.

We slept like angels, in nature's nocturnal silence. Boats chugging past at eye-level awoke us to a sunny day and a sun-drenched breakfast in the conservatory with the other guests, all of whom had slept soundly in beautiful book-filled rooms. Chickens strutted under the breakfast table as dish after dish emerged, each served with the informality and ease that mark the whole house. The plates and cups were antique, or just plain old. Peter wandered in and out, chatting amiably as he cleared a path among the chickens.

Peter revels in the unpredictability of his days. His funniest breakfast happened after Group 4, the security firm, decided to lodge two of their night watchmen with him; they were guarding the cars overnight at the Welsh National Rally. Peter christened one Fat Alun. Alun had only been out of the valleys during his years as a squaddie in the Royal Welch Fusiliers, and was 'everything phobic', especially homophobic. Peter fed them pies and beans, as requested, for breakfast and the same for their evening meal at half-past eight. On day three of their occupation he had a call from a man with a lovely voice saying 'Hi, I'm Charlie, do you have a double room tomorrow, because we want to come down and do some hiking.' 'Of course, come on down.'

Charlie clattered down the steps the next day and turned out to be a beautiful, cultured young man, an actor living in London. His partner was another, equally beautiful, Charlie, male and an actors' agent. When the two Charlies came down together the following morning and Fat Alun then tipped in after a night's red-eyed work, Peter closed the kitchen door and let them get on with breakfast. 'I expected blood on the carpet. Instead there was polite silence and phrases like "Can I pass you the salt, sir?" and "Another coffee, sir?"'

Later, Fat Alun pronounced them, 'Nice lads, those!' It turned out that Charlie the actor had been an officer in the Royal Welch Fusiliers.

Wales's treasures are scattered, but they repay the effort of finding them. I particularly enjoy stories of beautiful old buildings that have been hauled back from the edge of ruin, and Allt-y-bela in Monmouthshire is a fine example. It was built as a hall house in the fifteenth century, a cruck-frame building in which everyone lived huggermugger with the animals. In 1599 a wealthy merchant added a three-storey tower, the first in Wales, with huge, light-filled rooms. The central staircase is stupendous, built of solid baulks of timber, probably by itinerant shipwrights. For four hundred years the house slumbered and then, sagging and decrepit, was saved by the county council in the eighties. The Spitalfields Trust stepped in to restore it with old materials and skills, and then sold it on to Arne and William, who have added their own panache and energy, using timber to heat the house and emphasising the architecture in all their design decisions. It is a fine thing just to be there, let alone to sleep under those mighty beams. What county council could afford to help rescue such a building now?

The story behind a house, together with that of the owners, adds colour and depth to the picture. The same is true of landscapes. After reading *A Shepherd's Life* by James Rebanks, I now begin to understand what it takes to keep the Lake District hills going: the work and the intelligence, and the vitality of the traditions that enable the farmers to make the most of every gift that nature offers. During the foot-and-mouth chaos of 2001, those farmers lost many of their hefted Herdwick sheep, animals attached to the land by breeding and memory. When the disease had run its course the National Trust, the area's main landlord, teamed up with the Interface carpet company to create a special Herdwick carpet tile. We bought the leftovers to carpet our new offices in Yanley; every tile told the story of hefted sheep, of the National Trust's vision and of the government's monstrous confusion over how to handle the foot-and-mouth epidemic.

The current controversy about sheep-farming – its suitability for the ecological well-being of the area – is an unsettling one. George Monbiot, who lives in Wales, has raised the matter and the debate is still running. His view of sheep as 'woolly maggots' has gone down badly with those who see sheep as essential players in the landscape. George writes of 'shifting baseline syndrome', whereby we keep things as we know them or remember them, rather than as they should be ecologically. Our baseline shifts depending on who we are and what we wish to return to. Might Wales's ecology, and economy, thrive with more trees and 're-wilded' landscapes? The debate usually becomes, however, a familiar and unsophisticated case of a subsidised economy, in the shape of the hill-farmers, versus the ecology.

There is a good story, too, behind Ty-Mynydd, high up above Hay-on-Wye in the Black Mountains. John was building walls and damming streams with stone by the time he was eight, and his brother gave him twenty yards of stone wall to build when he was just fourteen. The die

was cast: John left school to be a dry-stone-waller. This love
for walls led him to hill-farming at Ty-Mynydd, but he was
missing a wife. A solicitous friend put John's photo in the
Farmer Wants a Wife section of *Country Living* magazine
and attracted seventy responses. Niki's letter won the day;
she drove down in a 2CV sagging under the weight of her
possessions, and never left.

'Our lives,' she says, 'run along slow principles. Our cows,
goats, sheep, geese and pigs roam free over acres of organic
pastureland. They live and grow at their own pace, calving
and lambing when they choose. The abattoir is only thirty
minutes away, so stress is minimised, and then the meat is
hung for a month – and believe, me, it is worth the wait.'
Niki and John are so unstressed and hefted to their land that
they, too, are worth the wait. They let your children run
wild, free and safe, and you want to do the same. Perhaps, as
our children are more and more irretrievably plugged into
the internet, we will be beseeching farmers like Niki and
John to show them another way – to unplug them.

From the perspective of Ty-Mynydd, and of wilder places
in Wales, the world can feel very safe. Lush, green hills
and unspoiled valleys seem to deny the existence of outside
threats. Yet Wales is no safer than the rest of the world. The
climate threats are global. Wales will know, as will we all,
more floods, strange weather patterns and species loss caused
by climate change. These things are hard to discuss or write
about for they demand too much of us, intellectually, mor-
ally, politically. Far better to deny them, or to ridicule them.
Or simply to turn away and carry on with life. Niki and
John are among those who have found their own response,
and I salute them for it.

My uncertainty about how to discuss climate change and the bewildering array of other looming crises was resolved for a while by our Fragile Earth series: the *Little Earth Book* and its sister books on money and food. The material was divided into chapters of about two minutes' reading – ideal for a session on the lavatory. Complexity, thus broken down, seemed less daunting.

One chapter in the *Little Earth Book* described how cod stocks had been devastated by over-fishing; from seas replete with cod off Newfoundland in the nineteenth century, there are now almost no fish to be had. Throughout the long decline we knew what should be done. Nothing was done, however, until recently, with modest results in the North Sea, where cod stocks are now deemed to be close to sustainability levels. We have done much the same with whales, with herring, with tuna and indeed with most fish stocks – now at perilously low levels worldwide. We then avoid deeper solutions to the problem by creating mini-'solutions', such as marine refuges and fish farming; the latter has a poor performance if judged by energy in versus energy out. Ninety-eight per cent of the krill we catch is fed to farmed fish, at the ratio of about five kilograms in to one kilogram out. The supply of krill – basic food for whales – has recently fallen, leading to a decline in whale populations. As has often been said, we are the only species capable of calmly arranging and then monitoring our own self-destruction. We know precisely, scientifically, how stupid we are being.

Other chapters in the *Little Earth Book* tackled issues such as debt, war, economics, energy, climate and happiness, all with the author James Bruges's masterful brevity and insight.

I began to understand the connectedness of all the issues. We sent a copy to every Member of Parliament, receiving eight thank-you letters (most of them from Liberal Democrats), but Parliament was unmoved. The Green MSP Robin Harper, however, launched the book in Edinburgh to great fanfare (one lone journalist in the rain) and used it frequently as a source and an inspiration, as did the University of Hong Kong and others. A barge skipper from Hungary vowed that if we were to publish in Hungarian he would devote the rest of his life to its promotion.

The *Little Food Book* did a similar job. Craig Sams, chairman of the Soil Association at the time and founder of Whole Earth Foods, pulled back the curtains on an industry that is corrupt and disingenuous. His introduction told the story of the closure of the macrobiotic bookshop in New York in 1966. The American Medical Association had taken against a philosophy that countenanced food as a source of good health. The sale of macrobiotic books was deemed to be illegal, and the shop closed.

The food industry, in cahoots with the chemical industry, has since then grown even more powerful, and more dangerous. It resists anything that threatens its profits, such as proposals to increase organic production, to tax sugar and salt, to curtail insecticides that threaten bee populations. It is happy for half our food, worldwide, to be wasted. During a crash in pig prices I learned that the contracts farmers had with the supermarkets were considered worthless. The falling price for pigs was – for the most part – passed on immediately to the farmers, whatever the length of their contracts at a higher price. Any threat of legal action would be met by the threat of future loss of contracts. The local-food renaissance offers some hope, as do changes in eating habits. These have affected Em and me at home in many ways. Em, a talented gardener, has an allotment where I follow orders and dig, and there is acute pleasure in eating food almost straight from the ground. Yet the underlying economic system continues to distance us from our food and its growing, and to undermine our agricultural system. A reminder for the sceptics among you: a third of the world's cropland has become unproductive in the last forty years.

David Boyle, an economics journalist, wrote the *Little Money Book* and explained how money is made, how different societies have treated it, how much a tool of central power it can be and, therefore, how much any attempt to escape its tyranny will be jumped upon. Witness the currency experiment at the little Austrian ski resort of Wörgl in the early thirties. The town was suffering from the Great Depression, and created its own currency as a way out. Unemployment fell and business began to recover, but the government felt its power threatened and after just over a year the experiment was closed down by the Austrian National Bank. In the USA to this day, local currencies are not welcomed by government; neither, I might add, are they in the UK, though there are some modestly successful ones such as the Bristol Pound. I wonder if they will flourish, and what will happen if they do.

The statistics behind such currencies are impressive: every pound spent locally generates up to four times more in the local economy. Most of the same pound spent in Tesco leaves the community. Many reasonable people find this hard to believe and continue shopping in stores that export their hard-earned cash. Then, over a latte in Starbucks, they lament the decline of independent shops. Another thought here for the sceptics: local currencies provoke us to think again about a system that allows 1 per cent of the population to have as much as the remaining 99 per cent. That is a good place to begin thinking about economics.

The books got off to a magnificent start with help from the Bristol area's great organic success, Yeo Valley. The Mead family have a farm below the Mendip Hills and have produced and sold organic milk and yoghurt for many years. It is now a £300 million-turnover company, generous to local and national causes. They advertised the *Little Earth Book* on the tops of millions of yoghurt pots, and we sold eight thousand copies within a few weeks. I delight in this sort of partnership between companies trying to do the right thing. We have shared projects with other small businesses, such as Howies, Kettle Chips, Dorset Cereals, Café Direct and Divine Chocolate, though it is hard to keep up as, one by one, small companies are gobbled up by larger ones.

An ethical structure for business, good in itself, is vital for the underlying health of an economy, though it is an idea that still struggles to gain credence. The Quakers have shown time and again how strong founding princi-ples can make a business successful, though most of the big ones (Rowntree's, Cadbury's, Lloyds, Barclays, Fry's) have gone the way of all flesh; most companies do, when they grow. The same is true of other companies founded on ethical principles: Ben & Jerry's sold out to Unilever, the Body Shop to L'Oréal and co-investor Nestlé, Green & Black's to Cadburys (itself swallowed up by Kraft), and Innocent Drinks to Coca-Cola. In the process, integrity and values have been lost and commercial value gained. Once companies are sold, their new leaders are rarely motivated by the same principles that drove the founders.

The challenge of structuring a business so that it maintains its values and purpose is fascinating. David Erdal, one of the pioneers of the employee ownership movement in Britain, showed me a possible way to exit my own company. David had inherited a paper company and often walked the factory floor to meet the workers. One day it dawned on him that all fourteen hundred of them were working hard just to make him, one human being, rich. It was a startling, if obvious, awakening, and he resolved to sell his shares at a reasonable price to the employees. The results were impressive, though the mill, the main business, eventually had to close after a long struggle to survive in a globalised paper-making industry. It was almost the last to close in the UK, largely thanks to the engagement of the workers. It was overwhelmed by overseas competition and the value of sterling in a globalised economy. No doubt the Asian mills that have taken over will one day be victims of the same globalisation that swills capital around the planet in search of the cheapest labour force. Each change carries heart-breaking consequences for communities, something that Donald Trump was able to exploit for his own purposes.

David told me the story of three small towns in Italy – and if you were baffled by my earlier suggestion that ethics underlie the real health of an economy, this may help. Town A was a normal Italian town, with a mixture of jobs and companies. Town B had both employee-owned companies and standard ones. Most citizens of Town C worked for companies in which they had an interest, for they were employee-owners. Now here is the fascinating thing: the social and health indicators in the three towns were radically different, to the extent that Town C had an average life expectancy of two years more than Town A, with Town B in the middle. The same was true for cardiac health, divorce, alcoholism, teenage pregnancy and many other indicators. Allowing for other factors, David's conclusion was that good business, especially when employees have ownership, reduces society's costs and increases well-being. Town C is an inexpensive town to run; that, surely, makes good economic sense.

Employee ownership is a fine idea, but is not enough in itself to ensure that a company behaves ethically and for the common good. That requires profound cultural commitment, drawing upon the decency that lurks under the skin of most people and most companies. It is therefore strange that the money-obsessed Anglo-American model of increasing shareholder value has got its teeth into British business culture. No wonder the French are keen to hold on to their own model, and the Scandinavians theirs.

This is, perhaps, one explanation of the success of so many of the special places that we work with. They are trying to do good work, whether by making their houses sustainable, by growing their own food, or by supporting their community. A pub in Dedham, Essex, has a room devoted to the sale of local allotment produce. Another, in Somerset, runs and hosts the village cricket team. Others are even owned by the community. Such places are more likely than others to prosper in difficult times, and are fresh air blowing in little gusts through a business world that needs change.

Penpont, on the River Usk west of Brecon, is a fine example of a house that has given back to the world around it. Gavin and Davina inherited it as an empty and beautiful shell, dropped their careers in teaching and tree surgery and set out on a long journey to turn the land into an organic haven. In the four-acre walled garden they grow fruit, vegetables, herbs and flowers for the house, and for local pubs and Brecon Theatre. Gavin has planted more than a hundred thousand trees and is supplying the fuel for an enormous wood-chip boiler that warms the house and all the outbuildings. This saves seventy tonnes of carbon emissions every year. The restoration of one building involved using sheep's wool as insulation. In a dozen ways they are bringing the community into Penpont, regenerating the woodland and giving back generously. Penpont seems to belong to us all.

Mad Hotels and Wonderful People

A good hotel owner brings far more to the lives of others than mere comfort and kindness. Imogen, the owner of Langar Hall in Nottinghamshire, was such a person. The house was once the home of the Scrope family. Shakespeare-lovers among you may recognise the name from *Henry V*:

> What shall I say to thee, lord Scroop; thou cruel,
> Ingrateful, savage, and inhuman creature!

Henry Scrope was involved in a plot against the king and lost his head. Imogen, centuries later and with a good head on her, inherited the house and wondered how on earth she could afford to keep it. She became as famous as any of

Langar's previous owners as she created, bit by bit, a hotel of a remarkable kind, elegantly beautiful and suffused with her personality. Imogen, known as Imo, reigned supreme and benign. Alec, from our office, tasked with photographing both Imogen and Langar, rolled up in his black leathers on a noisy motorbike and parked shyly under a tree. Still in his biking gear and heavy boots, he clunked his way into the house. He was met by Imogen behind her desk, looking severely over her spectacles at this unexpected leather-bound apparition. A smile slowly enveloped her face: 'Ah, you are on a bike. How splendid! Do park it here by the front door.'

Imogen's own words are a delightful record of her story:

Turning Langar into a hotel was not what I had in mind. I was ignorant of the hotel scene, having rarely stayed in one. Had I known what was involved I would not have opened the door. Those first two bedrooms and a few American visitors were the start . . . the good life I least expected. I love it. I have never wanted to go back to 'private life'. I can hardly remember an unpleasant guest and many have become friends. With their encouragement the house is more like a home. There is good wine in the cellar, celebrations, music and laughter in the dining room, and the house was never so comfortable or the rooms as pretty. The moat is stocked with carp and more trees have been planted. Next year you will be able to walk around the moat again, over bridges and through mown paths and picnic under the trees.

Her greatest gift was to convince everybody she met that they were her favourite human being in the world. Imogen died in an accident on holiday in 2016. Her death was a terrible loss for many, many people. A light went out, the sort of light that only a gifted and intensely human hotel-keeper of the old school can shine.

Richard and Sheila Johnson of Fingals Hotel in Devon showed us that, like Imo, one can run a brilliant hotel without sacrificing a shred of one's personality. Fingals, more a country-house party than a hotel, became a byword in the office for 'dotty but wonderful'. Nothing ran on time; meals were unpredictable and would last for as long as the conversation. Children and dogs were welcome, and I am sure a pet chimpanzee would have had a privileged place at the table. If Richard was seized by an idea he was off, perhaps dragging the guests with him out onto the river in his boat with a picnic. Behind it all lay generosity, a natural exuberance and a hunger for interesting encounters. Behind Richard stands, as stands behind every successful man, a fine woman rolling her eyeballs. Sheila, Richard's wife, is the constant *deus ex machina* in the life of Fingals.

On my first visit to Fingals, Richard took me on a bike ride to meet Jilly Sutton, a talented sculptor and painter who showed us an exhibition of 'local friends' in her studio. Around the walls was a seductive array of plaster casts of female breasts, each a faithful reproduction. It was a gallery of delights, reminders of the intimacy of this happy community. Richard recognised them all. We got back for lunch at four, a lunch that Richard was supposed to cook. The ever-patient hotel guests were used to this sort of whimsy.

Few of us would want to run a hotel, and Richard explained why. The biggest problem had been finding staff they could work and live with. Eventually they got a French chef, Eric, who stayed for eleven years. They put up with his little peccadilloes, such as coming out among the guests after slight misuse of the cooking brandy and holding forth in his atrocious English. He became part of the family and looked up to by the kids, probably as a source of good weed. While feeding a slot machine in a Totnes pub, he keeled over with an aneurism and died two weeks later. The family were devastated. His portrait now sits in the bar at Fingals and his ashes under a tree in the garden.

In the years that followed they had one chef after another: chefs who were drug addicts, even alcoholics, and one who stayed up all night in the bar on his first evening and only went to bed when Richard got up to lay breakfast. He then appeared to cook breakfast at half-past ten. All of them betrayed trust, so Richard sent an ad to a catering magazine:

CHEF REQUIRED. Small family hotel seeking chef to run our kitchen (into the ground). Must intimidate our young trainee staff and generally whip them out of shape. The successful applicant should ideally be alcoholic or a drug addict, and must be a chain smoker. Must be able to precook everything and then heat it up to order. Accommodation can be provided to make our lives hell 24/7. Wage can be supplemented with kick-backs from suppliers. No notice required when leaving, just a scribbled note left on the kitchen table – preferably on a busy evening.

The magazine refused the advert.

Another hotel that flew the flag for personality and eccentricity was Huntsham Court, a Victorian pile in deepest

Devon run when I knew it by Mogens and Andrea Bolwig.
I leaned heavily against the vast wooden front door to get
in, and wandered around the house seeking signs of life. A
fire burned in the grate, a CD played Oscar Peterson's 'C
Jam Blues', the vaulted hall was welcoming but devoid of
life. I found Andrea in her kitchen. The house was a triumph of chutzpah over commerce, a warren of grand and
modest rooms furnished with humour and panache. The
best room had not one but two grand pianos. Most had, as
lavatories, those Victorian thunder-boxes served by mighty
cascades of water from ceiling-high cisterns. My bathroom
had two cast-iron baths in front of an open fire, laid and
ready for action. I turned on the bath, applied a match to
the scrunched-up newspaper in the fireplace and soon had a
blazing fire at my elbow while steaming water gushed from
the mouths of taps grand enough to have served Queen
Victoria. It was generous and careless of practicalities. I told
Andrea how precious and bonkers such qualities were, and
her response reminded me of Cyrano de Bergerac: Cyrano,
the dashing hero of the play by Rostand, leaps onto the stage
to remonstrate with, and see off, the actors who were, in his
view, ruining the play. When the audience booed him he
threw money at them from the stage. '*Tu es fou!*' cried his
friend. '*Mais quel geste!*' he declared.

Behind these stories are people who believe in other
people, who pride themselves on putting people together.
At Fingals, running dinner on one long table brought about
many coincidences over the years. People would share intimacies with new friends. Once, Richard and Sheila sat next
to a woman who had just been beside her mother on her
deathbed. The mother had confessed that she was not her

only child. While a nurse in Southampton Hospital she had had an affair and got pregnant; her husband said he would forgive her if she had the child adopted at birth and had no further contact. This woman had made it her mission to find her half-brother.

'I used to work in Southampton Hospital,' said the doctor sitting opposite. 'What was your mother's name?' She gave it.

'Ha!' he continued. 'I knew of her, and I know who the child's father was. His name was Peter. He was a fellow doctor.'

'What?' she said, astonished. 'I used to call him Uncle Peter. He was having an affair with my mother all along?'

So she came one step closer to finding her half-brother over a dinner at Fingals.

Robert, one of our long-standing London B&B owners, had been mischievously insistent on me going down to Cornwall to see his bungy – his bungalow – in Portscatho. We had met in his Greenwich B&B while he was being filmed for Ruth Watson's programme, *The Hotel Inspector*. As the place was not a hotel I was called in to take Ruth's place for the day, an amusing experience with a man who takes things with a pinch of salt, whereas Ruth took herself rather more seriously. Her tastes were less eclectic than mine, more pro-fessional hotelier. The programme was a success, so Robert was branching out and had bought this bungalow.

Once an antique dealer, Robert has a flair for design, but the bungy nevertheless astonished me. From the outside it was as modest as bungalows can be. 'Bungy without, Chatsworth within' is his own description. Exteriors,

Robert reminded me, are no guide to interiors. In the lush sitting room are country-house sofas, portraits, a fireplace, rugs, good furniture. It is an optical illusion of grandeur, tongue firmly in cheek, framed at one end by a pair of pillars backed by giant swathes of fabric. You are dared to acknowledge your own pretensions. Beyond are two gaily decorated and comfortable bedrooms, one with an engagingly ridiculous and out-of-place four-poster.

Big, beautiful houses are gifts from history that we can all enjoy, but for our books and website we also revel in the unusual and the quirky – both of which are in decline. To meet one who has done his or her own thing, ignoring modern trends, is refreshing. Transforming a bungalow into a minuscule country house is gently to mock expectations.

Rule-breakers – well, I love them, and have been delighted by Canopy & Stars, our little company that finds and promotes the strangest and most unexpected places to stay. It is a ready-made community of rule-breakers. Finely sensitised to any support for my views (as one always is) I lit upon the words of the American writer and publisher William Feather: 'the man who doesn't know how and when to break a rule is a fearful pain in the neck'. Not much room for argument there. Canopy & Stars has a collection of places unconventional enough to please Feather: upturned boats, a five-roomed treehouse up an oak tree, an Iron-Age dwelling, converted buses and lorries, old train wagons and horseboxes, and a corrugated-iron chapel. Every visit lifts me briefly above any dark forebodings I may have about man's Pavlovian conformity.

Eccentricity and the unexpected are not preconditions for our approval; they just help. Sleeping in the attic of a

timbered farmhouse near Hay-on-Wye, I ducked my head
to avoid beams, stepped over cross-beams to leave the bedroom, and carefully avoided stepping through the floor
between the joists. It was an original and beautiful wooden
space, probably illegal as a bedroom for paying guests, but
the result was a memorable night nested in a forest of timbers. From my window I gazed out from my internal forest
over the sort of mist-shrouded tree canopy I had known in
Papua New Guinea.

I discovered another gem in Essex, the county next door
to the Suffolk where I grew up. Paul and Sam own three dis-
used gravel pits on their farm near Malden, two of which are
rented out for trout fishing. One winter Paul, bored, decided
to do something useful with his piles of old fertiliser barrels. So he built a raft from those barrels, and, almost as an
afterthought, created a little house on top. He then floated it
to the middle of the third gravel pond. The pond is fringed
with grasses and reeds, and with silence. Visitors stand on
a small pontoon that they pull by rope to the cabin in the
water's centre, where a meal – perhaps of Paul's smoked
fish – awaits. The cabin runs on solar power and there is a
fire pit on the bank near a tethered hot-tub platform. It is
a bizarre and wonderful project, an intervention that has
brought a little magic to a once-humble gravel pit.

The injection of imagination into ordinary places has
kept me fuelled for years. An artist, Hugh Dunford Wood,
moved to the Dorset coast, opened up his house to guests
and peopled it with his imagination: 'The house is my
canvas. I paint the furniture, hang paintings on the ceiling
and hand-print our wallpaper from my own designs. I make
the cups and the plates, the bread and the jams, the pesto,

the cheese and the fruit bowls.' He extracts the last ounce
of delight from every encounter, from life itself.

Erlend Clouston, in Edinburgh, also has that rare ability
to harvest the most from every moment. He and his wife
Hélène are an unusual marriage of France and Shetland.
Their humour, laced with historical and cultural references, gives their conversation an open-minded and liberal
tinge; views are expressed with a deceptive gentleness. For
breakfast on my first visit, Mozart had been recruited as the
background to a slow, thoughtful piece of culinary theatre –
an elegant and understated ritual. Every dish was Erlend's
own, each a new take on breakfast. Eggs were poached and
decorated with cream, chives and other herbs, or scrambled
among exotic fruits. Muesli made in the house came with
mango, goat's yoghurt, blueberries, fat currants and honey.
Toast was in unexpected shapes and flavours.

Erlend's generous and imaginative approach has, perhaps,
its roots in his childhood in Shetland, where strangers are
genuinely welcome. When I asked him about it he was
wryly analytical. It is, for him, all fun, and a little crazy. A
pact grows between proprietor and invaders, fuelled by his
food on the one hand, and their stories on the other. They
are a mixed and entertaining bag, Erlend told me: 'What
price the yarns of Stanley Kubrick's brother-in-law, the
King of Belgium's press secretary, a man who knew the
Beatles and now promotes BMWs, the Dutch estate owner
who ate tulips in the war? Dish-washing and soiled towels
are the metaphorical bullet holes in the ceiling: awkward,
but they come with the territory.' A little of Erlend's curiosity, character and availability will have rubbed off on each
of his guests. And theirs on him.

The character of a place, to which I allude so often, gives it vitality and life, and it is character, in our buildings, businesses and houses, that we are destroying at an alarming rate. We stand and stare impotently as it is wrenched from us. An editorial in the *Observer* of 3 April 2016 raged in lament at the passing of a café on Hampstead Heath, and its takeover by a café chain: 'brand tyranny . . . is the enclosure movement of our times. A cretinous brand-speak uttered by faceless stooges raised on corporate platitudes, in which "cost-effective" services and "customer feed-back" are cited as "desirable objectives".' Exactly!

Still, England can – IKEA notwithstanding – provide enough character for a lifetime of simple exploration. I have come late to exploring it, and life is not long enough. I revel in my English travels, especially now in my visits to Suffolk where I return often to see my mother and my elder sister Auriol, who lives in the old house with her husband Michael. They are devoted to the area. Auriol sings locally and organises events in the village hall, and they are both active in parish life. From the window of the cottage she built in the orchard, my mother looks down the length of the old garden wall and across green swathes of summer wheat. It is still a pretty Suffolk scene, even if shorn of some big trees and the farm animals of my childhood.

I hope you will forgive me a brief diversion, still in East Anglia, to Ely, where England's most ladylike cathedral soars above the Fens. H. V. Morton, in his *In Search of England*, thought that 'this sudden high hill crowned with its towered cathedral seen above the white mist of late summer is one of the most beautiful things in England'. I would add Salisbury Cathedral, rising from the autumn mists on the marshes, to his list. But I am in Ely to reveal the delightful origin of a little-used word: tawdry. St Etheldreda, who founded Ely Abbey, was also known as St Audrey. On market days at Ely people would sell cheap neckcloths of silk known as 'St Audrey's lace' or 'tawdries'.

Suffolk is best loved for its grey-watered shingle coast, for Aldeburgh, Benjamin Britten, Southwold and the marshes. But the inner Suffolk, of ruined castles and flint-towered churches, wood-framed houses and moated farmhouses, speaks tenderly to me. A visitor who has never seen Lavenham or Chelsworth, nor Hoxne, Laxfield, Long Melford or Clare, will have only half a view of Suffolk. Kersey, once famous for its rough-ribbed cloth that was soaked in the little River Brett that runs across the High Street, is now known for the imperious ducks that hold up the traffic. You might save Lavenham for an energetic day, when you know you can handle the visual burden of so many old Suffolk buildings. The size of the churches is explained by the old wealth of these once-successful wool towns. Blythburgh church grandly stands guard over the River Blyth as it slides, wide and grey, from the fields out to sea, past the river-worn poles marking the channel, each, perhaps, with a lone seagull standing sentinel.

My Suffolk is a gentle world of big skies over the estuary, of slow-ebbing water and flighting duck, of bird calls and beds of waving reeds, of geese wheeling against a Constable sky. The soft lapping of water against the side of my wooden dinghy was a sound of my childhood, and river mud was never far away. I would spend evenings on the marshes opposite Havergate Island, and there I scattered my father's ashes, for he, too, loved this place.

13

Eccentrics and Pioneers

The mere mention of the word B&B can spark distant memories of hatchet-faced landladies in grim boarding houses, net curtains twitching, Nescafé brewing, nylon sheets, hushed breakfast rooms, tomato ketchup, congealed fried eggs, UHT milk, sagging mattresses – and trouser presses. My own particular nightmare is that soul-shrinking moment when you enter the breakfast room to a hushed embarrassment, nobody looking up. A newspaper rustles, a spoon tinkles in a cup, nobody speaks. The young couple in the corner have run out of things to say to each other. The older couple did that long ago.

It can take an eruption, an invasion or an intrusion to break the ice. One B&B owner saw the ice being broken in an unusual way: a sparrow hawk whistled into the conservatory, having missed its prey outside, turned sharp left to avoid going into the kitchen, flew at eye level along the breakfast table where eight people had not said a word to one another, and crashed. Suddenly they all started talking and the most po-faced one got up, went into the kitchen and collected a pair of oven gloves to pick up the half-brained bird. She sat with it for ten minutes before it gathered the strength to fly away. Apparently her uncle repaired damaged raptors in the Pyrenees, so she knew exactly what to do.

Dogs, too, are ice-breakers and bond-makers. Em and I were once having breakfast in the slightly shambolic courtyard of a farmhouse B&B in Herefordshire when the owner's dog, the size of a large goat, approached the table looking for affection. Em allowed it to nuzzle her lap, then stroked its head, then found herself running her hand along its very long back. To her astonishment, it had somehow insinuated itself across her lap, its rear feet on the grass to her right, the front feet to her left and its belly on her lap. After breakfast, with a gentle movement, it untangled itself and shambled away.

There are occasions when, with animals, birds and other signs of throbbing life taking precedence over practicality, things tip gently into a sort of madness. Mrs Broomhead, whose amiably chaotic house in the Lake District won much affection from our office, was a keen gardener, providing meals entirely from her vegetable garden. But things began to go awry, and letters about her fluttered to my desk: about her 'filthy fingernails', her haphazard meals and, especially, about her eccentric husband. I wrote gently to ask how she planned to change, and she defended herself with the vigour of a boxing hare. Her letters were beautifully written, witty and engaging. She was a cultured soul struggling to bring order to herself, her house and to her dementia-afflicted husband. My resolve to drop her from the book was finally shaken, however, by a handwritten fax that spewed forth from our machine at great length and ended with '*Morituri te salutamos*' ('Those who are about to die salute you' – the phrase reputedly shouted to the Emperor by the losing gladiators in the Roman games). How could I stand firm after that? So I promised that an inspector would stay with her anonymously and deliver final judgement, after which she might well be among the *morituri*.

Nicola from the office booked in for the night and took her mother with her. Mrs Broomhead's fingernails were indeed a little earthy, but that was fine given the delightful aura of vegetable and culture in which she basked. The husband hovered at the table making strange noises and one of the guests, an odd man whose only chat was an under-the-breath mutter, had six dogs in tow and was to be avoided. Nicola and her mother escaped to their pretty bedroom and prepared for bed. Nicola made for the door and the stroll down the corridor to the lavatory, but odd scuffling noises could be heard on the landing, with under-the-breath mumbling. Nicola peeped round the edge of the door and then slammed it shut as she came face to face with the dog-owner. She is a brave soul, but even she succumbed to the madness of the moment. She and her mother treated the bedroom as a refuge, giggled all night and were relieved to find that the waste-paper bin was of solid metal, for they were not inclined to brave the journey down the corridor.

We do appreciate character, but this was just over the edge, so poor Mrs Broomhead became one of the *morituri*. Other places, perhaps equally over the edge, nevertheless survived in our pages.

St Hadit's is one, illustrated by a photograph of an old chapel in near-total ruin, with one wall and a lone door remaining in the former nave. St Hadit's is in Tatty Surplice Street in Edinburgh, where 'the verger was an optimist: somehow, by keeping the lone surviving door closed he thought he would exclude intruders. But there are few reasons to intrude. Much of the original charm has been sacrificed to modern minimalist tastes and the need to make space for random "objets", most of them thrown in by passers-by.'

Then there was Professor R. N. L. Idling's place called Surf's Up, in Cornwall. The photograph is of a decrepit hut perched over the sea and a tottering, sloping jetty down into the water. 'The super-rich may think they have everything: king-size beds raise you from your slumbers to tip you into the heated pool; luxury hotels perch over lagoons. But how about a Cornish hut with a brilliant and unusual device? The mere pull of a lever tips your bed towards the sea and propels you down a ramp into the thundering surf. Where do you imagine the RNLI got its ideas from?'

In our early days we had few boats in our books or website, whereas now there are canal barges and other miscellaneous craft. But we made up for it by writing about the special place to stay offered by Rear-Admiral and Mrs S. Odden, at River Bottom in Snoring-on-Thames. The photograph showed a long, wide canal barge on its side, half-submerged, and we described it thus: 'Feather-footed through the splashy fen you come – low-level view of the river from all rooms. A perfect riverside frontage, close to the flow. One room flows mellifluously into another; the sploshing of water is a constant backdrop sound and you may feed the ducks from your bed. Aquatic bliss with a touch of adventure.'

Booksellers encouraged us, and we reached new heights of silliness: one entry was for a turf-clad wooden hut, with saplings thriving on the roof. 'Sod it,' we wrote, 'why not include this extraordinary house? Man has met nature in rare harmony, taken it to his bosom and put it to work. Where turf, tree and tangled bush serve our purposes so elegantly, there is hope yet for mankind.'

Our spoofs rarely got us into trouble, but a couple did. The first was a once-pretty thatched cottage in Cornwall, its roof destroyed by fire. We named the owner Mrs S. C. Orched, and put her in a village called Burnt Norton, a reference to the T. S. Eliot poem that we thought most would know of. 'Have you ever been cooped up in a hotel without being able to open the windows? This charming cottage is an original solution, untouched since its last owners left, unable to cope with the heat. An interesting dark burnt sienna colour upstairs, and easy access to the roof.'

A local radio station called me, asking to be put in touch with the owners; we had published no phone number. 'I'm afraid there aren't any owners really, for it is a spoof.'

Silence. Then: 'But we want to do a piece about the house.'

'You can try, but there isn't such a house. It is, you see, a spoof entry – there for our own amusement.'

'OK – but let me speak to my manager.' A day passes, and the manager rings.

'I gather that you weren't able to help my presenter, but we are serious about wanting to do this interview.'

They wouldn't relent, so it went on and ended in anger on his part and embarrassment on ours, for we never intended to humiliate anyone. Another local news reporter became the second unintended victim of our spoofs. He had insisted on a press discount at a new place, Dan Dare Towers. This was a tall, slender tower surmounted by a disc-shaped object like a flying saucer. It could not possibly have existed anywhere as a workable building. We thought he might be amused, but his embarrassment became anger. I'd like to be able to say that we did give him a discount.

The insistence on character has brought us some wonderful relationships, few as entertaining as that with Peter Evans, whose barge Mike and I had stayed on during our cycling trip in Wales. Two grand ladies, whose names – Augusta Miller and Laura Ponsonby – are too portentous to ignore, arrived to stay with him. He was never quite sure why they came. 'L. Ponsonby, a pal of Prince Charles, uncle private secretary to George VI and great-grandfather Parry of Jerusalem fame – that sort of level.' It was a hot June day and Peter said, 'Look, if you don't want the chickens in we'll need to keep the door shut.' Ponsonby turned on him – no other verb will do – and said, 'I *always* have breakfast with my chickens. LEAVE THE DOOR OPEN!' Thus firmly in charge, she presided over breakfast with brusque efficiency. Cups and saucers were scattered all over the floor as sixteen chickens lined up on the table to be fed toast with honey, jam or marmalade according to the colour of their feathers.

Peter could only watch. 'Three days, fat chickens, no plates left,' he lamented later as he slowly returned his house to normality.

Chickens are now so popular that there is an International Respect for Chickens Day, organised by United Poultry Concerns. I gather that they don't like the idea of eggs being eaten, which stretches one's sympathy a little. I am all for respecting chickens, so long as they go on producing. Anyway, many of our favourite special places display chickens in the way that others display paintings. There are chicken names to be dropped: the Barbu d'Uccle, the benighted Rumpless Araucana, the Frizzle and the Faverolles, the Ohiki and the Orloff, the Silkie and the Sultan and the Yamato Gunkei.

Black Rocks and Marans strut their stuff at Beara Farmhouse near Bideford, and produce the eggs for a delicious breakfast. Once rambling and decrepit, Beara is now rambling and lovely. Richard and Ann are from Essex, which they left on a wave of despair, arriving in Devon on a wave of hope. 'When I hired machinery in Essex,' Richard told me, 'they always insisted on a deposit. Here in Devon they trust me. It is so refreshing.' The machinery was needed for eighteen long months of restoration and rebuilding, using stones from the old cowshed for the terrace and timber from a tumbledown barn for the porch. Richard has become a restorer of old things, and is usually to be found deep in wood shavings. He is now the owner of an old forge to which a blacksmith comes once a week. Part of the magic of Beara and places like it is the clash of expectations, the surprising comfort after expecting the raw interior that

might go with such deep rusticity. Raw wood, old materials, sophisticated modern design ideas and humour come
together seamlessly. The humour is essential if you have to
greet your immaculately clad guests while wrestling in the
mud with errant pigs.

The south-west seems to attract more than its fair share
of the UK's creatives, mavericks and radicals. It has always
been a rebellious limb of the mother country, the place
where John Wesley found fertile ground for his Methodism.
In the last century it was a Liberal power base, in those halcyon days when there was a strong Liberal Party to prod the
nation's conscience. Deep in the valleys of Devon I had an
evening bizarre enough for a Roald Dahl story.

It happened when I was running my travel company. I
took three middle-aged American women with me in a VW
minibus to explore the South-West, and from the beginning
they were unusually cheerful. An evening at Stourhead
watching the summer ballet was punctuated by their giggles.
Our picnic laid for four turned into a community event for
dozens, delighted by the unexpected feast and the mysteri-
ously available gin. On the way back I discovered the source
of the gin, and the giggles: each carried a baby bottle in
her handbag. They were running a discreet and convenient
mobile speakeasy.

The next night we stayed in Devon, in a house at the head
of a valley, and were invited to visit the 'resident Native
American' in his tipi. How could we resist? So we set off in
the minibus, the three women in their suburban mackintoshes and handbags – and their usual high spirits. The tipi
was a dark shape in the evening light and we approached
apprehensively across the meadow. I pushed open a low flap

and ducked in to a warm, candlelit space of cushions, an open fire in the centre and Splashing Waters, our Native American, awaiting in dignified chiefly pose. The ladies were still outside, giggling. It took some effort to get them to duck low enough to get through the flap and when they emerged, blinking, into the tipi they were like startled rabbits in mackintoshes.

I felt for Splashing Waters. This was not what he expected. But then, falling into amiable chat with him while the ladies settled, awkwardly, on the cushions, I detected traces of a Devon accent. His name was Kevin. At which point I lost the plot and the Monty Python-esque surrealism of it hit me. Try as I might, I couldn't think of Kevin as Splashing Waters any more. The three tipsy acolytes, for all their gin, had rumbled him too. We had to find an excuse to leave before our dignity dissolved entirely.

On the borders of Devon and Cornwall, overlooking the River Tamar, is the Old Count House, run by an unconventional woman called Trish. She has been known to welcome her donkey into the kitchen for breakfast. Trish, easy-natured and generous, had once booked a young couple into a room for the night and told them that she would be out to dinner. But she left a key for them, gave them detailed instructions and arranged to meet at breakfast.

Coming home late, Trish fell into bed, tired from her day and her dinner, but managed to get up as usual to make breakfast. She waited – and waited. The phone rang and her neighbour, a half-mile up the valley, said:

'Trish, I have a young couple here who expected me to be you, if you get my drift.'

'No I don't. What on earth do you mean?'

'They came downstairs a while ago and sat down at the table, waiting for me to give them breakfast.'

'But why don't you give it to them?'

'I've never seen them before in my life. They should have been sleeping in your house. And what I haven't told you is that when I came home from dinner last night and went upstairs, I found them sleeping in our bed!'

'What did you do?'

'We left them alone and slept in the spare room.'

Trish became one of our favourite inspectors. She has an eagle eye for a sense of humour in others.

The Tamar, a river resonant with significance as the barrier between Devon and Cornwall, widens out as it approaches Plymouth. As a family, we always whoop with joy when the car or train crosses the river. We feel a strong bond with Cornwall after twenty-five years of holidaying near Land's End, and now with a house in Redruth that Em inherited from her Uncle John. Redruth is a World Heritage Site for its mining; the place is so criss-crossed with underground tunnels that you must bore tester shafts under your land before you dare build: between Redruth and next door Camborne there are reputed to be ten thousand mine shafts. Our neighbour's project came close to collapse as a mine shaft opened up in front of his new front door. Thirty thousand pounds later he had capped the shaft and all was safe.

Between 1820 and 1840 the nearby parish of Gwennap was the richest square mile in Britain, and produced most of the world's copper. It was in the great Gwennap Pit, an amphitheatre dug into the ground, that John Wesley delivered some of his most stirring sermons, inspired by the subterranean misery of mining.

Redruth was once fabulously rich too, from tin, but also copper, silver and some gold. Its miners went all over the world to show others how to do it, but when the Cornish mines gradually gave up the ghost they left in even greater numbers to find work. A photograph at Redruth train station shows emigrating miners lined up on the platform, their distressed womenfolk on the road behind. It is a picture of human wretchedness, and the early industrial decline from which Cornwall has never recovered. The inheritance from those prosperous old days are count houses, engine houses and pumping houses – the last with their magnificent chimneys rising bleakly out of a scrub-filled landscape. Some of them are, at a distance, as magnificent as Inca ruins, and as thought-provoking.

Behind Redruth is the Carnkie Valley, whose old buddle-houses were built for the separation of tin from water in the buddles, circular depressions in the floor. There are a dozen chimneys, a stamp-house and a powerful sense of old buried energy and ingenuity. In Pool, between Redruth and Camborne, are a working pumping engine and a fine museum of mining.

Hopes remain for a renewed mining industry in Cornwall. South Crofty Mine has partially re-opened in the hope of a rise in world metal prices. A Canadian mining company has pumped in a huge amount of money – good for employment, but it is hard to be enthusiastic about men working underground again.

Pioneers thrived here: Richard Trevithick invented the steam engines that pumped water out of the mines; William

Bickford created the safety fuse; and William Murdoch created the gas that lit first his house and then most others in the Western world. Every time I walk down Redruth's handsome Fore Street I am made aware of this splendid past, and wonder what lies ahead. Now there are charity shops and places that sell plastic storage bins for the price of a sandwich, but little is static, apart from those chimneys. Cornwall can still dream, tinker with ideas about its future. A news item in January 2017 suggested that large quantities of lithium lying below the ground around Redruth may be extracted for use in lithium batteries. This could, if battery technology and use take off as many hope, be the beginning of another mining boom for Cornwall.

At the tip of the Cornish peninsula, forming the toe of Britain, is an ancient land called Penwith, with scattered Iron-Age villages, dolmens and stone circles. There are tombs and quoits from the Neolithic period, and twenty Bronze-Age stone monuments. Close to the well-preserved Iron-Age village at Bodrifty is a brand-new 'Iron-Age' roundhouse, a low wall of granite and mud plaster crowned with a thatched roof that reaches so high and yet is so low to the ground that it makes up most of the house. All this is born aloft by great timber posts. It was created by a local builder, largely out of archaeological curiosity and as an authentic reconstruction. His business-minded daughter persuaded him to make it more 'real' by getting people to pay to sleep in it. So an unusual venture was born, and you can stay there in modern comfort. What began as a two-week volunteer project ended with a two-year build. You never know what you have started.

Those who do their own thing, however mad, have my

admiration. In Carmel, California, I met a man who had built a clapboard house with twenty-three rooms, each of timber gathered from the beach and anything he could purloin. Corrugated roofs overlap roofs of rubber, plastic and wood. He even hauled the captain's cabin from a ship-wrecked freighter back up to the woods and balanced it on top of everything else, with a long ship's ladder to reach it.

It was a mad idea, too, to create an open-air theatre on a remote clifftop in Cornwall. But Rowena Cade, with the help of her gardener, lugged huge spars of wrecked wood, and tons of sand, up from the beach and laboriously created the Minack Theatre, now one of the most successful theatres in the UK. My stepfather George Sinclair, born and raised in nearby Porthcurno, was the widower of Rowena's niece and inherited the house in which she had lived with Rowena. For many years we spent the May half-term holiday there, one of the happiest weeks of the year for our family. Many thousands have watched plays at the Minack, wondered at the beauty of the setting and given thanks to the unregulated fantasy of one remarkable person who was there before the planners.

Penzance, the closest town to Porthcurno, has a hint of the frontier, and it struggles economically and culturally. But in 2016 the Jubilee Pool, an art-deco saltwater lido, was restored to its former glory. A handful of interested locals had pushed the project along, tapping into an underground longing to bring new life to the town. A new hotel/B&B, too, was opened in the old Penzance Arts Club, which had gazed forlornly over the inner harbour for years. The trans-formation is splendid: as I lay in my bath on the top floor I reached up and slid back the glass roof with one finger. It will attract new energy to the town and Susan, the owner, has thrown herself into community life with gusto. It would be good to see the fishing industry flourish again, and Cornwall less vulnerable to the vagaries of upcountry politics. Too much is asked of the art and surfing communities; they can only bring so much new energy. But when good people roll up their sleeves, change can happen.

14

An Attachment to
the Land

In the remains of the west end of Llanthony Priory snug-
gles a discreet little hotel, where I once stayed while
writing this book. The priory was founded centuries ago
by a handful of monks. Theirs is a moving story, for the
local Welsh were persistently hostile, to such an extent that
they retreated to Gloucester and founded a daughter cell,
Llanthony Secunda. Local hostility must have been bad
enough but I wondered, after a wet weekend there, how
they stood the rain. But they were, at least, below the great
escarpment of Offa's Dyke, one of the glories of Wales. Up
there I have lain in the sun and gazed east across the rolling
farmland of Herefordshire, while behind me the hills of
Wales receded fold upon beautiful fold into the west.

Paeans to Britain's natural beauty have filled libraries, and no wonder. Who can resist soaring beech trees, woodland shimmering with bluebells, a clear chalk stream tumbling over rounded rocks? But it is where nature and old buildings are in harmony that the country appeals most keenly to me. Jane Forshaw's twelfth-century Dunster Old Priory in Somerset is as much a haven for reflection and good company today as it was for the tiny monastic community who once lived here. The house is tight up against the north wall of the church of St George, given to the monks in 1090. The rood screen, mercifully untouched by the ravaging Puritans, separated the monks from the people. It is a stunner: fourteen fan-vaulted bays of tracery, sixty feet long and eleven feet high. The top of the screen is lavish with Flemish carving; the bottom has a display of panels of the utmost delicacy. It is one of the country's finest pieces of church carving and, as if this was not enough, there are fifty handsome bosses in the roof and another hundred in the south aisle. It is an almost theatrical performance by the medieval carvers.

The Dissolution cast the church and priory adrift, and dilapidation set in, helped by the regular theft of materials for building. The priory's continued existence as a B&B is a wonder and Jane has kept it simple: Venetian-red walls in the low-ceilinged living room with its fourteenth-century fireplace, and a four-poster bed upstairs, floating on an undulating oak floor. The walled garden is a serene setting for breakfast outdoors. Eggs and bacon, mushrooms and sausages hint at one form of bliss while shrubs, small trees and rampant climbers offer another. A tall mimosa greets you at the little gate, mature espaliered fruit trees line the path and then Jane's most formal touch: a square, mini-knot garden. You can wander through an archway into the church grounds next door. Jane is an entertaining and mildly eccentric character, more dedicated to stag-hunting and riding than to domestic maintenance, and is casual about living in a house with such history. I was instantly caught in its spell. You can ignore any number of cobwebs under the table if spiders have been weaving there since the Middle Ages.

A house whose natural setting has enchanted me since childhood is in Wiltshire, an old water-mill on the River Avon rebuilt by my uncle and aunt. The river-end of the house rests on its own island, the waters gushing under the sitting room and tumbling away beneath the wooded bank. Nature, again, was yoked to a building with marvellous effect, and I spent many happy days swimming there. But Wiltshire was not always so pretty and contented. In 1821 William Cobbett, the reformer and visionary who spent much of his life on a horse criss-crossing England as a lone social researcher, wrote witheringly of Wiltshire:

> I passed through that villainous hole, Cricklade ... and, certainly, a more rascally looking place I never set my eyes on ... Here and there a field is fenced with this stone, laid together in walls without mortar or earth. All the houses and out-houses are made of it ... The labourers seem miserably poor. Their dwellings are little better than pig-beds, and their looks indicate that their food is not nearly equal to that of a pig. Their wretched hovels are stuck upon little bits of ground *on the road side* ... It seems as if they had been swept off the fields

by a hurricane, and had dropped and found shelter under the banks on the road side! In my whole life I never saw human wretchedness equal to this: no, not even amongst the freed negroes in America ... this *Wiltshire* is a horrible county ... The land all along here is good. Fine fields and pastures all around; and yet the cultivators of those fields so miserable!

Castle Acre in Norfolk is extraordinary. The ruins, evocative as only ruins can be, date from 1090 and were the home of the first Clunaic monks in Britain. Cluny, the mother house in France, was arguably the finest set of monastic buildings in Europe and its ruin brings a lump to my throat. Only a tenth of it was left after the French Revolution. The Clunaics loved decoration, and you can still see how sumptuous Castle Acre once was. Wandering the ruins I could only imagine what had been lost to us through neglect and wantonness, but was rescued from the conflict of moods by some pilgrims who had gathered in the one surviving room of the monastery for their daily worship. They were on their way to Allingham via an ancient pilgrims' way, and gladdened my heart with their singing and optimism among the ruins.

My work has shown me the most bucolic of scenes and, within them, some very contented people. I have often been reminded of the wisdom of William Cobbett's dictum, 'It is not the greatness of a man's means that makes him independent, so much as the smallness of his wants.'

A great joy of the English countryside is its potential to surprise. With time to spare in North Devon one day, I followed the advice of Hilary Bradt, who had co-published a book about Devon with us, and visited the village of Lee. 'An absolute gem,' Hilary had written, and I knew she was right when I was swept into conversation with the landlord of the Grampus Inn. Bill had moved to Devon from Yorkshire and runs both the pub and a smallholding. He plays the fiddle with the local folk band, M'Larkey, too, and the pub buzzes with live music. It also acts as a shop for the slightly isolated villagers whose houses are scattered up and down the little valley. This ends in a small beach and a bay filled with rock pools. Bucolic indeed, even with no ancient church or priory.

Publishing *Go Slow England* was a special pleasure, an excuse to focus on people who have made slow living, and moments such as I had in Lee, central to their lives. I am no example, but we all need time to roam and to enjoy the unexpected – tricky in an urbanised world. What happens in the countryside is a mystery to most of us. I read once of a Victorian undergraduate, pompous and detached, riding his horse through cornfields in a sort of reverie. The farmer, whose livelihood this was and who was watching his family's income being ravaged, remonstrated with him. The student's response was 'I am sorry. I am not a botanist, you know!'

Years of wandering around Britain fill a man with a sense of attachment to this land, even to the very soil of it. Soil is at the heart and soul of our planet; we couldn't live without it. Our bodies are built from and sustained by nutrients found in soil. Civilisations rise and fall on how well they treat their soils. However clever we are with our silicon slivers and robotic wizardry, healthy soil remains crucial for food production, flood defences and our ability to tackle climate change. Yet every year we are losing topsoil in prodigious quantities: seventy-five billion tons of it worldwide. Twenty million hectares are annually lost to production. The statistics are hard to adjust to. Try this: in China, twenty-four thousand villages have been lost in the last fifty years from soil erosion, and it takes up to a thousand years to make an inch of topsoil. Knowing these things gives me a sharpened sense of wonder at the beauty I still see in Europe, and boundless admiration for those whose work builds back the soil.

I make a brief foray into organic farming here, as it has been such an inspiration to me. President Jimmy Carter's *Global 2000 Report* put the loss of soil at the top of the list of global threats. Since then, things have simply got worse. Intensive farming, upon which we lavish subsidies, takes nutrients from the soil without replacing them. The degraded soil is then propped up with fertilisers derived either from oil or mined minerals. No nourishment is involved. We all know something of the ups and downs of oil, but pay little attention to phosphorous, a key component of fertilisers. It is crucial for world food supplies and may only last another thirty years. The impacts of its decline will be wide-ranging and immense. Organic farming is a real solution, for it builds the soil naturally: for example, by using crops like clover and alfalfa which fix nitrogen from the air and pass it to the soil via decomposition or via animals. If you bear in mind that each of us contributes about ten tonnes of carbon to the atmosphere per year, a quarter of it via the food we eat (growing, distributing, etc.), then any system that reduces that tonnage should be attractive.

Americans contribute an average of twenty tonnes each and the Chinese less than five.

Organic farms that take guests have always added to our sense of publishing purpose. They are often run by people who have returned to the land, for example Thistleyhaugh Farm in Northumberland, which is run by a family hefted to its land, and whose children have returned: a family farm, enjoying a cheerful, bustling give and take. Most of us imagine that three generations under one roof would be a nightmare, but the Nelless family thrives, with extra company from their sheep, cows, pigs and poultry. They have their own little abattoir, a rare thing; about seven hundred small abattoirs were closed when the government insisted on expensive vets being in attendance all the time. There are now fewer than three hundred. The Nelless family see themselves as guardians of their animals and of the countryside, in stark contrast to the agricultural barons of East Anglia, whose industrial-scale farming I observed during a long weekend of harvesting in 2016. The assault upon the fields opposite my mother's house was military in its precision, in its use of tracked vehicles and clunky machinery. For four days the air was filled with the conversation-stopping roar of invasion. Later there was more invasion from large machines spewing fertilisers and pesticides, each one compacting the soil. If we are drenched with the wind-blown spray, that is our tough luck. We never saw a human being other than one driver in his high-tech cabin, and a well-dressed supervisor on his mobile phone.

Organic farming demands more of the farmer, not least extra ingenuity. I once saw an organic farmer's home-invented carrot-weeding device, a marriage of humanity and machinery. A tractor in bottom gear very slowly pulled a specially designed trailer on which lay, face-down, about a dozen workers, each weeding with his or her hands one row of carrots at a time. This ensured a thorough weeding and, talking to the weeders afterwards, I got the impression that they were enjoying the work and were well paid.

The contrast between productive and extractive farming struck me when I visited an Amish farm in Michigan. We were having lunch when their non-Amish neighbour dropped by to discuss soil: why was their soil so much richer than his? The Amish were coy about discussing it, but he insisted. So began a conversation that poured light onto the subject for me: on the regular use of manures and crop rotations, the avoidance of chemicals and a focus on building soil rather than depleting it. The Amish, of course, do all this better than most, eschewing heavy machinery in favour of horses. Their own carbon emissions are close to zero and they deserve our admiration. They also deserve our envy, if we heed the *British Food Journal*'s study of twenty vegetables that revealed that the average calcium content had declined 19 per cent in the fifty years up to 1980. Iron had declined by 22 per cent and potassium by 14 per cent. Would anybody valuing good health not choose an Amish vegetable over the intensively produced competition?

It is unfashionable to bring the Amish into conversation about agriculture or community, as we often see them as humourless – and tough on any of their children who don't toe the line. However, I was struck by their clever use of compromise. Thus, a telephone is useful, but not if it dominates your life; so they have one outside the house and only use it within limited hours. So with engines: clever beasts, but beasts nonetheless, so the Amish use them selectively: perhaps a tractor-engine on blocks to run other tools, or as the engine powering a bailer on the back of a horse-drawn wagon.

If I search for hope beyond the organic movement, I find it in the ideas about land reform gaining pace in Scotland. Lying on soft tussocks of grass among the great granite boulders near the Logan Rock in Cornwall, the Atlantic swashing in and out of the little bay below me, I devoured a book called *Soil and Soul* by Alastair McIntosh. He grew up on the Isle of Lewis and weaves his way between history, science, poetry and prophecy with the Hebrides as his geographical context. His thirst for justice links tales of English colonial land-grabbing with modern ideas for reform. He helped the people of Eigg to clear their laird from his own estate and become joint owners, and he later helped save a majestic mountain on Harris from becoming a super-quarry. The Scottish government has backed such reforms in a way that is unlikely to happen in England, and against inevitable hostility from the landowners.

In the Highlands, vast estates are still the norm: 432 people own over half of Scotland's private rural land, and estates of fifty thousand acres are not uncommon. The picture is almost colonial. But there are now more than 420,000 acres of the Highlands and Islands in community ownership, reinvigorating local economies and bringing people back to the remoter places. Government grants replace the many subsidies – for agriculture, forestry, nature conservation and other activities – enjoyed traditionally by landowners. I hope that this will bring back a focus on the land itself, the quality of it and its ability to feed us.

In 1976, the year Em and I moved to Bristol, a little

booklet entitled 'Chief Seattle's Testimony' took our small and embattled community of green activists by the hearts. Seattle was a great tribal chief, who in 1854 reacted in unforgettable prose to the United States government's offer to buy his tribe's traditionally owned land:

> The white man . . . takes from the land whatever he needs. The earth is not his brother but his enemy, and when he has conquered it, he moves on . . . His appetite will devour the earth and leave behind only a desert . . .
>
> You must teach your children that the ground beneath their feet is the ashes of our grandfathers. So that they will respect the land, tell your children that the earth is rich with the lives of our kin. Teach your children what we have taught our children, that the earth is our mother. Whatever befalls the earth, befalls the sons of the earth. If men spit upon the ground, they spit upon themselves.

William Cobbett would have agreed.

15

An Irish Honeymoon
and More

The big house revealed itself at the end of a long drive. Finding nobody to greet me, I entered tentatively and tiptoed around the ground floor. It was dark, so I reached for the curtains.

'Don't ye touch dose curtains, I tell ya.' I leapt with fright. 'If ye do, dey'll fall apart!' And indeed they were showing alarming signs of already doing so: clouds of disturbed dust, mingled with bits of velvet, settling around my feet. I headed for a chair, needing to gather my wits. 'And don't settle yerself there, either. It's got no seat in it.'

A small, determined-looking old woman stood in the doorway, one eye on me. The other was on the ceiling.

'Where is Henry?' I asked, standing cautiously, a

wary eye on the ceiling. Would it, too, be hanging on a thread?

'Ah, he'll be in bed, but you can go through and see him.'

'Upstairs?' I wondered aloud, thinking of woodworm and perilous banisters.

'No – through there, in the study.' Another tiptoed walk and I found him, lying prone in his farming clothes, welly boots at one end, flat cap at the other, looking for all the world like the prone Irishman of legend. But now the story takes a disturbing twist, for Henry was prone with good reason. He had an acute sensitivity to most chemicals, a result of dipping sheep in the organophosphates used by nearly every non-organic farmer. That morning a sales-woman had come to the house, ignoring warnings posted at the gate. One whiff of her perfume at twenty-five yards had floored Henry. It was shocking, and even more so as I learned about the history of this illness. Hundreds of farmers were in similar condition, but the government had refused to acknowledge the problem until the nineties.

When I met Henry I had just joined the Soil Association as a trustee. It was the beginning of a long and enriching journey among some of the most committed and delightful people I have met. Henry's story was well known and his experience was repeated across Britain. In the nineties, the Pesticides Action Network wrote 'There has been stoic acceptance by farmers of ill-health. But it is now acknowl-edged that there is under-reporting of pesticide poisoning incidents.' Since then, regulation has improved and sheep-dipping is no longer so dangerous. But it is a reminder of how wrong, and slow, governments and official bodies can be. Meanwhile, poor Henry was leading a bizarre existence, wary of any contact with chemicals, let alone with over-perfumed women.

Another example of official stupidity is the case of neo-nicotinoids, a pesticide sprayed on crops such as maize and oilseed rape. It is effective, but there is considerable evidence that it is also a main cause of bee-population crash, perhaps by disrupting their navigation systems. Bees are vital for about a third of pollination, so without them we are in trouble. In 2016 I listened to Peter Melchett, policy director of the Soil Association, describe the latest findings on toxicity levels in hedgerows and trees – areas we have always thought of as oases in the midst of arable barrenness. Those oases were ten times more toxic than the nearby fields. Peter, a veteran campaigner and farmer, was on the edge of tears.

The extent of chemical pollution on our crops is stunning. Water run-off from fields is so toxic that we are advised not to harvest mussels from rocky shores below fields after rainfall. I recently had to throw away a bag of laboriously collected Cornish rock mussels for this reason. Wildlife is in decline in rural areas. We know these things, and we are certain of the causes. The farmers and politicians who long argued that there was no need to limit fertiliser, pesticide and herbicide use are now crowing about how much such use has declined. This is why the Soil Association's independent voice is so vital. Meanwhile, many otherwise sensible people really believe that farm-fresh means farm-fresh and that free range means free range. I saw fresh vegetables from Kenya in Waitrose recently, as fresh as you can get – only nine hours' flight from Nairobi. One wonders, too, about Kenyan chemical use. My sister Fiona once walked among hundreds of dead flamingos on the edge of Lake Naivasha,

the result – some say – of the chemicals used in the flower
industry bordering the lake. A local campaigner against
excessive chemical use was murdered. Many believe it was
because of her efforts to expose the pollution.

So Henry, lying on his bed in Ireland, knocked flat by the
delicate chemistry of perfume, was just one victim of our
chemically enhanced system of producing food. At least he
was good-humoured about it, and accepted that the per-
fumed visitor was unaware that she was a walking weapon
of destruction. He had a take on life that was philosophical
and amused, the attitude that makes visiting Irish houses
such a joy.

Ireland's troubled colonial history has left it with a legacy
of people with strong views on almost everything, who
despise government and who do their own thing. History
has given Ireland, too, a lot of crumbling Anglo-Irish manor
houses as well as a good number of eccentrics who inhabit
them. One such morose, decaying Irish manor house was
owned by the most eccentric lady we have included in any
book. An earnest Dutch couple wrote to tell us of their experience. They arrived at teatime and were greeted by their
hostess wearing a bikini. She told them to put down their
suitcases and follow her. They had little choice but to agree,
and set off in puzzled pursuit of their scantily dressed hostess.
They came to a lane and were joined by several other, equally
puzzled, guests. Everyone carried a lighted candle, and one
was given to each of the new Dutch arrivals. This bizarre
procession finally arrived in a small field and was gathered
into a circle. All was revealed: they had been summoned to
attend a ceremonial, and very serious, burial. The deceased
was madam's cat. The bikini remained a mystery.

Dinner that night, let alone tea, was late, but so great was the 'craic', that Irish atmosphere or sense of fun, that nobody minded. Whiskey – for that is how the Irish spell it – was produced as a diversion from hunger and tiredness. Everybody got very drunk and even the staid Dutch guests joined in, but not before they spotted that their hostess was drinking with them rather than cooking their dinner. They manoeuvred her out of the room and into the kitchen, where they wisely stayed to keep an eye on her. Midnight arrived at the same time as dinner. This, naturally, was a moment for more celebration. Breakfast the next day came at lunchtime.

Ireland is like that; it can bemuse and delight in equal measure, as Em and I learned on our honeymoon in Connemara. We drove across Ireland in 1975 after our wedding in London, to a cottage owned by a middle-aged bachelor farmer called Michael, who was clearly delighted to have an attractive woman staying. He would turn up every evening just as we were settling down to our supper à deux. His battered head would appear over the half-open stable door, with a cheery 'Good evenin' to yer!' and we would put down our cooking pots and settle in to a long chat about the weather or the price of cattle. After a while, hunger rising, we would get back to preparing the meal and he would say: 'Well, oi'd better be goin'.' We would listen for the sound of departing heels. But silence. Finally we would say, 'Will you have a drink, Michael?' And he would reply, 'Well, oi don't moind if oi do.' He would eventually leave, but not before finishing at least one of our precious bottles of wine. We ate very late every evening. Our honeymoon was a good test of our marital tolerances.

Michael would complain of the toughness of farming life, and we listened sympathetically. Then one day I went for a walk above the farm and could see him working in his hay field. He would take his pitchfork to a small stack of hay, hoist it over his shoulder, stagger a few yards to another stack, dump it and then settle for a snooze. Every hoist was followed by another snooze.

One day Michael appeared, declaring with some portentousness that he was there to empty the Elsan chemical loo. This was just the sort of luxury treatment we hoped for on our honeymoon: the emptying of an Elsan. But we were happy that it was Michael, rather than us, carrying it to some carefully prepared distant place for safe disposal. Alarmingly, he returned only seconds later, Elsan emptied. We spent the rest of our stay tiptoeing cautiously around the garden, or avoiding it completely.

Our cottage was simple, of stone, with two rooms. In one was a bed, and in the other a sink, a table and an open peat fire, over which hung a cauldron. We had been assured of running water, and indeed the water ran down the hill past the house. We wandered the fields picking blackberries and mushrooms in their abundance to eat for our supper. It was a time for reading in front of the soft-glowing fire and for tramping the lush fields and inlets of Connemara.

There is no gainsaying Ireland's beauty, but there is much to say about the rash of bungalow building in the twentieth century. I was once introduced to the proud publisher of *Bungalow Bliss*, a compendium of about eighty bungalow styles, any one of which could be presented to the planners for easy approval and then be followed by the builders. During many a drive through verdant countryside, past lofty hills and aquamarine estuaries, I would be shocked by a display of pebbledash and concrete lions rampant, asphalt and PVC dormer windows. It is a heart-breaker for many sensitive Irish people; An Taisce, their version of the National Trust, has fought back with some success, but the damage has been done. I understand why the bungalows were built – by country people glad to escape the damp, dark houses of the past – but many an Irishman has wished for a magic wand to remove them and start again.

There is a group of three tiny islands off the west coast, opposite the Cliffs of Moher, to which, for our first Irish book, Simon Greenwood braved the choppy seas to inspect a potential B&B. Elsewhere I have described the bleakness of a breakfast room hushed by awkwardness, a place of solitary eating and fear of upsetting the landlady. Simon's experience on the Aran Islands was a model of the kind. Breakfast was served in a long thin room with two tables, each laid for one person, set as far apart as possible and facing the same direction. Simon ate looking at the distant back of the Japanese man at the other table. The landlady padded silently from table to table, whispering her questions: 'Nescafé? Milk? Butter?' and padding silently out again. Simon muffled his spoon, breathed softly, and afterwards slipped away like a fairy at a funeral. Heaven knows what the poor Japanese man felt about it.

Only in Ireland would one find Clarity Cottage, in Enlightenment Way, Ballyheaven, with linguistic flourishes that can only be Irish. The photograph reveals a fine tree growing in its middle, curtains of ivy hanging from the walls and a roof that has long gone: 'The greenest of green

Irish cocoons is here, the purest of fresh Irish mist is yours.
A place to discover the Truth of your Being and the firma-
ment. Never has the panorama of night and day, real and
spiritual, been so dramatically accessible within four(ish)
walls. Ah – the ineffable dampness of eternal Ireland . . . You
need only to stretch out a hand to pull back the screen of ivy
and plunge through the revelation roof into the twinkling
clarity above.'

Ether Real, the absent owner, is as enigmatic and elusive as tradition demands. Visitors to Ireland should expect
nothing less.

16

A Baroque Flourish

The motorway to Palermo had collapsed, so Em and I took a long detour across country. The concrete pillars must surely have been filled with the bodies of Mafia victims, or the cement mixed with pizza flour, or perhaps the reinforcing rods were made of spaghetti. This was, after all, Sicily, the land of the Mafia – a community enterprise still going strong after hundreds of years. Our ignorance of the place knew few bounds, so we were easy prey for fantasy. The fantasy grew stronger, and better founded, as we got to know Sicily better.

Carmelo was waiting for us in Palermo. He is a small mustachioed and twinkling man whom I immediately felt I had known all my life. An old friend who had stayed with Carmelo was whisked off every evening for ballet, opera and a round of parties that had left him dazed and happy, so we were looking forward to being with this legendary Sawday owner. The moment of arrival in a new house can be delightful and we were on cheek-kissing terms immediately. His flat is upstairs, on a ramshackle floor of the Bishop's old palace overlooking the Palazzo dei Normanni – a vicarious respectability that Carmelo enjoys. His vast dog is treated as a flatmate, though its nightly howling must infuriate the neighbours. Dog hair and dog smell permeate the rooms, but cannot outdo the overall sense of cultured, civilised, amiable chaos. Carmelo is a special case: casual, charming, loveable, uninterested in the trivia of hospitality like dusting, but passionate about the big things like good food, culture and conversation.

Devotion to the good things in life emanates from every corner. Carmelo teaches mechanics, but breathes a passion for dance and culture generally: stacked bookshelves, piles of art and ballet books, terracotta pots, little statues pf Carmelo's greatest love, Italy's once-prima ballerina Carla Fracci. Her worn pointe shoes hang from their ribbons all over the flat. Carmelo's devotion to Signora Fracci is touching, especially as he himself would never get off the ground in a *jeté*. Yet he has followed her all over Italy, partied with her, shared her tragedies and joys and become very close.

Carmelo's second devotion is to Palermo, and its cultural vitality. It is seedy in parts, crumbling after centuries of grandeur but there remains great dignity. Magnificent buildings, including private palazzi, can be seen at every turn. The Normans, who ruled in the twelfth and thirteenth centuries, were insatiable builders and even built two competing cathedrals, one in town and one just outside. The first was Monreale, completed in 1182 and an astonishing marriage of Normandy and Morocco, artisans from different religions working together to produce what some consider to be the most beautiful building in Europe. The young William II of Sicily built it to show his bossy bishop who was in charge.

Bigger even than San Marco in Venice, Monreale is a cathedral of golden mosaics, depicting biblical scenes, saints, kings and angels, with gilded motifs and lush decoration in Moorish style. The scale is heroic and the effect startling. As your eye follows this miracle from west to east, along ranks of simple columns between which reach dazzlingly decorated arches, your gaze comes to rest upon a colossal image of the Christ Pantocrator. The giant horizontal beams of the great ceiling are as elaborately decorated as the arches, and the walls are covered with mosaics of exquisite subtlety. The cloister is a covered arcade of 108 Arabic arches, a carnival parade of columns, alive with vitality and inventiveness.

Bishop Walter Ophamil, the bossy one, built the second cathedral, another bold mix of styles on a vast scale, just two years later in an expensive tit-for-tat. Thanks to endless tinkering down the centuries there are Arab, Norman, Byzantine, Swabian, Romanesque, Gothic Renaissance and Baroque flourishes in this one magnificent cathedral – uniquely so, I believe.

The splendid Palazzo dei Normanni, where the Norman kings lived, contains a treasure that touched me deeply. The Palatine Chapel was worked on by craftsmen from different religions and has a three-tiered arcaded courtyard, with each arch a delicately rounded masterpiece. Its size makes it accessible aesthetically, more so perhaps than the cathedrals.

Overlooking the palazzo, on Carmelo's plant-filled

terrace, we sat one evening among the urns, tiles and tables
and the lavish plates of food provided for the dinner party
that Carmelo was throwing for us. We drank Planeta wine
with the English woman who had married into the family
and was now reigning over a Sicilian wine empire. There
was the disgruntled widow of a Palermo princeling who had
fallen upon hard times and thus had to rent out most of his
palazzo. She felt 'terribly cut off' in her lonely apartment
at the back of the palace. Two entertainingly flamboyant
academics revealed that Palermo is behind most of Europe
in its tolerances. We mentioned the Mafia, the elephant in
every room, but they were all evasive. Perhaps they are,
understandably, as tired of the subject as we are of Brexit.
We had read *Gomorrah*, Roberto Saviano's grim exposé of
the Naples Mafia, and knew that the author was living under
armed guard. Mussolini had destroyed the Mafia before the
Second World War, only for the Americans, needing allies
on the ground, to reintroduce it before their 1943 invasion
of Sicily. Wherever we went we learned that the Mafia is
alive and well.

A little reading of history, however, reveals how Sicily has
been seized, plundered, exploited, yielded and then ravaged
again over the centuries, though never entirely subdued.
All this must have been, at best, irritating to even the most
mild-mannered Sicilian and it is hardly surprising that the
Mafia grew as a system of organised resistance. Italy was
only unified in 1861, and has suffered ample interference
even since then, so the survival of the Mafia is no surprise. I
am similarly unsurprised by the Somali pirates, whose early
behaviour was a response to the piracy on a massive scale by
Western fishing fleets, which were hoovering up Somalia's

fish stocks. That the Somali fishermen have turned violent, and then become a criminal power – as did the Mafia – is perhaps inevitable.

After Palermo, Em and I headed west to Trapani, a city ignored by tourists and travel books but snug with a Norman castle on its harbour walls and a fine Baroque centre. Thence we travelled by boat to the tiny island of Favignana, where we were met by the impossibly handsome Davide in his scruffy car – the sort of gruff-but-real island welcome I was familiar with in Scotland. We stayed in a house with views over the harbour and to distant Sicily, and with light touches of design-awareness inside: an antique basin, very old cupboards, polished cement floors and a vast slab of limestone for a table. We rented a scooter and explored the island.

One day, scooting slowly through the main marble-paved piazza, we skidded and fell. I gathered myself, manfully, to find that Em had disappeared. In a trice an Italian had swept to the rescue (of her rather than me), gathered her up in his arms – helmet still on – and cantered away to the nearest café. 'Put me down, put me down!' she cried, with little conviction and to no avail. Em was unharmed and fully alert, but the café owner raced out with his EU-regulation first-aid kit and plundered it for bandages to apply to this heaven-sent patient. A small group of onlookers and would-be paramedics gathered, and everyone was happy.

Favignana is abandoned by history. It was once at the centre of the tuna-fishing industry, one that after five hundred years had died in 2009, when the fishery closed. It still has a fine building to show for it: a *tonnara* the size of several football pitches and of muscular beauty, parading its great arches along the water. Here tuna were boiled and tinned, bringing wealth to the island and to the local Florio family. I swam across the crystal-clear harbour one day and climbed out of the water into the *tonnara*, through an arch reminiscent of Venice's Arsenal and into a cavernous room where old wooden tuna boats lay silent. Once they had been the platforms from which bluefin had annually been slaughtered in what was known as the Mattanza – the massacre. I am sad they were silent, but sad that most of the bluefin have gone too.

That magnificent tuna factory, proposed as a UNESCO World Heritage Site, must find another role. I fondly imagined, while I padded in my swimming trunks from one giant space to another, that it might become a Memorial to our Lack of Vision. It is always disturbing when an artisan industry leaves behind such a mighty monument after running amok and eliminating the very core of itself. Many old industrial buildings give off a faint whiff of nostalgia, along with regret for policies that might have been different.

The end of tuna fishing brought to a shuddering halt a whole culture in Sicily. The tuna had been sold in unsustainable quantities to the insatiable Japanese. The film *The End of the Line* revealed that even though bluefin tuna are heading for commercial extinction, Mitsubishi has invested in bluefin-fishing boats to catch the very last of them. Once they are extinct, and the last to die stored in the Mitsubishi freezers, the company can drip-feed the meat into the market as and when it chooses, at the sort of eye-watering prices that come with having something extinct to sell. To do this they have expanded their refrigeration capacity too – though as a sickening footnote, after the destruction of the Fukushima nuclear plant in 2011, the power supply to the Mitsubishi freezers was cut and the entire hoard lost.

One wonders if the world has gone mad. The International Commission for the Conservation of Atlantic Tunas sanctioned a bluefin catch of twenty-two thousand tonnes in 2009, the year the Favignana fishery closed, despite their own scientists having advised a catch of no more than 8500 to fifteen thousand tonnes. In that same year, the ICCAT revealed that populations had declined by about 75 per cent.

On a spare day in Favignana we motored out to sea with two fishermen on a *pescaturismo* trip, winding in the nets and extracting the fish, gutting them and then – as only in Italy – eating a four-course meal of those very fish, cooked by the boat's mate. It was all washed down with wine, limoncello, *dolce* and further gastronomic extravagance. All this was concocted on a single gas camping stove on deck. A handful of Chinese tourists were with us, but detached by language and observing the proceedings with a wide-eyed mix of awe and astonishment. A dignified older woman, who had demurred from the food and avoided the sun, suddenly erupted into a bold rendition of traditional Chinese opera before plunging into the sea fully dressed. She was driven, we imagined, to near-suicidal bewilderment with the excess of it all. But she came up smiling.

Favignana had hidden part of its magic: gardens created in the old tufa quarries, many of which are of Roman origin. Davide took us to a place of wonder created by a modest, gentle lady from Palermo who had planted *con vigore* in the ancient quarry network. A giant flame tree guarded the entrance to a garden that was a triumph of optimism over common sense. How on earth had she persuaded that vast tree to spread its wings in a barren, heat-soaked quarry below ground level? We strolled from one quarry to the next, through tunnels and past plants and trees that should simply not have been there. The *signora* had broken horticultural rules to produce a minor wonder.

Em, with yoga classes to teach, set off home still dreaming, I imagine, of being whisked away in the arms of a handsome Italian. I went to the westernmost point of Sicily to explore the *salinas*, the salt ponds just outside Marsala that once produced a hundred thousand tons of salt a year. The land bordering the ponds is pancake-flat, and beyond the *salinas* is an inland sea of azure serenity. Dotted about are ancient windmills that pump water in and out, and handsome-on-the-inside old farmhouses that are block-like and dreary on the exterior. Fontanasalsa is such a place, solidly functional on approach, and then a burst of colour and vitality as you enter the courtyard. The two women who run it are, as Michelin would say, 'worth the detour'. Maria was Sicily's first paediatrician and Ilaria had been – what else – a fighter pilot. Gentle yet commanding, they are rooted in their work on the land, firm in their convictions and gifted hostesses. The kitchen produced elegant but gargantuan meals as a matter of course, accompanied by the sort of animated food-related conversation that comes so easily to Italians. Ilaria was energetic in defence of Italian womanhood, and I could only agree.

Had the exteriors of those big farmhouses been more attractive they would, I learned, have invited envy and, inevitably, pilfering. As, later, I drove around the exquisite Baroque towns of south-eastern Sicily, I gave thanks that the tradition of exterior modesty had not taken hold in this corner of the island. In 1693 a terrible earthquake had destroyed the towns, and the Spanish king, who then ruled Sicily, ordered his favourite architect to design replacements – an architect's dream. (It made me dream of Ipswich collapsing harmlessly and being redesigned brilliantly.) The eight towns of the Val di Noto – Caltagirone, Militello Val di Catania, Modica, Noto, Ragusa, Scicli, Catania and Palazzolo – were designated a UNESCO World Heritage Site in 2002. They are of a piece, golden-stoned flourishes, with churches, piazzas, palaces and streets uncluttered by modern ugliness. One can become blasé about Sicilian Baroque architecture, with its voluptuous balconies decorated with wrought iron and supported by the heads of lions and putti. Buttresses are ribboned, gargoyles strut their stuff and mischief mingles with flamboyant humour. It all radiates a theatricality that belies the seriousness of the architecture. The devotional is mixed with the sentimental and the ostentatious – and why not?

I spent a few nights in Noto with our inspector in the area, Angelica, a tall, beautiful Roman whose life had become 'confusing' in Rome and who had taken refuge here. We would stop at the bakery on the street corner and chat with the twinkling ladies who ran it. Their twinkles always paid off, for we never left without an armful of pastries. Then we would bask in the golden-pink tufa glory of the piazza beneath the duomo before setting off for the beach, or to tread the ruins of the earthquake-destroyed old town. Angelica was distressed by the speed of my visit; how could I not 'see all the Baroque towns? And Syracuse?' she pleaded, appalled by my philistinism. The problem for a traveller in Sicily is that something stupendous beckons at every turn. Life is not long enough to know just this corner of Sicily. I never even made it to Syracuse, a failing that confirmed me as a philistine in Angelica's eyes.

17

Gondola!

Lord Byron swam the length of the Grand Canal in Venice. He also swam across the lagoon to the Lido. He found a physical freedom from the handicap of his club foot in his swimming, and inspired poets' swimming events all over Europe. When I gaze at the Grand Canal now, I imagine him weaving his way bravely among the boats. I have never seen anyone swimming in the canal. It would be unwise.

My parents took me to Venice in my late teens, to stay in the Hotel Accademia and to wander, enchanted, wherever I wished. The hotel has a terrace from which one can hear and glimpse the Grand Canal, surely the most ravishing feast of architecture on the planet – a 'gallimaufry' of it, according to Jan Morris. I was too young to take it all in. I still am.

Venice is mired in its own beauty. Dazzled, more than twenty million of us pour in every year. So do over 650 cruise ships, many bigger than the *Titanic*. Are we loving Venice to death? The buzz of the moment is the intrusion by these monsters. They tower above the rooflines and flood the city with consumers and sightseers. The city is divided between those who profit from the visitors and those who rate her dignity and beauty over commerce. I hope that one day Venice will ban the cruise ships, for they will slowly kill her. Each ship is a mini-city, bringing an invasion as terrifying in its distant consequences as a fleet of Ottoman galleys. Venice is part of a complex ecosystem and cruise liners enter this system as elegantly as bulls enter china shops.

Vanessa, one of our Venetian owners who also runs a restaurant serving slow food, was in despair as she talked of Venice's problems. Only about fifty thousand Venetians now live in the old town, as foreign buyers have snapped up the palazzi and most of the best houses. It is hard to find a shop that sells groceries. It is an unreal city, a shadow of its old self, condemned to primp and preen for the crowds of detached visitors – who will go away and on to Florence and Rome, or Athens, with their photos of the floodwater lapping at the feet of the Caffè Florian in St Mark's Square.

I once attended a lecture by John Julius Norwich about the Venice in Peril Fund, and was so moved by the plight of this city – one that belongs, surely, to the whole of humanity – that I offered myself as a volunteer after the talk. I had none of the skills needed, however, and slunk away feeling less than useful. But Venice does that to people. For decades alarm bells have rung, yet soon we will be urged to hurry, while the city can still be seen above the water, just as the alarm bells ring over Planet Earth. People hasten to visit doomed places such as the Maldives rather than campaign for the changes needed to protect them.

In 2012, when I was in Venice to meet Sawday owners, Em and I had an unexpected free day. The Biennale was still on, with exhibitions clamouring for attention throughout the city; we saw ancient stringed instruments, reproductions of Leonardo's machines, Madonnas and Titians and more Madonnas. We were awed by the carved and veneered choir stalls by Marco Cozzi in the vast Frari. The city itself is an exhibition, and we wandered through a whirl of architectural bravura.

We read Jan Morris's *Venice* devoutly and for the umpteenth time. It never palls. I urge every visitor to read it, for you will learn of the vastness of Venice's power up to the sixteenth century; of her duplicity, too. She persuaded the Fourth Crusaders, whom she was 'lifting' to a crusade, to drop in and take Constantinople on the way – and thus pay off the cost of their journey. Just a little diversion, yielding vast booty to Venice, such as the beautiful Roman Horses of St Mark's, now inside the basilica and replaced by copies outside.

Isn't it interesting that we so love traffic-free Venice, while insisting on battering our own cities with traffic? I sat next to a woman on the train who sang the praises of her serenely peaceful Venetian holiday while lamenting the parking problems in Bristol. The total absence of cars and lorries in Venice is one of the urban delights of our age. What I would give to hear of a city now being planned for the gliding of silent boats and the absence of cars. Bristol has several times lost the opportunity to create more space for water. The city centre, after a 92 per cent public vote in favour, was to be dug out to reveal the old dock, but traffic engineers and motor lobbyists prevailed and the traffic still flows. Limp fountains can only hint at the harbour waters below.

La Serenissima, as Venice has modestly called herself, was a nation of islands and of immense power, poised twixt East and West, Muslim and Christian, Rome and Constantinople. She was the mistress of the Mediterranean, haughty, detached, glittering and unfathomable. She lost her power in the sixteenth century but staggered on for three more centuries, applying make-up and partying as voluptuously as any power in Europe. She is still impossibly glamorous. Perhaps Britain will stagger on too, if less glamorously.

From the airport you may arrive by boat, swept along on a wave of dawning incredulity. From the railway station you step straight into the hubbub a few yards from the water and are swept into the vortex of beauty. You will find yourself drawn ineluctably to St Mark's Square, where you will blink and stretch your eyes in disbelief. For Napoleon, this great roofless room was the 'drawing room of Europe'; I prefer to think of it as a ballroom. If there is music playing in the Caffè Florian you may well sweep the nearest woman into your arms and dance her across the square, as I did. The magic of Venice works like that. Well, that was my excuse, and the rather startled Dutch tourist forgave my exuberance, I think.

After my first visit with my parents, I came to Venice as a student, working in my vacations as a tour manager and guide for groups of about forty American tourists. I tried to appear casual, but my face must have given away my delight at every turn. My enthusiasm carried me through a difficult moment when, alone at one o'clock in the morning on a pontoon with half a dozen stocky gondoliers, I tried to negotiate the price. The six gondolas we had hired for a merry evening of song and canal-gliding were about to cost me vastly more than we had agreed. My Italian was three days old, my experience not much older. The gondoliers had lost their jauntiness and were now serious, arms folded across their muscled chests, eyes narrowed.

'*Scusi, ma è troppo!*' I boldly declared. A cascade of Italian words and expletives overwhelmed me, but I stood my ground and tried again. Still, there is only so much one can do with '*Scusi, ma è troppo*'. I shuddered to a halt and, feeling my disadvantage growing and my knees wobbling, retreated while I had some dignity left. I resolved on that pontoon to learn Italian. I have learned recently that gondoliers annually can earn up to £120,000; had I known at the time I would have tried harder.

My language skills served me well many years later when, in 2011, Pope Benedict made an historic visit to Venice. While he was there I hired a water-taxi and was overcharged by such an astronomical amount that I protested. After feigning anger, the driver looked crestfallen: '*Ma il Papa viene a Venezia soltanto ogni duecento anni!*' – But the Pope only comes to Venice every two hundred years! How could I be so unreasonable as to deprive him of such a celestial opportunity to rob me?

In Venice with my elderly Americans during a university vacation, I hired an open boat, filled it with a case of wine and the bravest of them and set off to explore the canals armed with only a tourist map for navigation. This expedition would be unthinkable now, and was fairly unthinkable then, but I was in swashbuckling mode. We picked our way through the tiniest of canals and past astonished onlookers. Gondoliers said incomprehensible things to me, or things it seemed wiser not to comprehend. After an hour of Venice's nooks and crannies, we set course for the Lido, hearts full and case of wine emptying. The crossing was a choppy journey across the lagoon that had once been filled with the billowing sails of warships and traders, and the sound of creaking rowlocks and drum-beats from the galleys as they pulled into the wind and away to distant lands. When we finally came alongside a jetty we were more merry than competent, and one or two of my charges had to be hauled ashore by strong and kindly Italians. They proudly bore the bruises on their arms for many days: 'That handsome young Italian held me very hard.'

Our expedition came to an awkward and expensive end when our craft erupted from a tiny backwater to cross the Grand Canal at the only point where a policeman was stationed. From his cabin at the end of the bridge the policeman leaned over and stretched his cheeks to blow his whistle. But I was under way, surging forward into the canal and uncertain what the whistle blast was telling me to do. Two *vaporetti* were heading for me, one from the left and one from the right, and changed course in a vain attempt to avoid collision, their passengers crowding to the bows to see what was happening. They bumped each other lightly, and my little boat emerged from the melée unharmed. Luckily my charges were filled with wine and saw it all as entertainment. The policeman was not amused, however, and I was fined an eye-watering sum on the spot. I was too embarrassed to protest. Since that year, foreigners have not been allowed to rent self-drive boats.

A week in Venice is a backward glance to an era when beauty mattered, a summons to our better selves. It is an elemental truth that we benefit from beautiful buildings, the absence of noise, the dominance of space, and movement by other human beings rather than engines. The very word beauty is an outcast now, alien to planning applications, to urban schemes, even to most architectural writing. There is more attention paid to the space between buildings than to the buildings themselves. Functionality and efficiency are elevated above beauty, and we are hoodwinked again. Saddest of all, we forget how different things could be. Venice is different, and thrilling for it, reminding us that the motor car is not a beast that we have to tolerate. Town planners should all be required to spend a week in Venice every year, at their own expense.

Venice is full of surprises once you get beneath its skin. Our Venice inspector, Janine, found a palazzo called Ca' Gloriosa, whose big top-floor apartment belonged to an elderly Italian gentleman married to an English lady. The apartment was an irritant to the old man, who preferred his palazzo in Rome, but his wife insisted on renovating it. She found silk wall decorations, countless treasures from his parents' colonial days in Asia, the family silver, crystal glasses and a valuable Hayez painting.

In another palazzo, Ca' Nova, Janine noticed etchings by Canova and thought the palazzo's name must refer to the artist. But they were unconnected. 'So I was surprised to

find myself face-to-face with two huge Canova statues of
Hector and Ajax in the private quarters of the palazzo!'

Venice can still throw a good party. In the nineties I joined
friends for the Vogalonga, an annual event that brings
Venetians and visitors together, originally in protest at the
number of motorboats on the city's waterways. It is a non-
competitive race from St Mark's into the lagoon, around
the island of Burano and then back into Venice from the
north, down a long canal into the Grand Canal and then to
the finish: thirty kilometres, so a real effort. The boats are
all powered by human beings, which means a welcome day
free of motor boats. There are more than fifteen hundred
boats, and about six thousand participants in a jaunty chaos
of gondolas, rowing boats, canoes, dragon boats and crews
in every colour and livery. As they milled about awaiting the
starting gun, I wondered where the organisation was, but
it all happened in a very Italian way. There were no visible
officials, just people and boats: extra-long gondolas, 'shells'
with sixteen oars-people from three generations, women's
boats, old ladies' boats, canoes and kayaks galore. Spectators
cheer for any reason, and I watched a winning gondola lose
its place as the crew all stood up, grinning, with their oars
aloft to acknowledge the cheers of the crowd. It was the
happiest possible day.

Venice ruled over the whole Veneto and her wealth over-
flowed inland. The Riviera del Brenta carries travellers
through a villa paradise where rich Venetians built on
the canal to impress and to take their holidays away from
the intrigues and pressures of Venice. The magnificent

Palazzo Foscari, known as La Malcontenta, is by Palladio and there are hundreds of fine buildings, with palaces and great houses sometimes occupied by old families that have seen better days. Many houses are still richly decorated with paintings and sculpture. Janine was chatting to Alberto, one of our owners, in his house and there met the Contessa di Canossa, who invited Janine to her palazzo in Verona. The Palazzo Canossa is right in the centre by the river, nursing a grand past. In the former ballroom was a ceiling painting by Paolo Veronese, later decorated over by Tiepolo when the Contessa's ancestors had tired of the original. During the Second World War the nearby bridge was wired with explosives, and when they erupted most of the Tiepolo collapsed. But every tiny bit is catalogued and stored in crates, and some of them have travelled to exhibitions as fragments. I will no longer fret about the clutter in my own house.

Some of the great rail journeys of Europe begin in Venice. On my way back to Britain I have several times hopped off at Milan and taken the short ride north to the lakes, where nature and man have combined to produce a dazzling Romantic landscape. Roman senators would retire to contemplate their careers in villas here, and it has been a European favourite ever since. I have often wondered where I would spend my last weekend on earth. I choose Lake Maggiore and its tiny Isola dei Pescatori, only a hundred yards from the shore but a hundred miles from the real world. At one end is the little Hotel Verbano, with a garden that leads to the water, into which I would slip for a swim before breakfast, the water cold and clear. The buildings are unrestrained and elegant, the lake in the foreground and the Alps in the background.

Em and I have long known a handsome house on the eastern shore, La Polidora, whose owner, GianLuca, has created his own pine arboretum (pinetum) protected by the World Wide Fund for Nature. This is spread over a huge lakeside estate, with its own pebble beaches, acres of lawn and rare plants, woodland and silence. Following a morning on his beach, we joined GianLuca on a boat trip to lunch across the lake. After a crossing of silky smoothness the boat throbbed idly under a low stone bridge and into a tiny harbour fringed with attractive houses. I wondered how the Italians build with such consistent grace, and gave thanks that it is they who have inherited this paradise rather than others less aesthetically sensitive.

Although luxury can reduce me, like any man, to embarrassing obsequiousness. I prefer simplicity. There is a simple house on Lake Como called Fisherman's House from which you can almost dangle your feet in the lake. The pebble beach on which the old house stands is yours, and you can take the old rowing boat across the lake to Varenna. I can think of few more perfect places to write, to learn, or just to be. I am kicking myself for not going there to write this book.

The Veneto produces some of Italy's finest wines under the Soave label, and has also produced a delightful story. I am quoting directly from Simon Loftus, a childhood friend who became one of the UK's finest wine writers and the Chair of Adnams, the Suffolk brewery. He and his wife, Irene, were exploring the Veneto and, perusing our book, chose to stay in La Rosa e Il Leone:

La Rosa e Il Leone is hard to find, behind a high wall and tall iron gate at the edge of the village of Colognola ai Colli, but the gate creaks open to a romantic, over-grown garden filled with trees and columns and ruins and flowers, and then you discover that the garden is shared by two nineteenth-century houses, in one of which the sisters live; the other is occupied by their guests. Two of the three sisters were there, Valeria and Giovanna Poli, and they told us their story. Their father (an industrialist from Verona) had bought one house as a place to escape his womenfolk and immerse him-self in his books. His wife protested so he bought the second house and created this elaborate garden for her, also acquiring two small vineyards: one across the road and one at the bottom of the garden. After his death the sisters stayed on, offering its three big bedrooms to those, like us, looking for somewhere interesting to stay.

So we slept between the finest linen sheets, took breakfast overlooking the garden and explored the large house from top to bottom. Which was how I discovered the cache of wine –

I knew that the name of the place honoured the sisters' parents (his Lion of Venice, her Rose of Lombardy) so when I found a book, *La Rosa e il Leone*, lying near the wine I expected to learn of their history. But instead I read of Rosa Luxemburg and Leon Trotsky, and began to realise that Valeria was a frustrated revolutionary. This longing to find her own way of doing things prompted her decision to become a wine-maker.

In 2004 she decided no longer to sell their grapes to

the local co-operative, and for three consecutive glorious vintages, until the labour became too much for her,
she selected the best, late-harvested bunches, which she
dried on racks for several weeks until the sugars were
concentrated and the flavours complex, and it was time
to crush and ferment them. Valeria had the help of a local
oenologist, but she followed, almost step by step, the
instructions of the sixth-century sage Cassiodorus. He
it was who first delimited and regulated the vineyards
of Soave, and it is in his honour that Valeria named her
wine Cassiodoro.

But alas, that was that – for Valeria had no means of
selling the wine that she had so lovingly made, apart
from a few cases in her immediate locality. There it
stayed, slowly maturing in a cool room at the bottom of
her father's house, until I discovered it.

Down in the basement, Simon tasted it. He returned
upstairs in a state of barely suppressed excitement, for he
had found a wonderful wine and on the spot bought half of
it for Adnams, and then sold it on to his friends and most
deserving customers. I bought six bottles and treasured each
sip, not least because I treasured, too, the story behind it.

I cannot leave northern Italy without mentioning the
International Slow Food Movement, whose headquarters are
in Bra, to the north-west and close to Turin. In 1986, Carlo
Petrini, a food journalist, saw that a McDonald's was about
to open in Rome's Piazza Navona. This was a red rag to a
bull: for Petrini, McDonald's epitomises the mediocratisa-
tion of the food world and the dominance of the American

fast-food industry. Carlo resolved to fight fast food with slow food.

The other event that triggered Petrini's revolt was the near-collapse of the Italian wine industry when a Piedmont wine-maker was convicted of adulterating his wine with industrial alcohol. National sales plummeted by a third.

In 1989, the Slow Food Manifesto was launched, a clarion call for gourmets: 'Against the universal madness of the Fast Life, we need to choose the defence of tranquil material pleasure. Against those, and there are many of them, who confuse efficiency with frenzy, we propose the vaccine of a sufficient portion of assured sensual pleasure, to be practised in slow and prolonged enjoyment.'

In spite of this apparent hedonism, the movement is committed to promoting integrity and authenticity, and has established its own University of Gastronomic Sciences, whose courses include mouth-watering access to artisan producers and growers all over Italy: cheese-makers, bee-keepers, wine-makers, ham producers, olive oil-makers and others. Every November, in Turin, there is the Salone del Gusto, a slow food global feast for artisan growers. At the same time is Terra Madre, an international gathering of small-scale producers. I have known people talk of it all with tears in their eyes. No wonder, for it is the world's greatest display of good food.

The best conference meal I have ever had was at a Soil Association event in Edinburgh, when Scottish producers set up a Slow Food Fair in the conference hall. I wandered from stall to stall tasting and talking in a haze of food euphoria, and will remember until my dying day the single scallop dropped onto a hot skillet with a knob of butter, the cook telling me how he had plucked it from the seabed off the Holy Isle that very morning. I could see why St James was reputed to have arrived in Spain in a scallop shell, and why they were the preferred mode of transport for Botticelli's Venus.

Em and I had had a similar experience on Sark Island, where we ate scallops for breakfast having seen the café owner's husband emerging from the sea in his wetsuit, carrying them to the kitchen. I would eat one such scallop rather than half a dozen dredged ones.

Slow food is gaining pace, with old ideas that need to be re-articulated. It celebrates meals prepared with love and consumed at leisure, as in Italy, where life still stops for lunch. Italy has hung on to its local produce better than most. Until 1861 Italians were citizens of a state, or region, such as Piedmont, and this regional loyalty still drives passion about food. If you care about food, you will care where it comes from and who grew it. I still wince when a friend offers to share a roast Tesco chicken 'because it is fantastic value at £4.50'. I'd rather pay twelve pounds, very occasionally, and be sure it has had no hormones, antibiotics or added water. It will also have avoided a grim life cooped up with thousands of others in a dark room.

Michael Pollan's *The Omnivore's Dilemma* and Felicity Lawrence's *Not On the Label* are both powerful calls to rethink the way we eat. When I gave copies of the latter to my two boys for Christmas, they said: 'Now we understand why you have been banging on about these things for so long, Dad!' A significant moment for a father.

18

Elegance in Simplicity

W hy do we love the Italians? While pondering the matter for this chapter I remembered a surprising encounter Em and I had in Orkney – about as far from Italy as it is possible to be in the UK.

During the Second World War, five hundred Italian prisoners from the North Africa campaign were taken to Scapa Flow to build concrete barriers for the harbour. Two hundred of them lived in a Nissen-hut camp on the tiny island of Lamb Holm.

Nissen huts were an ugly feature of post-war Britain, and they can still be seen on (usually decrepit) farms. The prisoners approached the camp padre to ask if they might turn a couple of huts into a chapel. Permission was granted, and two huts were put end to end.

One of the prisoners was an artist, called Domenico Chiocchetti, and he gathered about him other prisoners with

artisan and artistic skills to create the chapel. A metalworker
created an altar rail from scrap metal found in the camp;
left-over cement from their construction project was used
to build an impressive façade, or west front. An old exhaust
pipe was used as part of the font; light-holders were crafted
from corned-beef tins. I found the ingenuity touching. By
the time of the Italian Armistice in September 1943, the
chapel was still not quite finished, so when the prisoners
were released Chiocchetti stayed on to finish his painting.
He returned twice in the sixties to do some touching up,
and the chapel is now a symbol of reconciliation visited by
thousands.

Am I right in thinking that only Italians would have done
such a thing?

My memory of that Nissen-hut chapel was triggered by an
Italian B&B owner once telling me that they can feel trapped
by their success. She lamented that they become *prigionieri
a casa propria* – prisoners in their own houses. Successful
owners have guests underfoot day after day, and looking
after them while wearing a constant smile can be wearing.
Private time with family is a rarity and the strain can crack
the boldest of façades. Giuseppe's eventually cracked.

Along the coast from Grosseto to Livorno, with a mountainous landscape directly inland, villages are few and far
between and dense woods of oak and cork-oak cover the
entire area. It is a nature-lover's dream, and the countryside of the famous Bolgheri wines. Our inspector, Claudia,
reached Giuseppe's house along a track leading to a large
stone farmhouse with five guest rooms. The inspection went
well, though Claudia noted that Giuseppe was hurried and
tense. He never introduced his wife, who was going in and

out of the kitchen, or his three children, but served a superb salad in the dining room. Claudia then settled in the living room to make notes while the family shared their meal.

The discussion in the dining room, about the lack of privacy in their lives, became heated. A marital yelling match began, punctuated with screaming and colourful Italian gestures, and continued out in the garden. The wife then rushed back to the table where the children were still sitting, and, with a fine feel for drama, smashed the dishes on the terracotta floor.

'I thanked Giuseppe and said we would be in touch, and then headed for the hills!' wrote Claudia, shaken by the experience. If one can bear a little drama, inspecting can be delightful.

In 2014, eight of our Italian inspectors came together at the Tenuta di Canonica near Todi. One was a stand-up comedienne married to a Roman, another ran archaeological tours in Tuscany. Caroline had married Lucca and settled among his family in distant Basilicata, while Katrina had lived in Sicily for years. They all had strong views on everything, let alone what constituted character and specialness. They had strong characters too – a vital ingredient for inspecting an unpredictable miscellany of houses.

Todi, with its near-perfect medieval piazza, could be seen from the windows of the Tenuta like a distant backdrop to a Renaissance painting. The windows themselves were pierced in massive walls that were part-Roman. Our medieval watchtower still frowned upon the fields beyond, as if it had not forgotten its original purpose. Daniele and Maria had peopled the house with portraits and guests, decorated it with period pieces and books, and rugs with bold Italian design. In contrast, one bedroom had pale blue walls, fine furniture, a Persian rug on an old tiled floor, stripped shutters and – untypically – a refined absence of art on the walls speaking more eloquently than any painting. Italians have a gift for making one feel part of their genius. Perhaps it is also the vitality of their language that draws one closer, or is it that they so clearly want you to like them?

We sat up late into the night discussing reasons for accepting and rejecting places. We disagreed amiably on the intrusion of IKEA, the value of good books on the shelves, of art on the walls. Is a bad painting done by the owner more acceptable than someone else's bad painting? What is a bad painting anyway? Are there general guidelines? Does a painting of a tree have more general appeal than that of a trumpet? Apparently one thing we all agree on, across cultures, is the appeal of the colour blue. Are dog-owners generally nicer people? Do people prefer to wander in and out of kitchens, or to be served from them? Does a sterile-looking bathroom matter if it is ultra-efficient? Does an antiquated bathroom, with character and clattering pipework, have special appeal any more? Leaning over the edge of the bath to select a book and then subsiding into hot, deep water is one of life's pleasures, even if the plumbing is of the protesting, unreliable kind.

As if to put competing views to the test, we went on to meet Marcello, a maverick Italian businessman with a Tuscan castle that cocks a snook to the hotel world. It is on the edge of a nature reserve, and Marcello awaited me, Toby and Nicole, our Italian 'ambassador', at the bottom of a steep track. Up we rattled in his old Land Rover, Marcello gesticulating and enthusing. The building at the ride's end could have been on Mount Athos: formidable, monastic-looking and on a huge scale. We stepped into a light-filled room built entirely in stone. Scattered about were colourful cushions, candles flickered in stone niches, a log fire blazed in the giant hearth, gentle music filled every corner. Upstairs, another corridor led to Marcello's tour de force: fourteen bedrooms, each a monk's cell but fashioned with a clever combination of austerity and luxury, all in stone again.

'Many couples like to go away separately, to charge their batteries without each other, so these rooms are for singles, not couples.' We were getting some marital psychology. 'To hell with market research; this is what people need, and they also need spiritual space. Come with me.' He took us to the third floor where he had built a chapel for meditation, reflection and prayer. Lunch was served on the terrace over-looking the forest, every morsel organic and delicious. The nature reserve stretched to the distance and silence hung over the house like an invisible net. Marcello had found his truth, and we were captivated. The building was to be off-grid, with solar panels hidden on the hillside behind the house, low demand for energy (hence the candles), the thickest possible insulation between the inner and outer layers of stone, and diligent recycling.

Not far away lived another character, David Edwards, who had often taken our American clients walking in Tuscany. He used to bring the exploits of Hannibal dramatically to life by beefing up his description of the Battle of Lake Trasimeno with fossilised turds he had brought back from the Empty Quarter in Saudi Arabia. He assumed they were from camels, but they passed as droppings from Hannibal's elephants which he used to 'discover' in the undergrowth. Another ruse was the unexpected chancing upon Italian porcupine quills, a prized trophy in the US. He carried a handful of them in his rucksack and would always 'find' some, which the walkers could claim as their own.

The Chiesa della Signora del Letto – Church of Our Lady of the Bed – was David's name for any church whose name he could not remember. But invented names were never as strange as strange clients, such as the woman who complained that the corridors in the hotel were not long enough. She liked to speed walk at night, but the corridors were too short for her to reach optimum speed. She regarded wine as sinful, so David would sit her next to the lady who liked a martini for breakfast.

I knew what he was up against. I once travelled for a week with an American woman who, throughout her meals, would sit up to her waist in a special plastic bag. She had a horror of draughts, and once also encased her head in plastic, so grim, apparently, were the winds blowing through an invisible crack in the window frame. It made conversation patchy. She had the mad forcefulness of Alan Bennett's Lady in the Van.

In spite of mad ladies and midnight walkers, or because of them, my walking-tour days in Italy were punctuated with exquisite moments, for which Italy has such talent. I persuaded my driver to take our large bus up to Monteriggioni, a tiny circular hilltop village untouched by the years. Giovanni protested, but up we went along a narrow and winding road, with me urging him on to greater daring. Within five hundred yards of the village there was an alarming noise from the rear wheels on a particularly tight turn. Giovanni and I got out to look, and found the wheels buried to their axles in mud. This, of course, was an opportunity: a farmer came to the rescue and towed the bus and all forty elderly occupants out with his tractor, offering me prodigious quantities of advice as Italians do so well. My American travellers thought that this was all part of the day's programme ... or so I like to think.

The walks in Tuscany also took me to Pienza, a town of such loveliness that I briefly contemplated living there. It is often called the Pearl of the Renaissance. I walked on the marble pavement slabs of the perfect cathedral square, surrounded by palaces, with the delicacy of a guest at a ball. Spitting gum or dropping litter would be unthinkable. Pope Pius II was born there and gave the task of transforming it from the village of Corsignano to the ideal of a Renaissance town to one architect: Bernardo Rossellino. It is still known as *la città d'autore*, the creation of one guiding intellect. As were those Baroque towns in Sicily.

Pienza, also known for its pecorino cheese, is in the famously beautiful Val d'Orcia, whose two main towns are also jewels: Montalcino and Montepulciano, both famous for their red wine. We organised walks from one town to the next, each step yielding another view of a Tuscany recognisable from faded memories of paintings. How hard it must have been in the Second World War for soldiers to fight their way up Italy from one town to the next, conscious of the damage being done. A British artillery officer called Tony Clarke was charged with the shelling of Sansepolcro in north-east Tuscany. He remembered reading that the town had one of Italy's finest frescoes, the Resurrection by Piero della Francesca, so he disobeyed orders and lobbed only a few shells in, reluctantly and nervously. The next day a young Italian boy breathlessly arrived to tell him that the town was empty of Germans. Not another shell was fired and the painting survived the war in perfect condition.

The British Army had a special squad charged with rescuing hidden works of art before they were lost to retreating Germans or the chaos of war. It is a moving story of cellars piled with hidden art treasures and just-in-time rescues. A big round painting by Ghirlandaio, who taught Michelangelo, was hidden in the Villa Canucci and used upside down as a mess table by German troops. It was rescued and returned to its proper place.

Before heading south to Puglia, after our inspector gathering near Todi, we had a masterclass from Giancarlo Polito, the economist, photographer, hotelier and chef *straordinario* – and enthusiast for all things edible and Puglian. He runs the Locanda del Capitano in Montone, a fortified Umbrian village, where he cooked a Puglian dinner that challenged more than just our sense of taste. One course involved holding a tiny bottle of frozen olive oil in one's hand, waiting for it to melt and be poured over the lamb. One can take the man out of Puglia, but not Puglia out of the man. He waxed lyrical about the region and meant every word. Italians defend their region as others might defend a lover – *con passione e con vigore.*

Puglia produces more olive oil than the rest of Italy put together, miles upon miles of olive trees marching through the rolling countryside like a disciplined army, the grape vines marching with similar purpose. The English are flocking to this landscape, some buying up old houses, *masserie* and *trulli*, and turning them into holiday lets or B&Bs. This mystifies me, for Puglia's landscape is no match for the rest of Italy.

A night at Il Frantoio provided part of the answer. A dull drive through olive groves from Bari train station, a bumpy ride up the track and then – an oasis. The courtyard glowed under a canopy of trees. Scattered about the yard were small groups of people chatting and drinking. The warmth of welcome was palpable, each table asking us to join them. Our bedroom within the massive walls of the farmhouse had old hats hanging off a line of hooks, photographs of previous owners and books about old Italy.

The gastronomic gauntlet was thrown down at dinner. We ducked the eight-course meal in favour of the six-course version. Here is the menu:

1. Panzerottini con ricotta e bietoline selvatiche – fried pasta with ricotta and wild Swiss chard.
2. Cicorielli selvatiche assise in cesto di pecorino – wild chicory in a basket of sheep's cheese.
3. Morbido di caprino allo zafferano con pere e composta di pere – soft goat's cheese with saffron, pears and pear compote.
4. Zuppa con funghi cardoncelli e fagioli 'Nasieddu rosso' di Sarconi – mushroom soup with Sarconi beans
5. Agnello con patate in coccio – lamb and spuds
6. I can't remember the last dish – but it was delicious.

This was an organic orgy, and nearly all homegrown. The wines were either Primitivo or Negroamaro, red and rich but easy on the head. But those six courses! And the foraging, the ingenuity, the integrity, the localness, and let me not forget the taste. Directing and stage-managing were Armando and Rosalba. For Armando, each ancient olive tree is a friend and he winced as the harvesting machine reached up and shook a branch. He is an old-fashioned paterfamilias, his staff devoted to him and proud of their Frantoio. One evening, normal service came to a halt as the staff gathered around the TV to watch a programme about local food. The guests put down their napkins and joined in, nobody minding the delay.

The two little towns of Monopoli and Polignano a Mare decorate the otherwise-dull coast near by, each with a white-painted old centre around the harbour steeped in bloodshed and invasion. The *passeggiata* was our entertainment, a survivor in spite of so much change in Italy. It is a time when the streets are leisurely with old men; they carry themselves like retired, but still important, village mayors. Women of all ages tutter and preen, some impressively upright on heels that would give me vertigo. Young men still strut their peacock stuff as they have for centuries – though nowadays less colourfully.

In Monopoli I twisted my ankle, a vulnerability that plagues me, but a kindly old man lent me his walking stick and thus brought me a step closer to those village elders one sees drinking coffee in amiably vacant-looking groups. As I grow older I am beginning to wonder how I can reproduce here the conviviality among old men that is such a feature of Mediterranean societies.

Our next stop in Puglia was Lecce, a sumptuous banquet of Baroque building in the soft, easily carved local sandstone.

Over ninety palazzi and forty churches grace this town so small that one can walk across it in twenty minutes. As in Venice, every turn reveals a new marvel. Our simple sitting room was itself a marvel, with a ceiling seven metres high. I was by now on crutches to cope with my ankle and would often skip a stroll, but Em insisted, one dusky evening as the street lights were beginning to flicker, on leading me, eyes closed, through the streets for about ten minutes. When I opened my eyes to the now-revealed illuminated beauty of the Piazza del Duomo I burst into tears.

Facing east across the Mediterranean, the Puglian coast has known more than the usual Italian share of history's turmoil. In 1554 Vieste was cruelly sacked by Barbary pirates from North Africa. Seven thousand citizens were taken as slaves, a dreadful fate. Some would be chained to the galley rowing benches and never set foot on land again. Others became servants, members of the harem, or labourers. Five thousand other citizens were executed before the pirates left the town. Curiously, the Barbary pirates got as far as Baltimore in Ireland in 1631, where they took more than a hundred men, women and children prisoner.

From Bari to Naples is a bus ride from rural calm to urban frenzy. Once in the city our bus shed its country ways and became fully Neapolitan. If there are just two lanes in each direction, what to do if both lanes on your side are jammed solid? Just use the oncoming lane, of course. We will surely die, I thought, but this was Naples, where luck trumps common sense. Thus began our stay, dicing with death, then a taxi ride that didn't, surely, have to do that grand tour of most of the city before getting to our B&B?

Naples, as we all know, doesn't work very well; it's noisy, dirty, traffic-clogged, corrupt and chaotic. Elena Ferrante's books have recently cast a warm glow over the city, but the future is grim, according to Roberto Saviano. Em and I were both glued to his *Gomorrah* while we were there, and saw a Camorrista behind every shop counter and bar. Half the shops in town are Camorra-controlled, according to Roberto, so we may have been half right. His analysis does explain the waves of rubbish lapping at every pavement. The Camorra controls waste management and waste disposal.

There is a comparison with Britain's waste system. It is not, as far as I know, in the Mafia's hands, but it is manipulated and thus controlled by the big companies that promote waste incineration. Once two hundred million pounds has been invested, say, in an incinerator – which pollutes, wastes heat and demands inexhaustible supplies of waste – there is no incentive to recycle. Thus many small, bad decisions flow from one big one. Is that corrupt, or just poor policy?

Naples was capital of the Kingdom of Naples, and for centuries, successive regimes invaded, controlled and embellished her, leaving behind magnificent buildings. The Teatro di San Carlo is one of Europe's finest, with five tiers of boxes soaring to a golden painted ceiling. We spent an enchanted evening there, Em occupying her own solitary box one tier above mine. This was an error, rather than grandiosity on our part, for we had lost each other in the pre-concert chaos. There are palaces and fine churches, a gigantic dock system (Camorra-controlled, again), and elegant shopping avenues. They cut through the long, dark alleys filled with hanging washing, carelessly parked children, tiny ground-floor flats, sordid workshops, scuttling dogs and cats. (A short story by

Graham Greene has an Englishman being crushed by a pig falling from a balcony in a Neapolitan backstreet.) Such is Naples: splendour and squalor intertwined.

Em tootled off to the National Archaeological Museum while I pedalled perilously around Naples on a hired bike with my crutch strapped to the handlebars. Cycling makes me reckless; I challenge the traffic and imagine the bike to be king, because I believe it should be. How I survived that day, in traffic renowned as manic, is a mystery. But sheer bravura took me the full length of the waterfront, pursued by motorists even more reckless than I, and down the back-streets of the poorest parts of Naples, ducking the washing lines, pursued by looks of pure astonishment. When I finally, and inevitably, fell off it was while stationary, and into the arms of a very surprised nun. She saved me from falling far, which is, I suppose, something nuns do naturally.

Em had the more elevating day, immersed in Roman art and being reminded that they were painting and sculpting with exquisite skill fifteen hundred years before Michelangelo. Before she returned, I drafted an article about my bike ride for a national paper and asked her to check it. 'I suggest you explain that the crutch was for your ankle before writing that you had strapped it to the handlebars.'

There is always a dog barking through the night in urban Italy, but night-time in the Bay of Naples has its compensation: an elegant seafront necklace of light reflected in the dark water. We are in a palazzo belonging to an absent Bourbon prince, observing rather than participating. The concierge sits in a glassed-in box by the entrance, doling out twenty-cent pieces for the clattering lift. Daylight reveals a different Naples. An old woman opens her balcony door and tours her pot plants. A schoolgirl takes the washing off the line, and a prim matron shoos away two scuffling cats. A well-suited businessman bursts through the French doors onto his roof, bearing a parrot in a cage. The man below lights a fag and leans out over the street. And then spits. Women stop to chat over their babies, ignoring the old crone sweeping the pavement around them. Schoolchildren skip along the street, and I see one steal a banana from the tiny grocery store below us. Traffic clogs, urges and slowly shifts. Screeching scooters break free.

Our last Italian dinner on that trip was the one meal without which any Italian holiday feels barren: Mama and Papa and elderly sister in a scrubbed café, serving simple food from a pencilled menu. It was cheap and delicious: fegato (lamb's liver) in onions and those oricchiette, little ears, from Puglia. Such elegance in simplicity – and so Italian.

My memories of Italian food are almost visceral. My first is of dinner in the home of Giovanni, the bus driver at Monteriggioni. I was goggle-eyed at the generosity, the plate of antipasto and then the *primo piatto*, lasagne. I love lasagne and this was the first time I had been served it in Italy, so after devouring the antipasto I demolished this too. Giovanni's wife Lola, a proud but nervous cook, hovered over me and urged me on with '*mangia, mangia*'. So I ate a second helping. It is an old story of foreign ignorance: the next course was not the dessert, but a gargantuan chicken dish. How I managed I cannot remember, but I was young, foolish and constitutionally stronger than now.

Giovanni was my first teacher of Italian, gesticulating wildly over pronunciation while I vainly reminded him that he was driving forty people at speed. He cared about his language: '*Ma, no, Alessandro!! Non si dice così!*' We would discuss grammar and tenses, spelling and dialect – most of it over my head. I tried to imagine a similar experience in England and could only picture the *Sun* stuffed into a pocket and a gruff discussion of the traffic. Giovanni was a true gentleman. One evening, in Florence, we learned that two old ladies in our group had been asked to share a double bed as the hotel had muddled the reservations. I asked Giovanni if he would give up his room and share mine, but he looked curiously reluctant. I pressed him, appealing to his innate kindness and Italian respect for older people, and he relented. When undressing for bed he had no choice but to reveal the reason for his reluctance: his wooden leg. He had kept this secret from his employers, and me, for fear of losing his job.

19

Human Towers and Other Catalan Phenomena

Friends described it as hovering alone above the clouds, and above the vultures too, with distant views to the Mediterranean. It was, we heard, quite unlike anything else. So I knew of L'Avenc from afar, and keenly wanted to see it. Then I read *A Castle in Spain*, Matthew Parris's charming tale of his family's love affair with L'Avenc and the journey they made to bring this Catalan jewel back to life.

The family of Matthew, an English broadcaster, columnist and former MP, moved to Catalonia and he would often hike along the lip of the plateau past an abandoned and derelict sixteenth-century farmhouse. Years passed and yet he returned to the area where the house still stood, battered by time but with dignity intact. The mad idea of buying it came to him and such was his enthusiasm that his sisters succumbed too. Both of them had Catalan husbands, so this became a family project. They could not have known it would put them under strain for years.

It was a form of obsession too, of course. The English have a particular vulnerability to ruined farmhouses; they have bought them all over Europe, pouring their youth and their fortunes into them. There is an amusing twist to the Parris story: they have, as if the house wasn't enough, built a hotel up there too. It began when Belinda Parris's husband, Quim, bought himself a digger to 'dig a hole to hide the cars in'. He couldn't stop digging – a problem with boys' toys – and by the time he had finished his cavern had space for forty cars. One can only be grateful that he had just one ordinary digger.

It all reminded Em of the opening of the mountainside in Robert Browning's 'The Pied Piper of Hamelin'.

> When, lo, as they reached the mountain-side,
> A wondrous portal opened wide,
> As if a cavern was suddenly hollowed;
> And the Piper advanced and the children
> followed,
> And when all were in to the very last,
> The door in the mountain-side shut fast.

The door opened automatically as we approached in the car, like a James Bond set. You drive into the mountain, walk through a glass door and a lift glides you up to the reception. The first person you encounter is Belinda. She has the gentlest nature, works indomitably hard and has strong ethical and green values. She and her sister campaigned for years to have bullfighting banned in Catalonia, and succeeded. She has planted organically all around the house and is keen that it be a centre for local cultural activities and environmental education. Belinda has borne the brunt of the family's enthusiasm for L'Avenc.

Egyptian vultures soar below you and above. The escarpments rise sheer from the valleys below, a thousand feet into the air like grand barriers to a lost world. The views are at least 180 degrees, fold after fold of hills and valleys beyond the range of your eyes. You are above it all yet deeply rooted in it, but behind the idyll is a distressing tale. The neighbouring farmer did all he could to sabotage their work, cutting off their water once they had begun the building; it took months of legal struggle to get it back. He did the same when they opened, with similar struggles. The battle nearly broke the family's resolve. Water battles are not uncommon in a country as parched as Spain.

Our stay up at L'Avenc was crowned by an evening of music from a young English pianist called Carl, who was there for the weekend. He produced a wild cascade of notes, his fingers butterflying crazily across the keys. There seemed nothing he could not play. It was a tour de force high up on a Catalan plateau, involving Noël Coward, playing with one hand and pouring brandy with the other. The Charleston had Em on her feet and performing like Ginger Rogers, so I later arranged for Carl to play at her seventieth birthday party. She came gaily, innocently, into the room to be greeted by Carl on the piano – a precious moment.

Catalonia has many jewels, and L'Avenc is but a modest one. The very word Catalonia evokes so much: Gaudí,

Barcelona, the language, experiments with food, the civil war, Salvador Dalí, Picasso, Miró, Gerona and a long historical connection to southern France. You cannot be in Barcelona for long without noticing how strikingly distinctive are Catalan art and architecture. You see Dalí's and Miró's ideas shimmering in the zany upper floors of workaday buildings, in Gaudi's Sagrada Família, in parks, bars and markets. The Santa Catarina market has more Catalan exuberance than seems possible in one place. It is one of my favourite buildings, a surprise at every turn with wood put to glittering use by a modern designer. A meal there in the evening stretches the eyes, the jaw and the imagination. The roof is a giant wave-shaped sail of coloured Seville tiles; the interior a temple to timber and gastronomy. The architects also designed the Scottish Parliament, another wonderful, if ruinously expensive, display of Catalan genius. Santa Catarina is a reminder of the power of an idea – in this case surrealism. It is a new way of envisioning a market, one that argues elegantly against the banality to which we, in the UK, have become accustomed.

The old quarter of Barcelona once gave me an afternoon of exhilarating spectator sport. In the Placa Jaume in the Barrio Góttico, filled to overflowing with people, I came across a Torre Humana – human tower – a uniquely Catalan contest with teams vying to pile humans on top of each other as high as possible. The tension reduced me to gibbering anguish. As I watched the milling of the crowd in the square a circle formed close to a building decorated with balconies and with people hanging from them, shouting their encouragement. The circle of squat, muscled men was surrounded and buttressed by the arms of others leaning in

on them. More, less chunky, climbed onto their shoulders
to form a second layer, holding each other round the waist.
One by one there followed more circles of diminishing
radius, up to six further layers in various combinations, the
higher the layer the lighter the people. The strain on those
on the bottom was almost unbearable to watch, each new
layer adding new strain and new tension. One man wobbled
slightly, looking close to collapse. I couldn't take my eyes
off him as the tower grew. He surely would bring the whole
edifice toppling down. But, grimacing with strain, he held.
Four boys were recklessly added, to the disbelief of foreigners in the crowd. Two smaller boys then stood wobbling,
impossibly I thought, on their shoulders, locked in arm's
length embrace. The last, and smallest, clambered up the
outside of the tower, gripping coats and belts, and appeared
on the slender shoulders of those two boys for seconds,
wobbling terrifyingly, before being whisked upwards – to
great cheering – by people leaning down from a balcony.
The others then rapidly unpeeled layer by layer, reducing
the pressure on the men below with each unpeeling. I was
weak with emotional exhaustion and relief.

It is a superb form of community bonding. Each team
comes from a different village or town. Sometimes the
towers collapse, with broken bones a frequent result. The
anticipation of collapse generates much of the excitement,
as each human tier adds a new level of fear and danger. I'm
not sure I can bring myself to watch it again.

The news from Catalonia is often of political ferment,
a no-longer-suppressed longing for independence and a
stubborn determination to celebrate difference from the rest
of Spain. I was in Barcelona in 1976, the year after Franco

died, and visited a book fair that was brimming over with publishing in Catalan. Franco had banned the language, but it had simmered beneath the surface and now boiled over in a torrent of new writing. There is something charming about Catalan, a gentle fusion of other Romance languages. It is soft, a susurrus, a whisper of syllables without harsh stops and consonants, whereas Spanish can cut the air. Intriguingly, it survives not only in Catalonia but also on Sardinia, in the little town of Alghero, a survival from four centuries of Catalan rule. If you have a smattering of French, Spanish or Italian you will enjoy Article 1 of the Universal Declaration of Human Rights in Catalan:

Tots els éssers humans neixen lliures i iguals en dignitat i en drets. Són dotats de raó i de consciència, i han de comportar-se fraternalment els uns amb els alters.

All human beings are born free and equal in dignity and rights. They are endowed with reason and conscience and should act towards one another in a spirit of brotherhood.

It is instantly recognisable, and I remember the delight with which I read it for the first time. I also tried reading *Babar the Elephant* in Catalan, but that was my limit.

Catalonia once stretched deep into southern France and is still more like a small country than a region. In the Pyrenees there are old villages with exquisite churches, nine of them in the Val de Boi – all early Romanesque and now a World Heritage Site. Each is worth a journey. In the mountains to the west of Gerona, where L'Avenc is to be found, are handsome towns and villages like Rupit and a vigorous rural economy.

Music is a recurring theme at our special places, such as one of them in the south, near a little town called Aracena, north of Seville. This is the land of gypsy flamenco, but it is also a world where the town brass band, with its drums and wind instruments and community pride, still matters. It is not unlike the tradition of brass bands in Welsh mining villages. The music connection here is between the band and one of our most engaging B&Bs, the Finca Buenvino. It was around the owners' dinner table that I heard this story; they knew the characters, and their daughter had become a member of the local band.

Ian Murray left the Scottish Symphony Orchestra, where he was principal bass trombonist, to play with the Seville Symphony. His daughter settled into the Aracena primary school, and Ian would drive down to Seville for his orchestral work. The town's wind band, once one of the country's finest, had shrunk to nineteen old men playing battered instruments and unable to read music. Ian agreed, to his own surprise, to be the bandmaster for the Easter festival in 1993. His orchestral colleagues came to help and threw themselves into the task of transforming the band. That year they won the regional championship and new players flocked to join. Within two years there were eighty players and they won the national championship. Ian opened a music school in the town and it grew quickly to two hundred students from the local area. Tragically, Ian died aged thirty-five of a heart attack, but in only a few years he had rekindled the energy and pride of a small town – and brought music to thousands. Janet, his widow, has built a legacy which now includes a concert hall and two music colleges – a senior and a junior. Imagine the same in Abergavenny.

The story of El Sistema, Venezuela's music-education programme, is similarly rooted in a belief in the capacity of music to lift ordinary lives to brilliance, or just make them sparkle a little. That, too, began with one man, José Antonio Abreu. Over the decades he has created many orchestras, especially among the poor. He has brought music to hundreds of thousands of people. The orchestras have taken the world by storm, bringing rapturous applause as far away from Venezuela as the Albert Hall. El Sistema is a miracle of the human spirit, as was Ian Murray's impact on Aracena.

Stories of one person, like Ian, changing a corner of the world have always moved me, especially when the difficulties have appeared insurmountable. Most of us think only of the difficulties. Churchill, whose contact with Spain was, I admit, minimal, famously dismissed those who argued against his mad scheme to build concrete harbours and float them across the Channel to France to back up the D-Day landings with 'Don't argue the matter. The difficulties will argue for themselves.'

In the wrong hands, however, the obstacles lead to failure, as we all know. One such personal failure was the Great Organic Bike Ride, which I dreamed up and organised as an autumn fundraiser for the Soil Association, across Spain from Bilbao to Barcelona.

The ride's name had a nice ring to it, and Toby, my son, and his cousin Sam were dispatched to research the route. They found beautiful places to stay, including a splendid organic farm, and thirty people signed up. I bought a fleet of bicycles, recruited guides and set off in my VW Caravelle minibus. It was fun for the cyclists, but costs were high and the organisational paddling below the waterline was frantic. Organic food was unexpectedly hard to find so we bought a small flock of chickens, cooked them and put them in our van-powered cool-boxes. We then ferried them in the increasing heat across Spain, vainly looking for the promised fridges at our campsites. They were either broken, or non-existent. A lot of organic Spanish chickens had to be discarded, an ignominious fate after their careful rearing. For the final humiliation, the driver of the Caravelle failed to top up the oil and the van died, to become a high-class home for live local Spanish chickens.

However, this bike ride was but a blip in my enthusiasm for Spain, which began when I was a boy. My cousin Sally had married Kiki, an engaging and sociable Spaniard who took me to my first flamenco performance. I was hooked. Kiki and Sally ran a campsite, at whose bar Kiki used to entertain the locals. We would go there for summer holidays and my delight in all things Spanish grew, so Sally arranged for me, a very English boy of sixteen, to spend three weeks with the Ortega family in Sitges.

The Ortega father was a retired Francoist general and disciplinarian who ruled his tribe of seven daughters and one son with military efficiency. The daughters were older than I and were all tantalisingly beautiful. Life with the family was slow, sun-drenched and routine-led. I had a siesta every afternoon, then would go to the beach and swim, consumed by hopeless longing for one or other of the daughters – or all of them. Dinner saw father at the head of the table, his daughters ranged down both sides. I sat at the end of the table with Pasqualine, the son. The evening would often end with one or two daughters flouncing out of the room in tears at their father's obduracy. England had not prepared me for such heat generated around a table, but my efforts to follow the dinner-time conversations, and communicate better with those girls, resulted in rapidly learned Spanish.

Spain in the fifties and sixties was still partly isolated from the rest of Europe. The Guardia Civil lurked everywhere, as did crippled veterans of the civil war. Old men often spoke with croaky voices, the result of smoking phenomenal amounts of cheap tobacco. Donkeys were commonly used for transport, and wine was bought cheaply from the barrel. The evening *paseo* was a key part of life. Everybody dressed up, and it was the best opportunity to find a potential spouse.

Later I came across H. V. Morton, whose *A Stranger In Spain* cemented my affections with that special gift of making the reader feel erudite too. Many years later, the opportunity to do our own book about Spain was impossible to resist. That opportunity came along in the shape of Guy Hunter-Watts.

Imaginative, maverick and generous, Guy launched himself into the job with gusto. He had restored a house in a small village near Ronda called Montecorto, an unremarkable place but with the best views of any I have seen in southern Spain. When I set out to visit him I was unaware that he had told the mayor that my visit would be good PR for the village. The two of them had concocted a plan: my bus was to be met on arrival by the girls' choir, and the mayor, dressed in his finest, would be there to greet me with a speech. All went to plan. The choir and the mayor, and the bus, played their part, and the girls sang their hearts out to the delighted but puzzled passengers who emerged into the Montecorto plaza. Ignorant of Guy's plans, however, I had dawdled and then taken the next bus. I arrived to an empty plaza; the choir and mayor had gone home, and Guy's standing in the village took a while to recover.

Guy had filled his house with music, books, bright colours and decorative flourishes from Morocco. It was unquestionably a special place to stay, and he took me walking in the Sierra de Grazalema, revealing to me a Spain of which most visitors are unaware. The rugged limestone landscape is cut with gullies and cliffs, and by a gigantic gorge with a colony of griffon vultures and walls of over a thousand feet. One landscape follows another, with more than thirteen hundred species of Mediterranean plants plus a well-preserved forest of Spanish fir. We ended our day's ramble with a meal of ham and eggs, Spanish style, a glass of *fino* and a round of tapas in Ronda – slow travel at its best.

Tourism on Spain's coastal fringe, however, is a very different picture. Each of those resorts has been a nail in the coffin of old Spain, of tradition and of human pace. It has also meant relentless economic destruction. Gerald Brenan, author of *South from Granada* and a writer who did so much to evoke the best of traditional Spain, would have wept at the loss. Tourism is an 'extractive' industry like coal mining, extracting material and profit and leaving when it wishes.

Staying with the locals is a good way to avoid such tourism. I have been whisked out by B&B hosts to watch flamenco, listen to a talk on an escape from German captivity in a local church, water-ski behind a Venetian taxi, enjoy Louisiana jazz in a rural community, gaze blankly at modern art, watch birds in the Doñana National Park and hike through sublime countryside. The unexpected can transform a run-of-the-mill experience, as happened to me in Andalucía.

I was staying, when running my own tours, in a remote farmhouse-hotel near Ronda, along with a group of classy American travel agents. They were there to see if I could handle their smarter clients. I had struggled to persuade them of the benefits of being in the countryside, on a real farm rather than in a smart hotel, and was, I thought, succeeding. We descended the hill at the end of a long mountain walk and heard a distant banshee screeching. Guy and I urgently pressed on ahead to find three men castrating the farm's pigs. There was carnage: blood everywhere, testicles hanging on the fence and the air heavy with testosterone.

In an heroic moment, Guy shouted 'Stop!' in Spanish to the knife-wielders who were in full castration mode. I feared for his dignity, and his testicles. They turned to face him, dripping blood from their long, sharp weapons. It was a stand-off, a Hemingway moment. Was Guy up to it? The Americans were closing on us, but still out of sight. I wondered how easy it would be to stop a bullfight by asking the matadors to desist. Finally, after a pause pregnant with porcine and male energy, Guy standing his ground, the men said '*bueno*' – and it was over. Guy then had to pay them off and rearrange the remaining castrations. The Americans were saved from witnessing rural Spanish life in the raw.

I wasn't suited to pleasing these wealthy Americans, pre-ferring to give them experiences I thought they should enjoy rather than those they wanted. Hoping to divert them with bucolic bliss, I would lay out picnics under fig trees rather than take them to McDonald's. I never prospered running

my own travel business. Any aspiring businessman will learn
that one's job is to give the customers what they want, and
I couldn't do it.

Speaking Spanish makes me feel almost Spanish, and has
underpinned my love for the country. I taught Spanish for a
year in London, which here provides a brief diversion back
to the UK.

My first day of teaching was a wet winter Monday. I
rode my scooter across London to school, looking forward
to using the tape recorder and film screen for the first time.
All was set up in the classroom, the boys lined up outside –
rowdy and barely manageable. I went in to check. The tape
recorder had been smashed. 'Someone must have put a boot
in it, sir.' I turned to the projector, switched it on and faced
the screen. There were gashes across it. 'Someone must have
slashed it, sir.'

It was frightening, standing in front of forty teenage boys,
unable to control them. I would long for the forty minutes –
spent shouting, cajoling, hectoring, punishing, sending out
of the room – to be over. I lasted two terms, enough to
finish my probation year, take my exams and qualify. But
just two terms of teaching took their toll on me and, aged
twenty-four, I abandoned my chosen career to head for
Spain. I dreamed of sitting in the caves of Granada with the
gypsies, learning how to play the guitar through a mixture
of osmosis and effort. There I would learn raw flamenco
from the people for whom it was life itself. I would begin to
understand, and perhaps even absorb, *duende* – the 'heart' or
'soul' of flamenco, without which one cannot do it justice.

I never got to Granada, for my father died before I left and

I stayed to see my mother through her distress and to deal with my own. For my failure to make it to the gypsy caves I, and flamenco, should be truly grateful. I would never have made a flamenco guitarist, and I like to go to bed early. But Spain had its tentacles around my heart.

20

Writers' Spain

There is a village in northern Spain called Santillana del Mar, flawlessly, impossibly pretty. The people grew so rich that for a while they didn't need to work. Each house is a small mansion, a *casona*, built between the fourteenth and seventeenth centuries with wealth from wool, agriculture and trade. The church, known as the *colegiata*, is a Romanesque jewel. There are no cars in the village. When I was there forty years ago, the evening would begin with the lowing of cattle and the plodding of hooves through the town as they came home from the fields, each one heading for its own home in the ground floor of one of the great houses.

'Jesus!' sighed one of my American flock, 'I wouldn't want one of those guys in my living room.' Those Americans might have loved Santillana, the pace and beauty of it, but in their own lives their needs were very different: convenience, speed, choice and 'stuff', therefore no room for cows in town, no car-free streets, no time to enjoy the peace. We destroy what we love. We now think of those cows as quaint, just a nostalgic reminder of our past. Yet we still depend on cattle, cattle that are not plodding anywhere now, just standing forlornly in feed lots among, perhaps, as many as twenty-two thousand others. This is our agricultural future, already flourishing in the USA.

Spain's agriculture is largely industrialised now, but still able to sustain magnificent landscapes, vast swathes of it unspoiled thanks to isolation over centuries and to Franco's focus on the *costas*. When tourists came in their millions in the sixties, they gathered in herds on the east coast, while the villages and the great hinterland remained largely untouched. Tourism passed by cities like Zaragoza, with its fabulous Islamic Aljafería Palace and two cathedrals, and León with its eighteen hundred square metres of thirteenth- to fifteenth-century stained glass cathedral windows. So little visited was Spain's interior that in 1928 the government, in a remarkably prescient move, created a network of hotels in ancient buildings to encourage people to stay. These were the paradors, a stroke of rare government imagination. Most are in uniquely stately buildings now saved from decay. I have stayed in many, most recently in the ancient university town of Alcalá just north of Madrid, a place to sleep away your last Spanish night before the flight home. The parador is in a seventeenth-century monastery school, with bold modern additions so handsome that I can forgive it the dullness that comes from state control. Em and I spent the evening at a jazz concert in the tiny old theatre round the corner.

Travelling on my own in Spain I always had a copy of H. V. Morton's book, and followed his advice to the letter. He wrote of a visit to the dark, squat cathedral of Burgos, where he chatted to the caretaker, Maria, who lived in a flat in one of the towers. She showed him the wicker figures in which people would parade through the streets once a year, one of them a monstrous female called Anna Bolena. Of course! It was the English Anne Boleyn who had supplanted their own Catherine of Aragon as Queen of England; they had turned her into a popular monster. Arriving in Burgos, my first task was to climb the tower to meet Maria.

'*Está María?*'

'*Quién?*'

'*María — la conserje.*'

'*Ah — se murió María hace veinte años!*' She had died twenty years ago! I had been so transported by the narrative power of Morton that I hadn't noticed that he was writing in the fifties.

When I passed through Burgos I was heading for the pilgrims' way a little further north, and came to a town called Santo Domingo de la Calzada. It was H. V. Morton who alerted me to the chickens kept high above the south transept of its cathedral. They strut behind a glass screen like preening curates, and have been there for centuries. Legend has it that a family of German pilgrims were 'set up' by the daughter of the inn-keeper who had fallen in unrequited love with the son. She maliciously planted a silver cup in his baggage; he was caught and hanged for theft. When his distraught parents returned from Santiago they found him hanging but alive, his weight borne by St Domingo. The local magistrate almost choked on his roast chicken when asked to release the boy, claiming that he was no more alive than the chickens on his plate. They, seizing their chance, rose from the plate, squawked and preened their feathers. The boy was cut down and returned to his family somewhat relieved; the rooster and the hen in the church are there to commemorate the legend.

Spain is a rich source of such tales. I am often asked about formative moments, stories and places from my travels, and Salamanca, in the León region, crops up regularly for me. It is a city to set a heart pumping. There are two cathedrals side by side, the 'new' one started in the fifteenth century. I stayed in a *hostal* on the Plaza Mayor as a student in the sixties and, having arrived in the dark, flung open the shutters in the morning to behold one of the great sights of Europe. It took my breath away – an extravagance of golden Baroque. For centuries, the plaza was used to display the magnificence of royalty and the church. Power needed to be paraded very publicly in those pre-social media days, and cynics suggest, too, that it was a grand idea to have a vast square in which to burn heretics. Nowadays the plaza resonates more happily with music and conviviality. England felt parochial to me at that moment; we have no great squares to compare, and I suspect that our villages, too, are the poorer for being without their plazas.

Salamanca had one of the world's four great universities in the thirteenth century. The others were Oxford, Paris and Bologna. There is a famous story about Friar Luis de León, vice-rector of the university at Salamanca, who was taken away by the Inquisition in the middle of a lecture and imprisoned. When released, after four grimly brutal and isolated years, he returned to the dais and opened matter-of-factly with '*Dicebamus hesterna die*' – 'As I was saying . . . '

It was Morton who told that story, but I have been appalled to learn that he was by no means the gentle, generous soul I imagined him to be. Michael Bartholomew wrote a book about him, which Max Hastings reviewed icily in the *Telegraph*:

> The shrewd, amiable lone traveller of Morton's narratives emerges in real life as a thoroughly nasty piece of work – vain, cynical, misanthropic, deeply anti-Semitic, with a penchant for grotesque sexual adventures.
>
> Michael Bartholomew embarked on his task as an admirer of Morton's work. As he explored his subject through his private papers, however, something close to revulsion set in. What is it about travel writers? This biographer's experience seems not dissimilar from that of Nicholas Shakespeare, a devoted admirer of Bruce Chatwin, who discovered as he wrote the Chatwin biography that, for all the man's famous charm, he possessed a notably unpleasant personality, and invented substantial parts of his books.

That was a shock to me, on both counts – Morton and travel writers – but I continue to admire Morton as a teacher and writer. I will keep an eye out for how his prejudices might have affected his writing – and, indeed, how my own affect mine.

Morton would certainly have been appalled by a recent

addition to our eclectic gathering of special places in Spain: the Resotel near Salamanca. It is an ultra-modern motel boldly sited on a garage forecourt, with the windows over-looking the petrol pumps. It squats in an industrial park on the outskirts of a bland village and, even more seductively, close to a motorway. Our adoption of the place shows us to have adjusted to the times, however. Juan Carlos García Regalado, the owner, is a journalist, well-educated and full of stories – and his father owned the garage. Juan once fol-lowed in the footsteps of Francisco Vázquez de Coronado, who led an expedition in 1540 from Mexico to Kansas. He wrote a book about the trip, and returned with a touching affection for America. American influence permeates the hotel; high-quality furniture and designs have transformed the interior. It is multi-coloured, zany, with pet areas and drinking bowls, local produce in the garage shop, an American-style bar and palpable pizzazz. Such unexpected taste in grim surroundings is encouraging. When the world is covered with asphalt and burger joints, there will still be room for hope.

Gerald Brenan's *South from Granada* has served, with Morton's books as well as the magnificent *Spain* by Jan Morris, as a background to my Spanish travels. I first read Brenan in the bath, at the Finca Buenvino near Aracena that I have already mentioned. The welcome from the owners had lifted me up and gently put me down on a cloud of good humour and good wine. I then had time before dinner to soak in a deep bath with views into the woodland around the house. In the woods pigs guzzled on acorns that would give flavour to the *jamón Ibérico de bellota* that they would later become. The bath was deep and hot, the evening balmy, the *fino* at my side delicious and Gerald Brenan was ready to entertain me.

A quick diversion on ham is needed here, for the Aracena area produces the world's finest. *Jamón Ibérico* is made from the Ibérico pig, an ancient breed marbled with a fat that lengthens and affects the curing process. The term *pata negra* refers to the breed's black trotters but is not a guarantee of high quality. The pigs just love acorns and can eat ten kilos of them a day, thus helping to preserve some of Spain's oldest oak-filled landscapes from development and change – for much of the oak is cork-oak. If you like to impress your friends, bring home a whole leg of *jamón*, though it may impoverish you. Their gratitude will be real, for each tender slice provides a succulent, and expensively precious, ham moment. It is also very good for you.

Sam Chesterton, who owns the Finca, is the great-nephew of G. K. Chesterton. A few kilometres south, Charles Wordsworth, direct descendant of the poet, has the Finca La Fronda, now run by his daughter. So Chesterton and Wordsworth spirits are alive and kicking in a remote Spanish sierra. (Chesterton has been proposed for canonisation by the Roman Catholic Church; Sam, as a good Irish Protestant, may have to bite his cheeks.) Close by, Rosamunde Pilcher also had a place, now owned by her son, Robin, also a novelist. Her novels, such as *The Shell Seekers*, have probably sold more than Chesterton and Wordsworth put together, so conversations deep in the sierra about book sales must have been animated.

Another character in our community of Spanish owners is Laurence Seidler. He and his wife decided to walk from Málaga to Granada using Spanish army maps. Stopping for the night, they found a room in Niguelas and his wife, exhausted, collapsed into bed while Laurence paid his respects to the local bar. He awoke on the straw floor to be told that he had just bought the ruin up the valley. Well, things could have been worse and they began restoration, but tiring of being a builder's mate his wife left him. He married a local girl and took twenty years to finish rebuilding the house. They now run the hotel with his mother-in-law. Laurence's taste is extraordinary, with antiques from all over the world and every corner designed as an experience. There is even a mini-cinema in the basement, with seats and carpets from an abandoned Odeon. Laurence himself is a miracle of psychological survival, for he has described his mother as a 'psychotic hoarder, prostitute and bigamist'. She was one of those mad old ladies who never leave home, keep everything that enters and live in unspeakable squalor. Her son has healed some of the wounds by cleaning and selling off some of his mother's detritus, and sharing his rare taste with others.

Carlos, who revels in getting to know the people behind the places he inspects, enjoyed a delightful coincidence on a visit to the countryside east of Jerez. He visited the spectacular La Alcaría, an estate of ten thousand hectares in the Alcornocales Natural Park. The aristocratic owners are Anglophiles and inhabit a rambling, ancient English-style house with a vast and ancient kitchen, lions – stuffed and mouldy – and a wild, overgrown garden. In the old sitting room Carlos spotted a picture of a familiar-looking man, the heir to the estate who had given it all up to become a priest in the UK. Father Alfonso de Zulueta became chaplain of the Holy Redeemer Catholic Church in Chelsea. Carlos had been baptised by him sixty years before. He sent the owners a photograph of their uncle holding him in his arms.

Many of our houses are up long and rough tracks, and lots of readers have left traces of engine oil on the rocks littering them. It is usually well worth the lost oil. El Añadio is up a four-mile track that wends its way across tree-strewn *dehesa* and up to the farmhouse, remote in the hills and beautiful. It is enveloped by birdsong and the lowing of cattle. The single-storey building wraps around an inner courtyard with a fountain at its centre. The farm rears fighting bulls, so this is an interesting place for an inspector who has signed many a petition against bull-fighting. The bedrooms are in the old farm manager's quarters, each with a wood-burner, beamed ceilings, Indian pieces, taurine prints, a few antiques. You eat overlooking the paddock where the young bulls are fed.

Our inspectors Carlos and Nicola arrived late at night to find a log fire burning and two bedrooms prepared for them, so they retired for a well-earned sleep. Carlos awoke early to a strange noise. Across a narrow back alley was a massive animal snorting and making very odd noises. This turned out to be a blind bull that was being cared for. Nicola suspected the noise was from Carlos's stomach and was awake from six in the morning until eight wondering whether to go in and nurse him, but the sounds were so strange she kept to her bed.

The bull farm was one of the biggest at the turn of the twentieth century. The then owner had three daughters and, lacking a male heir, sold it off. His wife then had a son. So he bought the farm back, but the son was killed in the civil war and the farm was divided between the three sons-in-law. These three also all lost their lives in the war, so the three daughters inherited the farm after all – and later his grand-daughter Maria. 'Grandfather,' she said, 'would be appalled.'

That story is a reminder of the unspeakable losses of the Spanish Civil War. Andalucía was a semi-feudal region with vast landholdings and an inevitable political backlash from local Communist and Republican parties. The fighting there was especially bitter, with the worst violence in, of all places, Málaga. It was chaotically defended by the Republicans, and Franco's invading army, with Italian and German help, easily crushed it. Citizens fleeing along the coast to Almería were slaughtered in their thousands. Every year there is a ceremony in Torre del Mar, a place now associated with the worst excesses of tourism, to remember the Caravan of the Dead. There is more to modern Spain than one might imagine.

I see sadness spread like a thin veil over Spain. The political upheavals of recent years, such as the rapid rise and fall of Podemos and other parties, have their origins in the civil war and the repressed decades that followed. The changes that followed Franco's death in 1975 have been confusing, with Spaniards reassessing their history, the roles their families played, the roles of the monarchy and Church, and their place in the modern world. Old tensions remain, yet it is a tribute to Spain's openness that democracy has flourished.

21

Basques, Business and Moors

After the civil war Spain, once the richest of countries, was poverty-stricken and isolated. Up in the Basque region, a lone Catholic priest resolved to create his own solutions rather than wait for the Franco government to provide support.

Don José María Arizmendiarrieta had been through the civil war as a journalist on a Basque newspaper, a dangerous job for Franco was hostile to the Basques. After seminary school he went in 1941 to Mondragón with a passion for social issues. Paying little attention to his priestly duties, he used redundant church organisations to set up clinics and social services. A school followed, and this led to Ulgor, a small co-operative business venture led by five graduates of the school. Next came a bank, and then other businesses. Now, over sixty years later, Mondragón is a byword for co-operative success, with over £34 billion in assets, revenues of £12 billion, seventy-five thousand employees, 260 businesses and fifteen technology centres. It is curious that we hear so little of this, for it is one of Europe's great business success stories. Arizmendi spent the rest of his life creating more institutions and support systems and died, exhausted by his work, of a heart attack. He deserves canonisation, but co-operatives don't appeal to a hierarchical and largely right-wing Catholic Church.

Mighty oaks have grown from these acorns in the Basque country. Mondragón offers hope to those who despair of business, and it generates keen discussion. Is it a widely replicable model? Who are most people working for? How can the sharing of risk and success best be structured? Do my family's values and my own differ from my work values? Would all economies benefit from sharing the risk and rewards? Mondragón offers a model that can change lives, and has, indeed, transformed a region.

Many businesses are extractive: extracting maximum benefit for owners, shareholders and directors, and extracting from the environment and their workers. They are, by definition, not sustainable. 'Start-up' has become a catchy, and misleading, buzz word; a lot of start-ups begin with dollar signs in the owner's eyes. Mondragón is evidence that successful business can be about many things beyond pure profit. I have met inspiring people, in Spain and elsewhere, who feel the same way and who live their principles at work as well as at home. When work and home are thus combined, the effect can be remarkable.

Dave and his Spanish partner Javier sold all in the UK and found an old house, El Gran Sueño, in a hamlet in Asturias. They rebuilt from scratch, putting in heat pumps and underfloor heating while adding sinews to the old bones of the ancient and very handsome house. Their commitment to sustainability goes deep and includes their food: fresh fish and home-made bread are staples. Theirs is yet another story of solid values, of bold decisions to move jobs, friends and country. Their rewards are, if not in Heaven, in a sort of Asturian paradise. They live close to several national parks in a part of Spain whose food is stupendous and whose villages are exquisite. The weather, however, reminds them of Yorkshire.

Their project was dogged from the beginning. Daily challenges, such as material costs doubling, work running over time and late starts, are familiar to us all. Others were more baffling. The municipality, Piloña, had been shaken by the economic crash, its declining population ravaged by unemployment as the downturn, *el crisis*, ripped the heart out of the economy. David and Javier had imagined that contractors would be queuing for work, but they weren't.

Even getting quotes was hard. Most builders didn't bother with a quotation, and those who did never chased Dave for a decision. The one they selected had to be badgered for a start date, to accept a deposit and then to send an invoice. (We have had the same problem with our plumber in Bristol, to whom I occasionally send money in the hope that it might vaguely match the sum owing.) Some contractors walked off site when they were bored. At one point Dave and Javier were left with two kilometres of tubing under their garden to serve the ground-source heat pump, and no contractor for the sixty thousand euros' worth of equipment to be connected to the tubes.

No contractor understood sustainability. Restoration, reuse and recycling were entirely alien concepts. Most builders wanted to demolish the beautiful eighteenth-century half-timbered house and rebuild from scratch. Sourcing organic food was equally difficult, a problem I had also experienced, during the Great Organic Bike Ride. When Dave and Javier opened in 2014 there was none locally. They were saved when a local Asturian opened a shop selling health foods.

The results, however, are magnificent. You would never know of the battle they fought, which is how it should be. Had Dave and Javier known more, they might have remained in Brighton.

Many owners come to us because they know we will admire their principled take on business and their involvement with local life. I take community cohesion seriously, for it can make for long life and general well-being. Malcolm Gladwell, in his book *Outliers*, writes of a town near Pittsburgh which had grown over decades of immigration from one slate-mining town in Italy. The positive social indicators, as they are called, mystified medical and social researchers: why did the inhabitants suffer so little from ailments and problems common elsewhere? The consensus, which took a long time for them to arrive at, was that community was the reason; the people felt they belonged, as they would in Italy, and had traditional social structures to hold them together.

*

Special places often sparkle with an extra magic that comes from the wider setting. Finca el Moro, in the hills two hours north of Seville, is alive with biodiversity. There are chestnuts, olives and handsome old cork trees, which are harvested every nine years and shelter the pigs that feed on their acorns. The grassland is rich with wild flowers (peony, cistus, gladiolus, iris), insects, horses and sheep; under the olive trees are carpets of grass, rosemary, thyme, oregano and flowers rather than the bare, over-sprayed earth you see all over Spain.* Nick and Hermione Tudor supply all the food for their guests, apart from basics such as milk and salt. Their *jamón Ibérico serrano de bellota*, sweet and succulent, comes from the predecessors of the two black pigs that were snuffling around outside our window. There are wood-burning stoves and solar heating, and a deep respect for the land. They have brought an abandoned farm back to life. Their place in the community was revealed during a recent stay, when it rained incessantly for at least a week upon Em, me and others doing a yoga course. During dinner Nick disappeared; he returned, looking pleased with himself, an hour later. The local police had asked him to rescue a car from a swollen stream with his Land Rover. He had clearly become an essential part of the local rescue system.

Just doing your thing well can endear you to your neighbours – or alarm them. Isabel, in southern Spain, felt that animal husbandry in her area needed a stimulus and that introducing a new farm animal might trigger changes. So she imported llamas from Somerset, driving them across France and Spain with a friend and her six-year-old son.

---

* There are even daffodils and snowdrops.

They stabled them for the night with an alpaca breeder in southern France, walking them in the woodlands before driving on. Isabel suspected one might be pregnant as she had been consorting with a male some time before, though llamas don't show their pregnancies well.

The two llamas, Rosanna and Benna, arrived safely and Benna gave birth ten days later. Soon afterwards there was a knock on the door from the Guardia Civil: Isabel had been reported by a local farmer for illegal crossbreeding of animals. Walking idly past, he had seen the llamas and assumed, sensibly, that the pony had been at the sheep, or that weird experiments had been taking place. Those animals could not possibly be natural. The Guardia had to be convinced too, but Isabel had her breeder's papers and all ended happily. The story made the Andalucía newspapers.

Another indomitable agent of change was Carmen Ladrón. She moved to Cazala de la Sierra in Andalucía to find that the fifteenth-century Carthusian monastery had lain empty for one hundred and fifty years. Carmen was so moved that she bought La Cartuja from, of all people, an Englishman called Harrington. He had done a little restoring and then abandoned the Sisyphean task. Buying it was entirely mad, for both of them; it was vast, ruinous, crumbling – yet magnificent. Imagine a large, brick church with triple-layered bell towers, arches forlornly gazing into great rooms that are no more: a dilapidated edifice of great dignity and history. Carmen concocted a plan and re-founded it as the Centre for Contemporary Culture. Year by year she brought life back to the old stones, decorating the bedrooms with the artwork created at the Centre and using income from the Centre to finance the gradual restoration. Even the frescoes in the main church were touched up and saved where possible. The old monastic cells make fine bathrooms now, disappointing those hoping for austerity. Years ago you might have been able to join in one of Carmen's *tertulias*, forums for sharing ideas, an old Spanish tradition similar to the French soirée. In Madrid, *tertulias* have often played a role in political discussion and dissent. But Carmen has moved on, taking her artistic and questing spirit with her. The monastery lives on, however, as a hotel.

Granada's ancient stones have survived better than most. The city held out as the last major redoubt of the Moors, then briefly became the capital of the new Christian Spain. It had more fine buildings than cities twice its size when Ferdinand and Isabella found it, and they gifted it with yet more. The view from our sitting room in the Hotel Carmen de Santa Inés reached across a choppy, pretty sea of tiles and white walls up to the mighty Alhambra. But Granada, like any old city, has its decay. From the bedroom we could see a roof hung with ancient tiles, between which sprouted a thin meadow of grasses and weeds. Clinging to the roof's edge was a tin gutter, fatally parted from the tiles under the weight of its composting contents and parted too from its own downpipe, which pointed into the void. This, to the winter-weary traveller, is not decline so much as a reminder of the endearing chaos of history.

In the Alhambra the Moorish sultans created, within the fortress walls, palaces of limpid beauty. The light-filled, lithe-limbed architecture seems to dissolve rather than buttress and reinforce. All is smooth, surprising, weightless – a reminder in this inane period of bigotry that Islam created a flourishing and civilised empire in Europe while much of Christian culture was still in its nappies.

These reflections came with a profound sense of ease in the Carmen de Santa Inés. Granada has many carmens, walled gardens celebrating the beauty of horticulture, of water and colour. We climbed the steps and alleys of the Albaycin, the old Moorish quarter, and entered the hotel through a wide wooden door; we found ourselves in a little courtyard within a square of columns holding aloft the two upper floors. Our bedroom was almost entirely of wood: a wooden ceiling, a bâteau bed and wooden floor, and shutters that opened to that Alhambra view. A fountain tinkled in the courtyard when we descended for breakfast, and another burbled in the formal garden. The Moors loved water and were ingenious in bringing it into their homes. There are still-functioning Moorish irrigation systems in the Alpujarras and in the Valencia region, and in Granada itself the water supply is much as the Moors left it. Many of those Moors, interestingly, came from Syria, where water supplies were similar.

Granada is a place where I immerse myself in the atmosphere by plunging into a tapas bar and losing myself in the crowd. Em was with me the last time I did so, and, even speaking no Spanish, enjoyed it too. A barful of Spaniards throbs with noise. They are Olympian talkers. The women, as all over the Americas, use their nasal passages to cutting effect and the men emit a guttural sound unique to Spain. My entirely unresearched theory is that while Spain was poor and isolated the smoke from cheap black tobacco wreaked havoc on the throats of male Spaniards. The resulting gravelly sounds have become the norm, though the alarming voices I heard in the fifties are now a rarity. Expatriate Englishmen, when imitating Spaniards, will often add a guttural touch to their voices to add authenticity.

The enveloping crush in the bar is part of the fun. Once you have waded to the counter and put in your ill-formed, confusing order, you burrow your way through packed Spaniards to a corner and await results. Invariably, although nothing has been written down, the order arrives exactly as hoped. Your neighbours shout at you and you pretend to understand, swill more *fino* or *rojo* than is wise, take in the riotous tumult of people and sound and then put in another order. It is shouted across the bar to a waiter, or to the kitchen. After an evening of this madhouse you tunnel back to the bar and ask for the bill. It emerges, a miracle of memory, accurate and without a hint of confusion. Then you begin the convivial process of excavating yourself. Spanish waiters are a species unto themselves – dignified, professional, confident and competent – and your equal whoever you are. (Manuel of *Fawlty Towers* was an amusing, misleading one-off.) This is a special Spanish quality, a sort of patrician pride that is infectious. I have encountered it in donkey-riding peasants, in castle custodians and courteous policemen. Ruling the known world for centuries must have helped.

Perhaps the bars of Granada are exceptional, for Spanish bars elsewhere can be grim and sterile places, a TV churning out its nonsense in the corner and drawing the vacant gaze of anyone there. I once spent a week in Galicia looking for places to take a group of artists, but abandoned the search after being depressed by countless such bars. It was raining too, as it often does in the north-west.

That rain, however, led to my best-ever meal in Spain. It was just a simple pea and ham soup, thick, home-made and served in a generous bowl by a large and amiable woman in her *hostal* high up in the Spanish Pyrenees. The building was of wood, with a mountainous fire burning in a medieval grate under low, smoke-blackened beams. I had arrived in the rain, in the dark and in very wet clothes after a miserable all-day cycle ride. It was a moment of exquisite and deep relief. Had the place been closed I would surely have wept. The soup and the *hostal*, in all their warm simplicity, made me feel like a traveller come home to rest. To complete my happiness, the landlady's name was Gabriella and her husband's Angél.

22

Turkish Hospitality

On the roof of the house, Hamish puffed and strained, sucking in lungfuls of warm Istanbul air and pressing them out through his old bagpipes. The sound he made was excruciating, but he was making it for all of us. Across the street the loudspeakers were aimed at us purely, it seemed, to keep us awake. Hamish was trying to compete, but was defeated by the inexhaustible loop of the muezzin's tape recorder and retired, exhausted.

We were in Turkey as vacationing students to explore the country in a Land Rover, but the car was such a bone-rattler that I escaped to stay with relatives who had settled on the coast at Gümüşlük, a tiny hamlet in the south-west near Bodrum. Uncle Ronald and Aunt Barbara had, after working with NATO in Turkey, built a house here. The work had been long and arduous, with camels plodding down daily from the hills with materials, but the reward was a simple house on a small enclosed bay of the purest blue. A Roman road was clearly visible beneath the water and amphorae were often found in the sand of the bay. The hamlet had no more than a clutch of houses, for this was 1966, before mass tourism in Turkey.

My stay there came during a time of tension, for Ronald had been accused by the mayor, whom he had considered a friend, of stealing antiquities. The accusation only had to be made – and it stuck. So Ronald and family had to leave Turkey, and their precious house. The last evening in Gümüşlük was to be a pre-supper celebration with all the neighbours – except for the mayor. We prepared drinks and awaited the guests. Every man brought his wife and children, mother, father and aunts. The numbers swelled until there was a line of patient waiting Turks along the walls, occupying every stool and makeshift seat. We scurried to and fro serving drinks – surprisingly, alcoholic ones, given the Islamic restrictions on alcohol that survived in spite of the secular society that Turkish had largely become. Time passed, then more time. Our own suppertime came and went, with no sign of a departing Turk. Ronald gathered us into the kitchen to see what we could feed them, but there was little food left. We were to leave the next day.

The solution was provided by the waiting Turks, who were eyeing the chickens pecking in the yard: chickens now destined for the pot. At a word from Ronald, several men launched themselves into the small flock with gusto. The squawking, the feather-flying and the neck-wringing were on an epic scale, and the cauldrons were soon overflowing with dead chickens. The resulting feast, for which we had to

wait a long, chicken-boiling time, was a happy and tumultu-
ous affair, boosted by more of the forbidden alcohol. When
the villagers finally left our heads were spinning, some of
us were clucking, and sleep was elusive. Our departure by
speedboat the next morning was fraught with headache and
sadness, and our immediate neighbours had to do without
the flock of chickens they had been promised.

The mayor, who had been the sole cause of our rushed
and emotionally fraught departure, moved into the house
as soon as we had left.

Another incident showed me how many forms corruption
can take. An American army unit were due to depart after
their stint in İzmir with NATO, and had offered their fleet
of almost-new ambulances to the Turkish Red Cross. The
latter, however, imposed so many conditions and asked for
so many extras that the Americans, finally exasperated by
demands for customs payments before the Turks would take
delivery, took the ambulances out into the bay and dropped
them overboard.

Nevertheless, Turkey was enthralling, with Ephesus
opening my eyes to the wonders of the eastern Roman
Empire. There are more than three hundred ancient Roman
and Greek cities lying in varyingly parlous conditions in
Turkey, more than any one nation can care for. The history
of Ephesus included the loss of one of the Seven Wonders
of the Ancient World, the Temple of Artemis, or Diana. (I
was less awestruck by Diana when I learned that she was
known locally as Cynthia.) It had been twice as large as the
Parthenon, with over a hundred delicately carved marble
columns. From the pit of the Great Theatre, a friend read
out a passage from the Letters of Paul to the Ephesians. We

sat on the distant top row and heard every moving word.

It was in Ephesus that I experienced Turkish hospitality at its most intense and euphoric. Wandering the streets alone one evening, and feeling hungry, I heard the sound of music and laughter. Drawn to it like a moth to light, I found myself in a walled garden and pressed to sit down at a table and join the feast. The first dish was followed by many others, and then the dancing began, long lines of men forming with their arms around each other's shoulders. I was gaily hauled to my feet and inserted in the line. It was a hell of a party.

My efforts to pay were met with astonishment. It was a private wedding party. But in spite of such extraordinary kindness I went no more to Turkey until many years later, when Oxfam came into my life.

While working with Voluntary Service Overseas in the early seventies, when I was helping to run the Papua New Guinea programme, I met hundreds of young volunteers whom I admired greatly. Most of them, once home, slotted back into their old jobs – often abandoning their energy and idealism in the process. I was keen to make use of their skills, so I approached Oxfam with the idea of providing volunteers for an emergency response unit for disaster relief. They liked the idea, and introduced me to an ex-ship's captain who had invented a way of building emergency housing out of polyurethane foam.

I should never have gone along with such an environmentally idiotic scheme. Polyurethane! But the system seemed ingenious. It involved a central unit the size of a horsebox – with engine, pumps and kit – being taken to the scene of a disaster, such as an earthquake. We would unpack the unit and mount two mini-hoists on the roof, one for each side.

From each hoist would dangle a rapidly erected octagonal hut made of bolted-together metal sheets. We would spray polish on the inner walls to prevent sticking, and then spray polyurethane foam onto the inside, the metal hut thus serving as a mould. The foam would expand and solidify in a moment, which is why it is now used by builders and DIY-ers to fill awkward gaps. We sprayed around wooden frames to create window and door openings. When all was done we would wind up the hoist, lifting the mould away to reveal a lurid, orange polyurethane hut. It was quick and ingenious, even if the work of spraying was horrible in the fierce Turkish heat.

The plan was, as we later discovered, fatally flawed. Polyurethane is a complex chemical and not readily available in disaster zones. It is expensive to buy and transport, and impossible to get rid of. It is, indeed, a disaster of its own. The lack of consultation all round, often unavoidable in an emergency, was also disastrous.

A dozen of us were trained, very badly, by the captain and we awaited an appropriate disaster. I scanned the news every day in anticipation, and it came in the shape of an earthquake in eastern Turkey, in the Kurdish mountains near Lake Van. Earthquakes, I was to learn, produce a peculiarly horrible form of suffering, with victims buried in the rubble, yet so close to the despairing survivors. The Turkish Air Force flew us in from Ankara and the army took us to the disaster zone, where we met local government officials and sized things up.

We had planned to take our kit into the mountains to build directly for the victims, but the army wanted us just to manufacture houses for them to distribute. This was a radically different concept, and I argued passionately against it. The army might misuse the houses, sell them, give them to their cronies. The victims might be left out altogether, or be asked to pay. The captain's response was simply, 'I am here to build houses and that is what I will do.' So I had a painful choice: to tag along with the madness, or to mutiny. I wanted to cable Oxfam to ask them not to ship the chemicals until we could get to the devastated villages, but in the end I couldn't find it in my heart to disobey the captain. I was too young, even at thirty, to put such a spoke in such a wheel. I regret it to this day; I might have saved Oxfam a lot of money.

The chemicals arrived and we began to manufacture our huts, though we were allowed, just to keep us quiet, to visit a few villages to discuss the project. Goats would be slaughtered and we would feast uncomfortably, sitting in a large circle, the interpreter acting as host, but no request came for our work in spite of the stench of dead bodies under the nearby rubble. These were distressing visits and the work down on the plain was unpleasant too, so much so that I volunteered to be in charge of the latrines rather than spray chemicals. Meanwhile, an attempt to persuade the general in charge to let us build in the villages ended awkwardly. In his tent, leaning back in my chair, I clashed with his portrait of the national hero Atatürk. It was a tense moment. All military eyes swivelled alarmingly in my direction, but then swivelled elsewhere and the moment passed.

We built eighty huts, stacked like so many Daleks on the dusty road. Then along came a wind brewed by the gods to torment us. It barrelled visibly across the plain for ten minutes before hitting us, giving us enough time to run about like startled rabbits, weighing some of the huts down with sacks and anything heavy we could find – including ourselves. The remaining Daleks began to take ungainly steps towards the edge of the road and then tipped, one by one, until the wind got underneath them and launched them into the air. Aghast, we watched our village of laboriously created huts fly away. As they crash-landed they scattered orange debris far and wide.

Dawn revealed columns of ants winding their way up the hills carrying bits of orange polyurethane. Or were they people? One way or another, most of the debris ended up as part of a house, or a goat hut, or a compound. At least it was used, albeit in scraps. Just one hut was taken by us and the Turkish army to a village they needed to impress. The by now familiar feast of goat's meat barely tempered the humiliation.

When we departed we had installed just that one hut, and left behind all of our equipment, so the project can rightly be called a calamity. It turned out that our interpreter was a Marxist who, unaware of Oxfam, thought we were a private capitalist company; he did all he could to block us. The army never intended to provide the stricken villagers with housing, because they were Kurds, potentially rebellious, and the earthquake was an opportunity to rehouse, and thus control, them down on the plain. The Kurds and the Turks, of course, are still at each other's throats. So our project fell foul of a toxic mix of local ignorance and local politics mingled with our own ignorance and macro-politics. I now take it as gospel that intervention by outsiders will usually fail to some degree. It is not unlike interfering in a troubled marriage. You do so at your peril.

One day in 2004, I had a phone call from a Turkish writer and publisher called Sevan Nişanyan.

'Did you receive the copy of my Turkey hotel guide?'

'Well, yes. So sorry I haven't thanked you.'

'Never mind. But I want you to publish it in English.'

'We don't publish books by other people. We have to do our own research.'

'That is not correct. This is a book you must publish. I am coming to see you next week.'

'No, don't do that. I am busy, our office is deep in the countryside, and I need time to think.'

'Well, I am coming!' he declared, and the call ended. It was bonkers, so I forgot about it. On Monday morning, when I walked into the office there was a short, plumpish, good-looking gentleman having a cup of coffee with Annie. Sevan was not a man to be deterred, as we discovered later; he was a Turkish Armenian with a long pedigree of intellectual and political dissent. He had even been imprisoned, briefly, for refusing to use concrete when restoring his ancient Ottoman house. It was inside prison that he found the time to write his guide to Turkish hotels; it had been a considerable success in Turkey, but there was no way we could publish it as a Sawday guide.

Sevan, not to be defeated, invited us out to see his hotel and B&B choices for ourselves, hoping that if we learned to trust him we might yield to his pleadings and publish. He had matchless charm, a prodigious grasp of history and culture, intelligence and commitment. We relented, and Annie travelled to Turkey, learned to trust Sevan's choices, and we published his book as *Special Places to Stay in Turkey*.

It was a terrific failure. On the very day of publication, a bomb went off in a Turkish resort. It was also ahead of its time; independent travel in Turkey hadn't yet taken off, and indeed is still a rarity.

Our relationship with Sevan wobbled when he, a married man, brought his mistress to stay with Em and me in Bristol. It was, even for a pair of liberals, awkward. But my interest in him has been quickened again: while researching this book I discovered that he is in a maximum-security prison for objecting to the state's right to pursue critics of Islam. The technique used by the state was to avoid a political confrontation and just gradually accumulate trivial charges against him for violations of, say, construction law. When Sevan offends the authorities politically, they rake up the construction charges and whack him with them, piling up the sentences until they amount to as much as twenty years.

Sevan's construction work in Şirince, a handsome village abandoned by the Greeks and then by the Turks, has been transformative. He has rebuilt some of the Ottoman houses, created a hotel and attracted visitors. The fact that he is an Armenian, let alone an outspoken one, is almost certainly his biggest handicap in a state that still refuses to acknowledge the Armenian genocide. And now he is in prison, for doing what many of us would be proud to have done. As a fellow guide-publisher and erstwhile green builder, I am humbled.

Working on our book with Sevan was an education on Turkey. It is not easy, with so much negative publicity, to keep a sense of the country's vitality and multi-faceted culture, so I will do a whirlwind tour to the places Sevan showed us. One of the first was the Hotel Empress Zoe in

Istanbul, a glittering surprise to first-time visitors, especially if they have forgotten how long the Ottoman Empire lasted. It is made of two old townhouses in the heart of the city, with a minaret-style staircase. They are marvels of tasteful styling and joining them is a little gem of a garden. The survival of these old houses is a relief from the frenzied pace of change elsewhere in a city being transformed by hectic and barely regulated development.

If you know only Istanbul you are missing an astonishing variety of old towns and some places to stay that match anything in Europe. Alaçati is a wonderful little town inland from the Greek island of Chios, transformed by the efforts of Mrs Öziş, who set the standards with her much-imitated hotel and other restored and redesigned houses. Hers is a natural, simple, unaffected style, colourful and richly textured. Taş Otel is a sturdy old stone house in the neoclassical mould, with blue casements and a milky-blue stairway. (Could blue, so rare in the UK, not bring a little sun to a grey Britain?)

Another fine old town is Selçuk, close to Ephesus and topped off with a perfect Byzantine castle. Nilya, a sort of hybrid B&B/hotel, is hidden behind high courtyard walls in the old quarter. Mrs Kaytanci and her husband, once a senior civil servant, settled in this sleepy Aegean town to treat guests with the easy kindness that is natural in this country but amazes visitors from stiffer lands. The bedrooms surround a peaceful arcaded court, and below the hill lies the grand sweep of the plain of Ephesus. To the south is Didim, a dull modern place but home to the Temple of Apollo, an earthquake-shattered Greek monument of great significance. Didim's sturdy stone Old Medusa House stands in a lush Mediterranean garden close to the temple. At night, you can slip into the temple grounds and rejoice in the two-thousand-year-old marble – or weep at what it must have been before the earthquake.

In the very south-west corner of Turkey is Demre, whose Roman theatre in nearby Myra is a stunning survivor. There is a basic family-run *pansiyon* on the sea in the archaic Kale, a village so completely enmeshed with Lycian antiquities that it is hard to tell which bit of masonry is two millennia old and which is new. There is no traffic: street and court-yard merge together and the whole village feels like a large living room.

Many will have heard of Cappadocia's cave-churches and houses, roughly in the middle of Turkey. The Elkep Evi Cave House in Urgup has a private terrace carved into a nook of the cliff and a gorgeous view over the Cappadocian dreamscape. There are carved-in-the-cliff towns and vil-lages all over Europe, such as the gypsy caves of Granada and the cliff houses of the Loire and the Dordogne. But these are of a different order and, as this is Turkey, Cappadocia's history is rich with thousands of years of conflict and developing civilisation. It was even a military power in its heyday.

Antik Belkis Han is a splendid stone house of the type that has almost disappeared from the once-beautiful city of Antep. It was saved from the wrecking squad – just the sort of thing that Sevan would do, and be incarcerated for – and refurbished in loving detail by Ms Karabiber, a painter, activist and businesswoman of infectious vivacity. Not far away is the Roman town of Zeugma, most of it now under water from a dam-building project.

This was not the Turkey I expected: the Ottoman architecture, the old towns, the Roman remains, the fascinating
and richly cultured people. Then many years later I went to
south-eastern Turkey for a walking holiday, and saw another
aspect of this extraordinary country. Lycia was one of the
great powers of the eastern Mediterranean and yet little is
now heard of it. Great chunks of Lycia, such as the Nereid
monument – a charming and sculpture-packed building
of temple shape – are in the British Museum, revealing a
sophistication of Greek dimensions. We walked one day
along a two-thousand-year-old aqueduct made of huge
interlocking stones. None of us could quite believe that this
was neither Roman nor Greek. Lycia had, throughout our
long lives of reading and education, been ignored – and here
we were touching vestiges of its greatness.

Lycia, as all great powers, had its full share of tragedy.
I was brought up with the story of the mass suicide of the
Jews at Masada, 960 of them flinging themselves off the
cliff rather than yield to the Romans. Some say that they
killed each other to avoid the forbidden suicide; but it is a
dreadful tale. Then, in Lycia, I read of the siege of Xanthus
by the Persians, and the way the women and children gathered together in the temple to be burned alive before the
surviving men made a suicidal last charge. Such stories add
depth to one's understanding of a place, in the same way
that living people add depth to their own places with their
histories, their conversation, their personalities.

It was on this holiday that I sprained an ankle again and
had to abandon the walk. My party left me behind as they
walked on, and I was hungry. There was one house near by,
so I knocked on the door. It crept open to reveal a woman

in her thirties, and a small child. I rubbed my stomach and looked hungry. The woman disappeared, and returned with her husband, who invited me in and solemnly pulled up a table and chair. There was a short silent interlude before the wife returned with lunch. They watched while I ate, an awkward experience I have never quite grown used to. When I had finished I slipped them some money – which they accepted shyly – and hobbled out. I wondered how an elderly Turk, rubbing his stomach, would fare at the door of any of my friends in England. Or even at mine.

Turkey offers us its own experience of history, its own culture – or series of cultures – that can speak to us with little influence from Europe. I hope that she never joins the EU. Just on the edge of Europe, close enough to touch, she is a cultural gift to the world; yet on another level, while Sevan and people like him languish in jail, Turkey's influence on us might turn out to be baleful.

23

On the Holy Mountain

T he village was abandoned, the roofs gone and only a few swinging shutters and doors hinted at a more animated past. Em and I trod paving stones worn by the feet of villagers over many centuries. Each street led neatly to another, to a square or a church. It was clearly once prosperous and well ordered, and had been left in a tragic rush. The inhabitants of Livissi, after years of persecution during which many thousands of Greeks were deported, tortured or sent on forced marches, were given just twenty-four hours to leave by the newly triumphant Turkish government of Atatürk.* Thus ended, in 1922, over two thousand years of Greek settlement in Asia Minor. The upheaval was vast, with more than a million Greeks from Asia Minor forced

---

* Atatürk was, it must be said, responding to an invasion by the Greek Army.

to resettle in Greece, and three hundred thousand Turks having to come home from Greece. Livissi remains empty, some say, as a mark of respect by the local Turks who refuse to repopulate a place abandoned by their friends and neighbours. It is a moving reminder of the trauma that reshaped Greece, and of the sensitivities that shape Greek responses to the world. If they feel unreasonably burdened by the current financial and refugee crises, it is no wonder.

The story of Greece doesn't get better until long after the Second World War, so it is natural to sense the layers of history behind every encounter one has there. In Crete, in 1975, Em and I met village elders who would gleefully mime the slitting of throats and the shooting of parachutists as they drifted to the ground during the German invasion. Being British we were, much to our relief when contemplating the alternatives, made to feel welcome. The British were still treated as wartime saviours, though some historians berate us for our military incompetence. Luckily, Paddy Leigh Fermor's book *The Cretan Runner* has rescued our reputation and allowed us all to bask in his glory. He kidnapped a German general and was chased with his Cretan partisans through the mountains. It is a great story and we landed on the island wearing our admiration for the brave and ill-treated Cretans on our sleeves.

We knew that the Greeks are hospitable, but inviting ourselves to an evening meal in a private house was a genuine error, if not my first. In those days Loutro, to which we came by boat after a magnificent day's walk down Samariá Gorge, was scattered among the rocks, many of the houses standing alone against the setting sun. It was hard to see any shape to it all, and we wandered awhile, hungry from the walk, looking for a café or signs of food. One house was bigger than the others, at the top of a rock-strewn mound. Such was the general air of conviviality emerging from the three tables of old men outside it that we experienced that familiar traveller's relief at finding a restaurant, sat down and ordered. Em, whose minimal Greek outshone mine, asked for a menu, but the woman who had welcomed us reacted with puzzlement. There was no menu, but in Greece you often eat whatever is on offer so we pointed at the food the old men were eating and she disappeared to the kitchen. We waited but moments before she returned with a dish of goat's liver bubbling hot in a rich brown sauce, succulent and delicious. The woman, who now so sweetly served us, had cottoned on to our gaffe and went along with it. The evening turned gay with laughter and misunderstandings, and for both Em and me it was, and remains, one of the best meals we have ever eaten – which shows how atmosphere and context are vital to the enjoyment of a meal. I have also, since then, learned again and again how poverty and generosity often go hand in hand. So we are resolved to be kind to unknown foreigners intruding upon our meals. (We are, as yet, untested.)

That day of walking down the Samariá Gorge turned out, as I have described earlier, to be significant in our lives. It showed us that we should leave London, and Bristol beckoned. After the walk and our goat's-liver dinner, we returned to Xania, on the north-west coast, for a night in the Imperial Hotel on the harbourside, a ramshackle old place with a battered but heavily made-up face. In the morning we were awoken by the sounds of vigorous slapping. Peering groggily through the windows we watched two fishermen rotating their arms like windmills, each rotation bringing a small octopus crashing down onto the harbour wall. Were they killing them, stretching them or softening them? I'm not sure, but I felt for the octopuses.

We returned to Crete in 2014 for a yoga holiday and stayed again in Xania, now overwhelmed with tourists. The exquisite Venetian lighthouse was still there at the end of the harbour wall. We ate on the harbourside, served by an unusually sophisticated waiter who earned a trifling salary as an air-traffic controller and needed to boost his earnings. The crisis had laid waste to people's finances and many were returning to the land: Greeks hold tightly to their rural roots and return to them when the going gets tough. Yakis was philosophical about it, for he had a family smallholding just outside town where he grew vegetables and kept bees. That gave him a sense of self-sufficiency in a topsy-turvy world.

The part of Greece least affected by the economic crisis is probably the part that has for centuries detached itself wholeheartedly anyway: Mount Athos. Monasteries all over Europe have been abandoned in the past centuries, but Mount Athos and Metéora remain as refuges for those seeking an ordered spiritual life. They are remote, a challenge to reach. I have never been to Metéora, but photographs of monastic buildings clinging to the highest pinnacles are captivating. Mount Athos is different: constitutionally independent, isolated from the rest of Greece by a border and with the wisdom to stay so. It is three times the size of the island of Jersey, with twenty monasteries, about three thousand monks and a number of *sketae*, or daughter houses. There are also hundreds of remote hermitages. Most of the monasteries are also cultural and artistic centres, preserving and encouraging the arts. The Monastery of Iviron, for example, has a famous icon, the Panagia Portaitissa, and some sumptuous architectural features and frescoes. There is a silver lampstand with thirty silver lemons, plus a library of more than fifteen thousand books and two thousand parchment manuscripts. It is no wonder that Athos has had an immense influence on orthodox art.

The whole area is called the Holy Mountain, and it really does feel sacred. There is no space for the braggadocio and delusion of the outside world. This is deeply reassuring, a living reminder that humans are capable of creating communities of holiness in a cynical secular world. There is more to it, of course, than this. Farming is a major part of monastic life and the monks are famous for their organic produce and for their maintenance of rare plant species. Athos is a laboratory of conservation, nurturing ideas, plants and traditions that may serve us in the future.

I spent a week there in 2012 with friends from Bristol. We walked from monastery to monastery, staying the nights as guests, motivated by a mixture of curiosity and admiration. My curiosity had been aroused further by the story of the sudden flight of a friend's Greek hairdresser from London, leaving a note on his shop window declaring 'Gone to Mt Athos'.

Mount Athos is a provocative place to be, for it challenges many of our modern assumptions about how the world should be ordered. The buildings are semi-fortified structures, some of them of great beauty, all different. One, Simonos Petras, is perched upon a rock over the sea; another, Vatopedi, is like a village, with a population of monks from all over the Christian world. Our guide there was Brother

Constantine, large, boisterous, chuckly and French, only recently joined after a life as a restaurant owner in London. He still seemed to enjoy a good chat with 'the clients' – unusually, for most monks kept their heads down and greeted us only if they had to. They have, after all, fled the world of casual chat. I kept an eye out, meanwhile, for a monk who looked like a London hairdresser – tricky, for they become more visually alike as their beards and their hair grow.

We discreetly attended vespers. The chanting was hypnotic, part of a thousand years of unbroken tradition. The monks sat in deep pews to the side, coming up to the altar or lectern one after another to recite, read, pray. It was hard for us to understand the services, but just witnessing them was very moving. Dinner afterwards would be silent, our group seated self-consciously together, with readings by a monk. Each monastery had its own traditions, but always served good food, often with a glass of its own red wine. The Mount Athos diet is famous for ensuring a long and healthy life, largely free of many problems such as cancer, diabetes, heart disease, strokes and dementia. The monks eat no meat, a little fish, lots of pulses and spices such as dill, onion, garlic and cumin. Some days each week are reserved for a more austere diet.

The absence of stress may also contribute to longevity and well-being. Simplicity, structure, companionship, hard manual work and the constant presence of Mother Nature must play a part too. And faith, perhaps?

We slept in dormitories, or simple shared rooms, in the guest quarters under the care of the guest master. Sometimes we shared the bathrooms with monks, which I was unaware of until I emerged from the shower to startle

some monks into alarmed retreat. We would get up early
for the morning service and then breakfast on eggs, bread
and coffee. Then we would file out of the monastery for the
day-long walk to the next one. The countryside is thickly
wooded, well-tended in places by the different monastic
communities and often within sight of the sparkling sea.
We succumbed to temptation one day and plunged naked
into the water, only to be admonished by two passing
monks. We were embarrassed to have broken their rules. To
have insisted, even among ourselves, on our right to do as
we wished in a free world would have been inappropriate.
This was their world.

Some of the paths between the monasteries have been
neglected during thin times, and a British charity, Friends
of Mount Athos, has walkers working as volunteer path-
clearers and builders, encouraged by their patron, Prince
Charles, who loves the Holy Mountain.

At a particularly handsome monastery, with wooden balconies cantilevered out from high defensive-looking walls
and not unlike monasteries I had seen in Ladakh, I was taken
by the excellent English of the small, twinkly-eyed, grey-
bearded monk who looked after us. He didn't respond easily
to questions about himself but I did tease out of him that he
had run a small business in London, was without family, and
had arrived recently. That was my hairdresser, surely – but
I hadn't the heart to say so, for he had left London to start
afresh and anonymous in another world.

What is the Mount Athos community there for? Or, as
people ask me cynically, what is the point? It is a question
that will enrich debate for centuries to come, even if it
doesn't preoccupy the monks themselves. They are there to

worship their God. However, there is a secular response: it is an example to us all, while the rest of us are destroying our life-support systems with reckless consumption and leading lives shorn of meaning and purpose. The communities of Mount Athos are sustainable; they produce nearly all their own food and energy, living lives so materially simple that they demand little of the ecosystem. The rest of us depend on others to sustain us, whether through accepting our pollution or producing and buying goods. But this is to state the obvious. Among the many roles of a monastic community is the keeping open of a door to the possibility of God; to explore other ways of being, of knowing ourselves. Not one of us was a practising Christian, yet the devotion of so many fellow men touched us deeply.

The fact that no living female creatures are allowed there, other than those one cannot control, such as mice (and cats to chase them), is mystifying to outsiders. It can hardly be sustainable, surely? But the population is replenished by a fairly reliable supply of monks.

Those of us who secretly hoped to spot a crack in the monkish carapace of perfection were satisfied to hear that there had been near-conflicts between monasteries in the not-so-distant past. One community, Esphigmenou, had even hung banners to protest against the visit of the Ecumenical Patriarch of Constantinople, whose remit they would not accept. Not every monastery is beautiful. The Russian foundation, Panteleimonos, was, we were glad to see, even a touch vulgar. Too much new money.

*

Greece's hinterland, like those of Spain and Turkey, is ignored by most travellers. Our book, put together by the delightful and half-Greek Michael Cullen, revealed spectacular places to stay. I drove with Em from Salonika all the way up to Zagoria, in the far north-west near Albania, to see its mountains and famously handsome villages. On the great Macedonian plain, whence Alexander the Great had once sallied forth with his armies, we saw one result of EU membership: countless abandoned warehouses and small factory buildings. Applying for funding for business ventures had been too easy, and the results were lamentable. We were to see more of this in the villages, but first we saw something magnificent.

Alexander the Great's father, Philip, was buried in Vergina, the ancient capital of Macedonia, and his tomb has been preserved in an underground museum. Em was particularly entranced by his gold crown, the most delicate, intricate and exquisite work, a poetic intertwining of acorns and leaves – almost art for art's sake rather than a symbol of power.

We stayed in a local hotel whose owner we had described in our book as a culinary genius. The hotel was gloomily empty and as we stood forlornly at the bar a small voice rang out from the back of the room: 'Are you Alastair Sawday?' I turned to see a young woman approaching us with outstretched hands, bubbling with enthusiasm. Anna Colquhoun was here to learn cooking. She was driving a Land Rover from England to Turkey, and then all around Turkey, equipped with the relevant Sawday books, studying food. I was ridiculously pleased, not least because her father had coached my rowing eight at university – with little effect. We had a superb meal that night produced by her and Dimitris in the hotel kitchen, two masters of the art of cooking, a special treat in a country where good food can be elusive. Anna has gone on to make a name for herself as a chef, food writer and culinary anthropologist.

Zagoria is a mountainous region far from the Greece of islands and whitewashed buildings. Here the villages are of big handsome grey stone houses that look prosperous and well ordered. The mountains are dramatic, not unlike the Dolomites, and there is fine climbing to be had. We were keen to hike up one particular mountain to reach a wildflower meadow with a small lake, the Dragon's Lake, on the edge of a very high, steep escarpment. We loaded ourselves with food and after a long, hot morning of zig-zagging up a wide slope to the distant top reached a small plateau dominated, to our surprise, by a modern-looking mountain refuge. As we staggered in, our rucksacks heavy with food, we were asked: 'Would you like stew or spaghetti for lunch?' It was similar to that humiliation on Snowdon when we Scouts had found the party of elderly ladies already admiring the view with a cup of tea.

One reason for the apparent prosperity of the Zagoria villages was, again, the EU's generosity. A house owner would apply for a grant to convert a modest house into a hotel. There was rarely a proper business plan, and even more rarely any real intention to create a hotel. Countless houses had been upgraded this way, left empty for the requisite number of years, and then declared failures. At which point, the owners moved back in to their restored houses. These things shaped my own response to the Greek crisis. A corrupt Greece being fairly disciplined by Germany? Or unfairly bullied? Or heroic little Greece struggling yet again to be itself, give or take a little corruption, burdened by history and outside pressure?

Greece, or those of its citizens who care about its environment and its autonomy, is battling on many other fronts, one of which is in Halkidiki, the northern region from which springs the peninsula of Athos. The Canadian mining company Eldorado intends to mine for gold there and the locals want to stop them. It is an epic struggle, one that has gone on for decades. It is even possible that the local community will win. They know that profits would be expatriated and run through a subsidiary in another low-tax country, as happens with many international companies. Yet again, for the Greeks, it is them against the rest.

At the beginning of this chapter I wrote of the heartbreak of the Greek exodus from Asia Minor. A second heartbreak was the suffering of the Greeks during the Second World War, and then for many years afterwards during a vicious civil war. The role of the British was not one of which we can be proud. Churchill, a committed monarchist, poured resources into supporting the monarchy and the establishment against the progressive left and the communists. All this in a country broken and impoverished by a war of which it had wanted no part, but into which it had been dragged by Mussolini's invasion. So it is painful to see Greece yet again overwhelmed by outside forces and tens of thousands of migrants for whom life has become impossible in their own countries. Greece, I believe, bears no responsibility for this last great migrant crisis, but bears much of the brunt. It is hard for those who have lived a long time to see their country torn yet again. But Greece has been with us for a while and will keep its head; and it still has much to teach us.

24

Sawday Raj

The heat overwhelms you, voices and arms reach out and pluck at your sleeve, arms, legs, hair. Unmanned, you see your bags bobbing away upon a strange head into the chaos of people and taxis, and you allow yourself to be pulled along in pursuit. Resistance is futile. You have been captured by India, and you will love it.

Thus it is upon arrival, and thus it has always been. Everything is new. My first rickshaw driver used his foot as a brake. There was no other way, so it was logical. India breaks every rule we have learned, yet captivates with its sensuality, colour, noises and surprises. All life is on display; the expected and the unexpected happen on the street. There is room for astonishment, but not for shock or disapproval. Mark Twain summed it up: 'Nothing has been left undone, either by man or nature, to make India the most extraordinary country that the sun visits on his rounds.' A first-century Greek traveller, meanwhile, wrote that 'in India, I found a race of mortals living upon the earth, but not adhering to it, inhabiting cities, but not being fixed to them, possessing everything, but possessed by nothing.'

As an introduction to the living theatre that is India, I tell the tale of a Sawday inspector called Dave Ashby. His first encounter with religion stretched his mind wide open to whatever else the country might throw at him.

There had been a steady procession of wrapped bodies making its way down the stone steps to the river and many were set down on the muddy, litter-strewn shore to await their pre-cremation immersion in the sacred waters. Up above, on large platforms, several pyres were in full flame, the shrouds and bright decorative wraps all but gone and the shapes of the bodies distinct among the stacked logs and flames. At one end a fire was all but over and the priest was raking the ashes with a stick. He stopped to pick up another stick and, using the two as crude tongs, pulled a charred pelvic bone to one side. He then made his way down to the river with the bone, the deceased's family following him. At the water's edge he stopped, chanted a prayer and made to cast the bone into the water. He turned to one side and, rotating, slung it outwards in a wide arc. Missing the river completely, the bone sailed through the air and landed in a large wooden boat. There was a scream and the boatman, who had been asleep in the shade at the bottom of his craft, leapt to his feet clutching his arm. Cursing roundly, he leant over the side and plunged his scalded forearm into the water. The priest stood rooted to the spot, as did the family. The boatman, now recovered somewhat from his injury, launched a torrent of abuse at the priest. The priest retaliated but, clearly in the wrong, did so in a more placatory tone. Tempers cooled, as did the pelvic bone, which was retrieved by the priest. With pride a little restored he carefully placed it this time into the waiting waters, his duty finally done.

Dave sipped his chai and reflected that only in India could one be peacefully asleep in a boat one minute and the next have a scalding hot pelvic bone land on you.

The Sawday relationship with India began with my great-grandfather George Sawday, the son of a piano-maker in Sidmouth. George left to make his mark in India as a Methodist missionary and spent sixty years in Mysore, where he devoted himself to medical and educational reform. He died there in 1947, at the age of ninety-four, after building a school, a hospital and clinics – all funded largely by the admiring local maharajah. The maharajah's palace has a vast mural depicting the durbah, which features one white face: George Sawday's. He was a white-bearded figure much loved in Mysore and was held up to us children as a legendary figure, a missionary to his core but the sort of man who would nowadays be called a pioneering social entrepreneur. My mother adored him. Perhaps his missionary zeal came down through the family and explains some of my own zealotry and that of my youngest sister. Fiona founded what became the national family planning organisation of Swaziland, and has worked in international maternal healthcare ever since. Her son and daughter, Sam and Zoe, are continuing the tradition – both in Africa.

One of George's two sons, another George, was my

grandfather, the dentist from Weybridge, and the other son, Uncle Sam, was in the Indian Civil Service and something of a man-about-Calcutta. He was an expert in finance, played the piano, threw parties with enviable panache and had a lover called Madame Rahim. He never married or had children with her, I am told, though I half expect one day to encounter someone in Calcutta with the long Sawday face. But he did leave the family name behind. Fiona had dinner with a young Indian at the Calcutta Club, and when he gave her his card she saw that his firm was called S. K. Sawday and Co.

My own relationship with India began with my birth. On 6 August 1945, the US dropped an atomic bomb on Hiroshima. The previous day my mother had dropped me onto a bed in a wooden house in Gulmarg, fourteen thousand feet up in Kashmir. The local newspaper featured my birth, not as a minor item on the back page but in a paragraph firmly above the one about the bomb, thus reinforcing my mother's sense of my significance. For the previous twenty-eight years there had been no European baby born in Kashmir. Ten days after I arrived, another English baby was born in the very same bed. Nicholas Wright now lives just ten miles from my mother in Saxmundham, and is a firm friend.

When her labour began my mother summoned the Indian army doctor, who came by horse. He was used to severing limbs rather than umbilical cords, but his presence added substance to the occasion and distracted mother from my father's weeks-late arrival. When he finally appeared, he was unimpressed. 'Is this it?' My mother threw a stale samosa at him.

Why was my mother in Kashmir? My father had been posted to Persia with the Queen Victoria's Guides of the Indian army, to guard the oil wells, and was killing time while awaiting the German army. Luckily it was stuck at Stalingrad, otherwise it would have swung south to take the oil fields and my father might not have survived. By all accounts, my father's time in Persia was an innocent and tedious life, punctuated by duck-shooting expeditions and skirmishes with local Kurds. I have recently discovered a letter from his colonel thanking him for his discreet and effective role in setting up a brothel for the troops, under the medical eye of a plump Indian doctor called Dr Singh. Singh eventually had to be removed when it was learned that his visits to supervise were more personal than medical. My mother was a touch coy about all this and I suspect that my father would have been even more so. Anyway, mother was far away in Lahore at the time.

The colonial British would escape the summer heat by heading for the hills, where the cool and the natural beauty made up for the discomforts. The government, too, would decamp and wind its weary and encumbered way up into the mountains to spend the summer in Simla. Kashmir, even higher in the Himalayas, has an ethereal beauty. Without the war between the Muslim people and the largely Hindu Indian army, it would still be taken for Shangri-La and submerged under waves of tourists. Those who have stayed on a houseboat on the Dal Lake at Srinagar have touched the heavens. The boats are pastiches of English architectural styles – Tudor, Edwardian, Victorian – on water. The Maharajah was fearful that the English, once established, would take over the country and so forbade them from building houses, so the houseboats were an ingenious response, a sort of Himalayan Surbiton-on-Water. Any English person over the age of sixty would feel at home here, for the boats serve roast beef and semolina and custard, much of which must end up in the lake. The mystical forces that have forever, some believe, kept the lake 'clean' are also presumed to deal with the semolina and custard.

In Britain, a month before my birth, there had been a landslide electoral victory for Clement Attlee's Labour party. The new government, living up to its promise to end the Raj, quickly demobilised the army in India. My father, to qualify for a free passage home with the family, returned on an early troopship to demobilise in the UK. Thus, in a rush, ended the Sawday presence in India, and with the hasty withdrawal of the army the British lost their capacity to stop the slaughter that accompanied Partition.

Our now out-of-print *Special Places to Stay* book about India jogs my memories, as do others on the bookshelves at home: *Through the Sikh War, Forty-One Years in India, The Siege of Krishnapur, The Men Who Ruled India.* Em's Uncle John, whose bookshelves were heavy with such titles, had been on the North-West Frontier during the Second World War, speaking Pashtu and gathering intelligence with the Kochi Scouts. My childhood was richly studded with characters from India, such as Jacky Morton, who, aged twenty-five, had stormed the walls of a desert fort at the head of his police force. My friend Ian Battye comes from the Fighting Battyes of Indian army fame, and I can see the fight in him still. In the days when a few thousand British civilians ruled many million Indians, character and chutz-pah were essential. Six of the Battye brothers were present in Delhi during the Mutiny. One of them, Wigram, died leading his regiment in a cavalry charge in Afghanistan.

Reading my mother's diaries recently, I came across a story that reveals much about her. Travelling on a train to Lucknow with my year-old sister Auriol, she was keen to get back from the dining car to her carriage (there was no interlinking corridor) to breastfeed. The train was scheduled to stop at the next station, and so Mother planned to get down and walk along to her carriage, but the train careered straight through, leaving her with two hours to wait until the next stop at Lucknow. Nowadays a mother would feed right there and then, but that was not done in 1943. So this mother pulled the communication cord, the train screeched to a stop, she descended blithely to the track with Auriol, walked ahead and climbed into her carriage. Nobody seemed to mind, she assures me.

In the twenties my father, another George, went to Calcutta after university to work with a jute-trading company, but lost his job in the Depression and came home to train as a lawyer. Life in Calcutta had been a colonial paradise, but also an orgy of shooting tigers, leopards and assorted other victims. (I am stricken with embarrassment now when challenged over the animals he killed. One tiger 'survived' on the floor of the family home in Suffolk and a leopard hung on the wall.) He lived in chummeries, where bachelor Englishmen shared a house-with-servants, and his social life seems to have revolved around clubs and elegant balls. So back to Calcutta he went, as a lawyer this time, meeting my mother who had been sent out by her parents at the age of nineteen. He was fourteen years her senior but she was besotted, and remained so for the rest of their largely happy marriage. India lives on in the family as a vivid memory for my now very elderly mother, and in family words like *nanga punga* for 'naked'. *Nanga* is Hindi for naked, and *punga* is a rhythmic, child-friendly addition.

The troopship carrying the family home in 1945 sailed away from India through the Red Sea and the Suez Canal, a long voyage in tropical heat. My mother, separated by army rules from her husband, made such a fuss that the captain gave her a cabin where she could breastfeed me, entertain my father and, I imagine, stay out of the captain's hair. We ended up in Suffolk, where my father joined a solicitor's practice in Halesworth and my parents bought the old and derelict farmhouse Carlton Rookery. There began decades of happy family life and my childhood world.

The ship in which my mother had sailed to India in 1938 was called the SS *Conte Rosso*, built in Scotland but owned by Lloyd's of Genoa. She was beautifully fitted out in the Italian manner and the crew gave my mother an entertaining voyage. The skipper even invited her to his cabin for an authentic Italian experience before she was lost to India, but 'I was a good Scottish girl.' The *Conte Rosso* became an Italian troopship and was in 1941 part of a heavily defended convoy bound for Tripoli when it was torpedoed off the coast of Sicily by a British submarine with the loss of thirteen hundred lives. The submarine commander, Lieutenant-Commander David Wanklyn, earned a Victoria Cross for the sinking. Had the Italian soldiers arrived in Africa the British would have devoted themselves to killing or capturing them, of course, but the sinking of a ship filled to the gunwales with human beings does churn up impossibly complex moral issues.

*

I am conscious that my India is more colonial than modern, but, given my roots, publishing *Special Places to Stay in India* was a natural for me – though more nostalgic than commercial. Our son Toby, then aged twenty-two, was dispatched to 'create a book about India for us', and sheer chutzpah triumphed over inexperience. His adventures along the way were often hilarious, and he matured quickly. Em and I joined him and his girlfriend Miriam for a few weeks as they explored places in the Himalayas and below.

We began in a Lutyens-style house, Tikli Bottom, outside Delhi. Who could resist a house with such a name? The architect had created a dream solution to the heat, with air currents and breezes driven by design and cunning to avoid the need for air conditioning. When, in spite of all this design brilliance, we awoke in the morning having carried our steaming beds out onto the roof to avoid the sauna within, we found ourselves in good company. Our hosts were out there too, feeling a touch wistful about their architect's fee.

One of the people we met at Tikli Bottom was Barbara, a solidly middle-class English woman in her fifties. She had arrived in Delhi some years earlier, expecting to tour the country with two other women. She waited, but they never arrived. The taxi they had arranged was there to meet her so she set off alone, grandly in the back like a memsahib, with a small, handsome Indian driver. By day two, embarrassed to travel so imperiously, Barbara climbed into the front seat where conversation was easier. By day three she was sharing her own story with the driver and hearing his too, and the following day she was no longer missing her friends and joined the driver that night in his bed. By the time the tour ended she had been captivated by him and by India, so they married. She learned to take India's surprises on the chin, such as finding their wedding bed, or charpoy, next to other charpoys filled with the extended family down on the farm. This was a far cry from polite Kensington, not least when she had to rise before dawn to 'use' the fields. Wisely, she kept a small flat in Delhi and, as a morale-booster for herself, had her hair done once a week at the Imperial Hotel.

The taxi for our tour with Toby and Miriam was driven by someone alarmingly youthful. We explored the foothills of the Himalayas, staying in a tiger camp, an old colonial bungalow run by a retired Indian colonel, and a little house in the hill station of Ranikhet. A tiny old Nepalese man burst into our bedroom to light the fire, just two feet from our pillows. On went the logs, on went the petrol and on went the match. Up shot the flames, and then died again to be revived by further waves of petrol. Then our genial arsonist disappeared to light the fire under the water-heater.

We also stayed in pine forest, in a house that was unusually clean. After leaving a bit of a mess in the living room we would return to find everything in order. Only upon departure did we discover that the cleaner merely tipped the rubbish out of the window. We had been looking for a quiet spot in the forest for a picnic and had to sidestep a plastic bag rolling downhill towards us. This method of waste disposal is an old Indian trick, which we witnessed again on a train journey.

Opposite us sat a family that enchanted us with their smiles, their manners and their neat and tidy way of eating their meals. They insisted on giving us titbits. As we worked our way through our own meals, wrappers and

waste collecting around us in disarray, the family fastidi-
ously collected their own detritus into a plastic bag. As we
approached a station, the father sealed the bag and headed
for the door. Impressive, I thought, he is even going to get
off and put it all in a waste bin. He stood by the open door
and as the train pulled out tossed the bag on to the platform
and carefully closed the door.

Before leaving for India I had asked Ashoka, an overseas
development organisation, for contacts. Ashoka functions
by selecting local pioneers and subsidising them to focus
more on their work. It is an impressively effective system. In
Chennai we made contact with an Ashoka Fellow called Dr
Mutu, who was working with local tannery children. They
had been sold by desperate parents into semi-slavery in the
tanneries, where they would stand knee-deep in urine (used
to soften and tan the leather) for long periods. Dr Mutu had
long conducted a campaign against this, which led to him
being hounded by the tannery owners and even arrested.
Undaunted, and now supported by Ashoka, he set up roof-
top schools for the children and micro-credit schemes for
their mothers, so they could afford to educate, rather than
enslave, their children. It was impressive and moving, and
his hospitality to us was undeserved. He arranged a visit to
a school, where we were fêted and garlanded regally. Every
one of those children would, were it not for Dr Mutu, have
been working in a tannery. That day was worth the three
weeks we had spent on our own. It also reinforced, for me,
the wisdom of the drive behind our books: bringing people
together. That is travel at its best.

Unable to repay Dr Mutu's generosity, we showed him

what we thought would be a useful energy-saving device, one that we use at home for casseroles and which has saved lives and energy in Africa: a hot-box made out of a cardboard box, with scrunched-up newspaper – or even rice husks – as insulation. This device, known in Africa as a wonder box, works brilliantly for cooking pulses and stews, saves precious firewood and avoids the tragic accidents that often accompany open-fire cooking. He and his staff expressed polite wonder, but probably thought it was too simple to be of any use.

Toby and Miriam pressed on with research for the book and were enchanted by what they found. I was impressed by their determination to stick to their guns when I listened in on a conversation Toby had with Vikram Oberoi, head of marketing at the famous Oberoi hotel chain. Vikram had invited Toby to see their glittering former maharajah's palace on a lake in Udaipur, upon which eye-watering quantities of money had been lavished.

'Well, Toby, what did you think of it?'

'Wonderful place, Vikram, but not quite right for us.'

'What! What on earth can you mean?'

'Well, perhaps you have just spent too much money on it.'

'There is not such a thing as spending too much money . . .'

'Well – perhaps not for you. But it can overwhelm ordinary mortals.'

A far cry from the Udaipur palace is the former Himalayan kingdom of Ladakh, now in eastern Kashmir. In 1994 I led a party of sixteen there under the aegis of Journeys, a small company I set up to be the UK's first eco-friendly travel company. We intended to avoid the tourist industry and learn from direct contact with local people. It is tempting, when travelling in a country as alien as India, to reach for the familiar. Those who are wary or nervous retreat to Western-style hotels, safe but unchallenged. That is a shame, for all over India people have opened their homes to foreigners or created small hotels where you feel safely part of the country. There are treehouses, villas, camps, palaces, cottages, bungalows and forts, up mountains and rivers, in cities and countryside. The variety is bewildering. You can adopt any role you wish: collector of human experience, idler, imperial dreamer, yoga disciple, massagee, meditator, adventurer, wanderer, self-improver, artist – India can absorb all your fantasies and offer a thousand more. Journeys attempted to add environmental awareness to the exotic mix of learning that India provides.

'Travel with a fainter footprint' was the Journeys message, and we arranged our travel through the Ladakh Ecological Development Group (LEDeG), set up by my friend the eco-warrior Helena Norberg-Hodge. They had recruited their own Women's Rural Development Group to act as our hosts and guides. We took the train to Simla and then a bus over the mountains to Leh, the old capital. The bus journey was ghastly: diesel fumes pouring into the bus, many suffering with altitude sickness, all of us terrified by the driving. At one stage the driver decided that taking a fast run at a small gap between a crashed bus and the edge of the mountain road was the best way of getting through. We have a curious tolerance when being transported in other countries: 'Oh, the driver must know what he is doing, for he is a local. One should have confidence.' We clench our buttocks and sit tight, yet a glance over the edge of the road often reveals the carcasses of other vehicles that once carried the confident. In this instance, we got out and walked rather than risk catastrophe in the bus.

Ladakh is a desert country over ten thousand feet up in the Himalayas, irrigated by glacier run-off and, until the seventies, inaccessible other than by air, foot or animal. It was Helena who lured me there with her book *Ancient Futures* and her promise that we would be not only enchanted but rewarded by the civilising values of the people and their culture. She was right. The Ladakhis are Tibetan Buddhists and the region is known as Little Tibet; there is that gentle, self-effacing, accepting nature that comes with Tibetan Buddhism. Ladakh had clung precariously to its values in the face of cultural assault from India and the West. Helena was instrumental in this. She had lived there for long winters as the only European woman in the kingdom, to learn about this unusual world. Why, for example, did people smile? Was it a Ladakhi sign of detachment? Was it a habit with cultural significance? Did they smile in pity? Was it, even, a sort of rictus brought on by winter winds? Finally she realised that it was because they were happy, and that is a difficult phenomenon for cynical Europeans to accept.

So why were they happy? Maslow's hierarchy of needs tells us that shelter, security, friendship, good food, time and health are higher on the list than money, status and power. Ladakhis had everything they needed. Their houses were solid and handsome; they grew their own food, using their own human waste in the compost; they had time to dream, socialise and play; their surplus children could go to the monastery or convent yet still be active members of the family. Child mortality was high, and for us that would be a serious chink in the armour of happiness, but surviving children lived to a ripe age. There was no insecurity from not having what others had; they all had roughly the same. Helena felt that she had found a balanced and contented society, one that lived within its means and within the limits of the ecosystem. She resolved to spread the word and help the Ladakhis secure themselves against destructive change. Hence LEDeG and the Women's Rural Development Group. An example of Helena's work was the bringing of small-scale hydroelectric power to the villages in preference to imported, and expensive, power from India. She also taught Ladakhis about the West, about our insecurity, poverty, materialism and loneliness. Tourist literature and the media give false images of our cultural and material success.

Helena lodged us with some of her Ladakhi friends and we were touched by their warmth and openness. The sweetest moments were often the least promising, for example the act of contributing our own waste to the common pool. A corner of each house was devoted to this: a two-storey tower within the corner of the house, with projecting platforms equipped with a spade and some sawdust. You cantilevered yourself out and performed, even if someone else was doing the same a floor higher (but not, I hasten to add, directly above). No embarrassment, just modest pride in one's contribution. At the end of the winter the resulting compost would be taken to the gardens to boost the vegetables. These were magnificent, and must have played a role in the general robust health.

The houses were big, with thick walls, wooden-framed windows and a flat roof for social gatherings and for drying the crops, for it never rained in Ladakh. No rain for thousands of years, yet it has just begun to happen – a result, scientists think, of climate change. If it happens frequently it will be devastating.

Ladakh is, of course, now quietly going the way of all flesh: increasing commerce from India, Nike shoes, branded sunglasses and jeans, youth unemployment, urban drift, imported food and energy, crime and dissatisfaction at their new perception of themselves as 'poor'. The narrative that we have sold worldwide, that Western methods should be emulated, is tragically effective. We have even convinced ourselves. Bhutan, another Himalayan country, understands that and has committed to a brave attempt to subvert the narrative. They know that they are under cultural siege and have devised methods, such as heavy payments from tourists, to deter thoughtless visitors and generate extra income to shore up local institutions and resilience.

Changing the narrative is perhaps the only way we will emerge intact from the story we have told ourselves, and spread to others. Perhaps the tide will turn as we in the West begin to understand that our successful economies, dependent as they are on growth and relentless extraction, are flawed. They are generating catastrophic changes, undermining our ability to survive on this planet. Should not the very first criterion for judging an economic system be its impact on the planet? I find it heart-breaking that the Ladakhis and the Bhutanese will suffer with us all, innocent of the crime of eco-destruction. My time in Ladakh gave me much to ponder.

Our journey back was fraught with uncertainty, as the once-a-day plane never arrived, neither then nor the next day, leaving Monday's and Tuesday's stranded passengers poised to join Wednesday's in a rush for the limited seats. The maths was unsettling. So I gathered the group together to agree a way out: stay put in the hope of extra flights, or leave by taxi (a two- or three-day journey) to Srinagar, and thence to Delhi. The consensus was for a taxi ride.

Hailing a taxi to take me from Paddington to Marble Arch is one thing, but taking one nearly three hundred miles from Leh to Srinagar felt extravagant. But there was no viable alternative. Descending back to Simla in a bus, after our grim, semi-asphyxiated ascent, was not an option for us. So we gathered five taxis and set off deeper into the Himalayas. That journey is another story, punctuated by scenes of river mud packed onto overheating engines, a taxi breaking down and its passengers squeezing into the other four, and mountains of breathtaking beauty. But we made it, finally, into a Kashmir that was, as my birthplace, significant for me. We stayed on a houseboat on the lake and, between roast beef lunches with semolina and custard for pudding, plotted a hazardous return to Delhi.

Sadly I never did get to Gulmarg, for the Indian army, inexplicably, wouldn't let me go. This was hard to bear after a lifetime hearing stories of my high-altitude birth. I had to settle for the hope of returning another year.

25

Quakers and Refugees

How can one not love a country that treats your imagination as a plaything? Fantasy mingles with reality until the two are indistinguishable. Only in India can a simple village in an arid and poverty-stricken region turn into a fantastic place of palaces and unimaginable luxury at the turn of a corner.

It happened to Em and me in Chettinad, a small area of about seventy-five villages in Tamil Nadu. The Chettiars were a wealthy group of families who made fortunes through money-lending and gem-trading. Later, following the British into newly conquered lands such as Burma, they made further fortunes from banking and from exporting teak. They are no longer wealthy, but their village palaces are their legacy, often empty or under-used and as opulent as anything in Rajasthan. There are thousands of them, one hundred alone in the village we saw. Imagine houses entered via one courtyard after another, through avenues of giant carved teak columns polished to a shimmer.

Our taxi took us past squatting families, dust-covered shacks and mangy dogs, and then turned left into another world. A boulevard stretched into the distance, lined on each side with vast houses, many in imitation of European styles: French châteaux, Palladian villas, Scottish castles, Tudor mansions. Marble was imported from Italy, crystals from France and mirrors from Belgium. A lavish sycophancy was evident in statues of English administrators and public figures decorating the façades. I still cannot quite believe that it was real, not an extravagant film set. We wrapped our arms around a few teak columns, yet we still didn't feel entirely earthed. India absorbs its fantasies and makes them real.

In spite of my birthplace, and a few visits, the deepest contact I have had with India was, strangely, with another distinct group: her émigrés-turned-refugees, the Ugandan Asians. From India to East Africa came thousands of Indians in British imperial days. Some were indentured labourers, building railways and working in plantations. Others, mostly from Gujarat, came over as merchants and prospered mightily. With their ethic of hard work, family cohesion, frugality and building for the long term, they had an advantage over the Africans, for whom business was novel. By the seventies many Gujarati families had business empires, owning sugar mills, factories, chains of shops and plantations. Their wealth removed them from their African fellow citizens, to whom they were often less than generous. When Idi Amin came to power and needed scapegoats for his home-made economic chaos, he picked on the Asians and ejected them from the country with just twenty-four hours' notice. Twenty-four thousand came to the UK over a few days in 1972 and were housed in resuscitated military bases all over the country.

At that time, I had just abandoned teaching again, after my two years at Charterhouse. I was keen to explore new ideas, and briefly considered working with George McRobie, who ran the Intermediate Technology Development Group. George had been close to Fritz Schumacher, the author of *Small Is Beautiful* and an inspirational figure for many young environmentalists. I often wonder how things might have been had Schumacher not died, for he had the ear of government ministers.

However, I needed a bigger change and offered to help with the Ugandan refugees. I reported to the volunteer HQ in London and was sent to an old RAF camp in Somerset called Houndstone to 'get on with whatever was needed'. The camp had been hurriedly revived, partly by the local Women's Royal Voluntary Service, who were heroic in their efforts, willing to do anything. I saw them roll up sleeves and clean lavatories, push-start vans of clothing, care for children and marshal adult volunteers. They brooked no nonsense and were selfless. I saw one splendid lady teach a group of women, who tended to squat on the seat with little sense of accuracy, how to use the lavatory. I hastily left the room as she unbuttoned her tweeds.

My employers were Quakers, I later learned, but they kept that quiet. That is the Quaker way: intelligent, informed and committed, but with no trumpet-blowing. I was soon running a hockey team, teaching in the temporary school, helping to track down spare houses in the area and generally being a friend to the refugees. Asked to point in the direction of Mecca by a group of Ismaili Muslims, I gestured vaguely east and hoped for the best. There were no lightning bolts.

We soon came across the natural spirit of enterprise that had given the refugees such an advantage in Africa. One couple attached themselves to us volunteers and bent over backwards to help. They were charming, knew everybody in the camp and were strangely un-pushy about their place in the queue for housing. We eventually discovered that they were in no hurry to leave for they were running a prostitution business inside the camp. I have no doubt they have since prospered.

The follow-up work after a refugee influx is, of course, the difficult bit. Housing, schooling, social services, the health system – they all have to be attended to. With Britain in its own housing crisis, it was hard to find spare houses without rattling political cages; but the Quakers were respected and listened to in their communities. When Houndstone closed, Bristol Quakers asked me to help the families they had settled there. This was perfect for me: a wide-ranging job with people, and freedom to get on with it. A score of families were settling into Bristol and I was to help them in any way I saw fit.

Befriending them came first. I ate a lot of samosas and some fine meals, and drank tea in gallons, but I never got used to the women hovering at the table or in the kitchen while we men ate. I made naïve mistakes, such as settling a family into a remote house on the Avon. They abandoned it within a fortnight. What for me was glorious isolation with river views was for them aching loneliness with nothing but the water to look at. The government made the same

mistake, settling families in villages throughout the countryside, only to find them leaving to be with their friends
in the cities – as we all would. As I write, I see governments repeating the mistake with refugees from Syria and
Afghanistan.

My main success was a gesture with unexpected consequences. Mr Majothi had been a shop-keeper in Uganda and
was miserable with nothing to do. He came to me with a
twinkle in his eye and asked if he could borrow fifty pounds
to pay the rent on his first shop, a grocery store. Thirty years
later I was on Radio Bristol talking about the environment,
and Mr Majothi heard me. He tracked me down and rang:

'Mr Alastair, I am so happy to find you.'

'Mr Majhoti – how nice! What has become of you?'

'I am now proud owner of Bristol Sweet Mart in Easton.
Very successful. Everybody shopping here. Please come to
visit me.'

'How wonderful – of course I will.'

Ah, I thought, perhaps I will get that fifty quid back! I was
intrigued, and keen to see him again. I got a warm reception
in the office of his impressive emporium and then a cup of
tea with a samosa. I occasionally bump into his family, for
he has now died, and they never fail to remind me how vital
was that first loan. They are a successful group, the Ugandan
Asians. Perhaps what was most needed in those early days
was a loan to get them back on their feet.

Years later Em and I sent our children to a Quaker school
and began to attend Meetings. The Quakers are a remarkable community, where service to others is built into their
way of being. There are only about twelve thousand of them
in the UK, yet they are influential beyond mere numbers.

Quakers were conscientious objectors during both world
wars, founded the School of Peace Studies at Bradford
University, and have always campaigned devotedly, and
behind the scenes, for peace. In 1947 they won the Nobel
Peace Prize.

Their Sunday Meetings, to which we used to go, are
quiet, reflective times when anyone can speak if moved to
do so. We have found Meetings helpful in times of crisis,
such as the looming invasion of Iraq. It was an unsettling
time, all of us plagued by doubt and ignorance but pain-
fully aware that conventional, violent response would be
pointless. A Quaker woman living in Baghdad was there
as the invasion began and described how a cruise missile
that had, according to official reports, 'destroyed an enemy
target with pinpoint accuracy' had actually destroyed her
local primary school – which had been full of children. She
was spirited out of Iraq by the authorities. Talking of these
things as equals in Meeting helped us deal with our dismay
and distress at the invasion.

The Quakers believe there is 'that of God' in us all, hence
the rejection of the idea of a minister or priest. They are
more attracted to experience than to theology, to democracy
than to leadership. They are a force for good, and I grew
a little when with them. Perhaps I will return, influenced
again by a wife whose instincts for quiet reflection are
stronger than my own.

India and the Quakers had a long and fruitful relationship.
Gandhi was influenced by them; some remarkable Quakers
worked alongside him. Samuel Stokes, a prominent Quaker
who ran schools in the Indian hills, went to jail in Gandhi's
support. Marjorie Sykes was a friend of Gandhi and lived in

the Quaker village of Rasulia, in the Narmada Valley. The campaign to save the Narmada from drowning under dam-building has been a long one: Marjorie Sykes was active in it long ago and was an early advocate of sustainable agriculture. She also ran a school. Perhaps the best-known English Quaker in India, however, was Laurie Baker, a pioneering architect of low-cost, sustainable building techniques. His later years were spent in the hills of Kerala. His biographer writes that Baker's 'acceptance of the frugal style of life . . . stems perhaps from his Quaker background. The rigorous Quaker upbringing, with its emphasis on simplicity and austerity, its rejection of all ornament and luxury as sinful self-indulgence . . . ' That could be Gandhi.

My brief work with the Quakers, my birth in India, great-grandfather George's work in Mysore, and then my time with the Ugandan Asians – all seem to fit together. When in Kerala I was unaware of Baker's work, but the state still has more than its share of ground-breaking, progressive ideas, mostly via a gentle form of communism. But this doesn't mean that Kerala is necessarily easy to get along with. Jeremy Fry, the father of a Bristol acquaintance from another old Quaker family, built a palace in Kerala and, piqued by the state's failure to value his work, dismantled it into twenty-six thousand pieces in order to move it to Tamil Nadu next door.

Em and I were in Kerala for a while, first at the hippy village of Varkala, where beer was served surreptitiously from teapots and yoga started and ended every day. Before I knew Em, yoga had been a mystery, entirely outside my male, public-school experience. Bit by bit she has gently worn away my natural resistance to it, leading by example and teaching yoga herself. She is supple, disciplined and open-minded in ways that remain beyond me. Eventually she persuaded me to go to regular classes. I now see how profoundly yoga can alter one's body and one's mind. I still feel like a beginner, but have a growing awareness of my body, my health and my place in the universe. Standing still in a yoga position, eyes closed, one's concerns, petty vanities and trivial ambitions shrink to their rightful size. If yoga were part of our culture and education I believe the world would be a saner place. Years of yoga have made Em a wiser person than I, and stronger too. She fell off a ladder and cracked her pelvis in 2016, a frightening accident. Her rapid recovery had much to do with her yogic discipline and awareness of what her body needed in order to recover. I still have much to learn.

I could learn something of silence, too, from Em. I have grown up with noise, conviviality and conversation, and am ill-adapted to silence. I know that the silence of a yoga meditation refocuses and soothes. Sara Maitland wrote a beautiful exploration of it – *A Book of Silence*. It delivers a simple, yet complex, message about its extraordinary power. Silence offers, she writes, a return journey into the 'seed-bed of the self', the place where much of our self swirls and bubbles and yet cannot be articulated. It is where we are, but hard to reach.

Varkala was followed by a stay in Fort Cochin, where Toby had found several places for our India book. It is a town with deep roots in both colonial and Indian history. In the nineties a tiny Jewish population still attended their eleventh-century synagogue, but now only a handful of Jews are left. There is something uplifting yet depressing about the last people of a group, the last speakers of a language, the last residents of a community. Cochin Jews now constitute a tenth of a population of eighty thousand Indian Jews in Israel. Only about five thousand Jews are left in India. The Cochin Jews were once rich and energetic, dominating the Indian spice trade. Many Indians are proud of the Jewish thread running through the fabric of their society and are battling to preserve what is left.

The Jews of India have provided several great Bollywood stars, such as Pramila, born Esther Abraham and one of the all-time greats. Curiously, the Jewish community also furnished a military hero of the terrible war between India and Pakistan over the independence of Bangladesh, which sent ten million refugees into India. The war was negotiated to a rapid end by a Jewish Indian officer, Lieutenant-General J. F. R. Jacob. Alone and unarmed, he brokered the surrender of the Pakistani army's ninety thousand men, demanding unconditional surrender in exchange for a protected retreat, or they would face the full might of the Indian army. He had just three thousand troops available. That is the spirit which has several times got the Israeli army out of trouble.

Cochin, the spice capital of India, has lines of handsome old godowns, warehouses filled with sacks of spices and foodstuffs stretching from one distant end to the other. We enjoyed plunging our bare arms into sacks of ginger, peppers, cloves and cumin, luxuriating in the feel and smell of such bounty. We stayed at the Old Courtyard Hotel, sleeping in a vast bed floating on a sea of wide polished teak floorboards. Below us was a whitened, cobbled courtyard with plants and a stately old mango tree. Even the lavatory worked, in a cantankerous sort of way. I spent a lot of time in the bedroom as I had broken two ribs while demonstrating my punting technique on the backwaters. I was grateful for Em's devoted care and for any small mercies, of which India is a rich provider: the smells of incense wafting up from the courtyard, the warbling sounds of chatter among the hotel staff, the geckos scuttling across the ceiling.

Kerala has long been communist and better governed than most, with the highest literacy rates in India. We met some remarkable people there, such as Vasudevan, who ran the Tasara Centre for Creative Weaving, with his five siblings, a few children, some dogs and a ceaseless wave of energy – much of it from visiting artists and resident weavers. We were encouraged to create in whatever way we cared, but not to be idle – the very antithesis of Vasudevan's idea of a useful and happy life: 'Mr Alastair, you must know that happiness comes from busyness. We are all working hard here so we can create beautiful things.' The place was eccentric, happy and bustling, and we loved it. The weavings were sold worldwide, and displayed in Tasara. We were briefly part of another man's dream.

Another of our hosts, Dr Gopala, invited us to join him one evening – not for a drink but for a conversation. This was a wholly new sort of invitation for us. He had a 'conversation hut' in his garden, in which he would offer his guests a range of topics before they settled on their choice. He was erudite and interesting, more rewarding than a gin and tonic – though that would have been welcome too. In India anything is possible, and acceptable.

Being a European in India can be like being a very active spectator at a wild and unpredictable theatrical extravaganza, one that never stops. It is also a particular experience of privilege, just from being outside the complex struggle that is daily life for most people. Most of us emerge from India enriched in unexpected ways, touched by encounters with people more sophisticated than ourselves, kinder, more generous, wackier and more open-minded, people whom we will never understand, with layer upon layer of culture and insight.

Another lesson taught to us by India is that there is vitality in diversity and virtue in simplicity. India's modern rulers, in their hectic rush to Westernise, turn their backs on their country's own native genius at their peril.

EPILOGUE

Slow Travel

Shakespeare's King Lear, wandering demented and distraught on the heath, asks Gloucester: 'No eyes in your head ... yet you see how this world goes.' And Gloucester, who has been blinded, answers, 'I see it feelingly.'

I am writing this in a Cornish café, looking across a wide bay towards St Ives. Shadows chase each other across the water and the surf sparkles. As Em and I strolled along the beach our cups ran over, and now we are enjoying a most traditional pleasure – a cream tea. Sun, water, peace and beauty – perhaps even cream – are eternals. Trends, technology, self-guided cars and assorted digital devices are out of place, for us, here at this moment. Travellers will always delight in simple things, will rebel against being told what to enjoy and buy, will defy trends and relish surprise. So as travel publishers, of books and a website, we will continue to stand behind those who rebel, defy and relish – and those who have tales to tell.

The real traveller opens himself up to experience and plunges in. The happiest travellers are those who travel lightest, free of preconceived ideas and fat suitcases. And who travel slowly.

I recently met two remarkable women who have rekindled my affection for slow travel – in this case for cycling slowly, and seeing the world at close quarters. Kate Rawles was about to set off from Panama to Patagonia on her self-built bamboo bike, alone. Philippa Cox had just returned from a lone cycle journey of eight thousand kilometres from northern Norway to Gibraltar. Both carry their camping equipment and sleep wild when they can. Once I get over the thought of the discomfort and cold, my spirits are quickened by their exhilaration, the sheer beauty of the journeys, the encounters with remarkable people, the time they created to do this and that the rest of us work so hard to find.

I think I shall set off around France on my bike next year, from one special place to another. What could be better?

Acknowledgements

The focus of this book is the story behind my travel publishing, rather than my life – much of which remains unmentioned, together with many of those whom I love and admire. Even when shedding light on my travels I have, rather than drown readers in a tide of unfamiliar names, remained quiet about most of those who have helped me. I have had kindness and hospitality, advice and ideas on a huge scale. I have been supported, too, by a large and forgiving family and a network of friends and staff, all of whom deserve more than my silence during the writing.

The many names that follow form an unwise and belated attempt to thank those behind the travel story, unwise because it will surely be incomplete – the peril faced by all writers.

The shaping of this book has been benignly guided by my delightful editor, Richard Beswick, from whom, in cahoots with my agent, Kate Hordern, emerged the initial idea. Deeper in the wings waited Zoe Gullen, whose copy-editing took my breath away. My lifelong infatuation with the humble comma was exposed, as was my dangerous addiction to the hyphen. Worse, or better, was her gentle improvement of my careless spellings of place names and people – and much else. I salute her.

Em, my wife for over forty years, has too often had to watch me depart for yet another trip to Europe. Her love and friendship, humour and wisdom have inspired me and given me fresh perspectives. Toby and Rowan, our sons, whose individuality is a source of pride to me, should have been better fathered but have emerged triumphant: Toby as Sawday's MD and Rowan as Dizraeli, the rapper – challenging and entertaining. He greatly improved some of my writing.

I have written far too little of two of my three remarkable sisters, Auriol and Fiona, both of whom have visited many special places – as have other family members. A person to whom I owe a life of gratitude is Annie Shillito, who worked alongside me for twenty-nine years in close friendship. She was the greatest, and least acknowledged, of gifts to my travel-publishing life. Ann Cook-Yarborough was another such gift. Further sparkle was provided by Painton, Jane Ryder, Simon, Nicia, Nicola, Sarah, Lady B, Jo, Jules, Siobhan, Wendy, James, Ann, Guy, Susan, Sheila and Sandra, Andrew, Gonz, Chris, Jane Warren, Florence, Krysia and so many more who deserve to feature here – such as Rachel Fielding, Lynn and Emily. A longer list would be indigestible, though I will risk adding Russell, Tom Bell and Tom Dixon, Bella, Eliza, Quentin, Caroline and Sue and Ian Miller. Then there are the inspectors and owners of the special places, hundreds of whom have inspired me and many of whom have become friends. I cannot begin to mention names, like those of Pru, Lise, Jeannie and Sam,

Aideen, Henrietta and Bas, David, Peter, Janine, Pippa, Richard and Linda, Georgina, Monica and Lucinda. Those who have joined in more recently, or who have contributed greatly – such as Sally and Christine – know who they are. I owe a special debt to Jackie and Emma, and apologies to the many whom I have mistakenly not mentioned. Lastly, Toby's replacement of me in the company's driving seat has enabled me to write this book, the company to modernise and continue doing its good work, and the celebration of special people and places to survive in a more modern form. It has not been an easy ride, and I am proud of him.

My part-time environmental activism has been shaped and encouraged by the views and experiences of many others such as: Jonathon Porritt, Ivan Illich, Brian Price, Fritz Schumacher, Richard St George, Keith Hallett, Lester Brown, Charles Secrett, George Monbiot, Helena Norberg-Hodge and John Page, Helen Browning, Charlotte Mitchell and Craig Sams, Patrick Holden, John Grimshaw, Nikki Jones, James Bruges and others, including the Worldwatch Institute, Helen Browning and many other organic farmers. If I had to pick one book to thank for igniting a lifetime of interest, it is Schumacher's Small Is Beautiful. It should be required reading for us all. As I steam gently into my eighth decade, I owe much to the many young people whose commitment to social and environmental change continues to ignite me. My generation has left them a heart-breakingly steep hill to climb. They need our help.